New Orleans

AltaMira Studies in Food and Gastronomy

General Editor: Ken Albala, Professor of History, University of the Pacific (kalbala@pacific.edu)

AltaMira Executive Editor: Wendi Schnaufer (wschnaufer@rowman.com)

Food Studies is a vibrant and thriving field encompassing not only cooking and eating habits but issues such as health, sustainability, food safety, and animal rights. Scholars in disciplines as diverse as history, anthropology, sociology, literature, and the arts focus on food. The mission of **AltaMira Studies in Food and Gastronomy** is to publish the best in food scholarship, harnessing the energy, ideas, and creativity of a wide array of food writers today. This broad line of food-related titles will range from food history, interdisciplinary food studies monographs, general interest series, and popular trade titles to textbooks for students and budding chefs, scholarly cookbooks, and reference works.

Appetites and Aspirations in Vietnam: Food and Drink in the Long Nineteenth Century, by Erica J. Peters

Three World Cuisines: Italian, Mexican, Chinese, by Ken Albala

Food and Social Media: You Are What You Tweet, by Signe Rousseau

Food and the Novel in Nineteenth-Century America, by Mark McWilliams

Man Bites Dog: Hot Dog Culture in America, by Bruce Kraig and Patty Carroll

New Orleans: A Food Biography, by Elizabeth M. Williams (Big City Food Biographies series)

Big City Food Biographies Series

Series Editor
Ken Albala, University of the Pacific, kalbala@pacific.edu

Food helps define the cultural identity of cities in much the same way as the distinctive architecture and famous personalities. Great cities have one-of-a-kind food cultures, offering the essence of the multitudes who have immigrated there and shaped foodways through time. The **Big City Food Biographies** series focuses on those metropolises celebrated as culinary destinations, with their iconic dishes, ethnic neighborhoods, markets, restaurants, and chefs. Guidebooks to cities abound, but these are real biographies that will satisfy readers' desire to know the full food culture of a city. Each narrative volume, devoted to a different city, explains the history, the natural resources, and the people that make that city's food culture unique. Each biography also looks at the markets, historic restaurants, signature dishes, and great cookbooks that are part of the city's gastronomic make-up.

Books in the Series
New Orleans: A Food Biography, by Elizabeth M. Williams

New Orleans

A *Food Biography*

Elizabeth M. Williams

ALTAMIRA
PRESS

A division of
ROWMAN & LITTLEFIELD PUBLISHERS, INC.
Lanham • New York • Toronto • Plymouth, UK

The publisher has done its best to ensure that the instructions and/or recipes in the book are correct. However, users, especially parents and teachers working with young people, should apply judgment and experience when preparing recipes. The publisher accepts no responsibility for the outcome of any recipe included in this volume.

Published by AltaMira Press
A division of Rowman & Littlefield Publishers, Inc.
A wholly owned subsidary of The Rowman & Littlefield Publishing Group, Inc.
4501 Forbes Boulevard, Suite 200, Lanham, Maryland 20706
www.rowman.com

10 Thornbury Road, Plymouth PL6 7PP, United Kingdom

British Library Cataloguing in Publication Information Available

Library of Congress Cataloging-in-Publication Data

Williams, Elizabeth M. (Elizabeth Marie), 1950-
  New Orleans : a food biography / Elizabeth M. Williams.
    p. cm.
  Includes bibliographical references and index.
  ISBN 978-0-7591-2136-2 (cloth : alk. paper) — ISBN 978-0-7591-2138-6 (ebook)
  1. Cooking, American—Louisiana style. 2. Cooking—Louisiana—New Orleans.
3. Food habits—Louisiana—New Orleans. I. Title.
  TX715.2.L68W546 2013
  641.59763'35—dc23

                                                              2012034857

♾️™ The paper used in this publication meets the minimum requirements of American National Standard for Information Sciences—Permanence of Paper for Printed Library Materials, ANSI/NISO Z39.48-1992.

Printed in the United States of America

To Rick
Thanks for taking this journey with me.

Contents

~

Series Foreword

Big City Food Biographies

Cities are like living organisms. There are nerve centers, circulatory systems, structures that hold them together and of course conduits through which food enters and waste leaves the city. Each city also has its own unique personality, based mostly on the people who live there, but also the physical layout, the habits of interaction, and the places where people meet to eat and drink. More than any other factor, food defines the identity of so many cities. Simply say any of the following words and a particular place immediately leaps to mind: bagel, cheese steak, muffuletta, chowda, cioppino. Natives, of course, have many more associations—their favorite restaurants and markets, bakeries and donut shops, pizza parlors and hot dog stands. Even the restaurants seem to have their own unique vibe wherever you go. Some cities boast great steakhouses or barbecue pits, others their ethnic enclaves and more elusive specialties like Frito pie in Santa Fe, Cincinnati chili, and the Chicago deep-dish pizza. Tourists might find snippets of information about such hidden gems in guidebooks; the inveterate flaneur naturally seeks them out personally. For the rest of us, this is practically unchartered territory.

These urban food biographies are not meant to be guidebooks but real biographies, explaining the urban infrastructure, the natural resources that make each city unique, and most importantly the history, people, and neighborhoods. Each volume introduces you to the city, or reacquaints you with an old friend in ways you may never have considered. Each biography also looks at the historic restaurants, signature dishes, and great cookbooks that reflect each city's unique gastronomic makeup.

These food biographies also come at a crucial juncture in our culinary history as a people. Not only do chain restaurants and fast food threaten the existence of our gastronomic heritage, but we are increasingly mobile as a people, losing our deep connections to a place and the cooking that happens in cities over the generations with a rooted population. Moreover, signature dishes associated with individual cities become popularized and bastardized and are often in danger of becoming caricatures of themselves. Ersatz versions of so many classics, catering to the lowest common denominator of taste, are now available throughout the country. Our gastronomic sensibilities risk becoming entirely homogenized. The intent here is not, however, to simply stop the clock or make museum pieces of regional cuisines. Cooking must and will evolve, but understanding the history of each city's food will help us make better choices, will make us more discerning customers, and perhaps more respectful of the wonderful variety that exists across our great nation.

Ken Albala
University of the Pacific

~

Preface

I have been studying the history of the food of New Orleans in one way or another since I began to eat. In this way I am like every other person lucky enough to have grown up in this city. I have a bit of old Louisiana and new New Orleans in my personal family history. But on both sides there is an appreciation of food. Food—eating and sharing it—is associated with the happy times as well as with the sad ones. Food is love; it is worship; it is celebration; it is condolence; it is memory; it is identity. And when I say food, I include drink. Whether it is coffee or spirits or other special drinks, New Orleans takes care with anything that involves flavor.

I am particularly pleased with this opportunity now to write the story of the food of New Orleans, because after the flood caused by the failure of the federal levee system following Hurricane Katrina, the sense of place established and held together by eating in New Orleans has been undergoing a huge change of emphasis and focus. It is now both more grounded in tradition and looking forward to the future. Change itself is certainly not something to be avoided. It has been the city's ability to bend with change, ever adapting, that has allowed it to maintain such a rich and nourishing cuisine. I have no wish to stop change. But I do want to remember where we have been. An appreciation of the past will allow us to march forward with an understanding of the continuum to the future. Because I choose to continue to live in New Orleans, I will probably change with the city. So with full disclosure I admit that my attempt to tell an accurate story may be to no avail. It is likely that my own opinions, formed as I grew up and tasted, formed as I traveled and tasted, and informed by some investigation of history have colored the way that I present the story of the food of New Orleans. So in that sense this is also my story. Despite that I have tried to confine my voice to this section.

I am not unlike so many New Orleanians. We live in a city with a sense of place, a sense of history and character. It is not Anywhere, USA. That sense of place seems to bind all of us. Growing up in a sensuous city allows a person to appreciate the senses, without realizing that you are. When I was a child, I thought everyone cared about smells and sounds, sights and textures, and most of all taste. I think that every New Orleanian grows up with this swirling sensuousness all around him. Since so many of us denizens of the city remain in New Orleans for our entire lives, whether from inertia or lack of opportunity, many of us fail to appreciate how special it is here. Without having seen how others live or eat, we have no point of comparison. It takes the outsider to come here to appreciate the wonder of it and to make us see what we have taken for granted. Those of us who leave often return, drawn back to deep flavor and a need for a grounded place. I had my awakening in Augusta, Georgia, where I foolishly ordered Trout Almondine at a white tablecloth restaurant in 1975. I should have known that fresh trout might not be readily available there. I was served fish sticks—literally previously frozen formed rectangles of fish—with chopped almonds and dried parsley on top. After recovering from the shock of it, I realized that I was not in New Orleans anymore.

In addition to my good fortune regarding my place of origin, I was born into a half-Sicilian family. My grandmother, Elisabetta, and my grandfather, Francesco, were Sicilian. My mother was first generation American. She grew up speaking the Sicilian dialect, learning English when she went to school. She was a part of the large Sicilian community in New Orleans. Because she was my mother and the family culture-bearer, I learned to eat, appreciating food and family in New Orleans, with a Sicilian twist.

My father brought old Louisiana French and a bit of Alabama cracker to the family. That meant there was a country sensibility in his attitude, as well as an appreciation for simple things. Because my father wasn't Sicilian we spoke English at home, and I didn't spend my entire growing up years within the Sicilian community. We, my brother and I, moved in and out of it. Sometimes we attended family gatherings redolent of garlic, lots of shouting, huge hugs with those awful cheek pinches, and more Sicilian dialect. At other times we quietly visited fields and dusty roads, where we ate meat pies and corn bread. My Alabama grandfather made the best angel food cake ever. He beat the egg whites by hand. I still have his angel food cake pan. He also drank coffee that he dripped one cup at a time and poured into warmed cups. He grew the very best peaches in his backyard. But mostly we lived in a middle class urban American neighborhood riding bikes, watching Saturday morning television, and going to school. I have eaten my share of TV dinners and fast food. I am not a purist.

As I have grown up, traveled, and matured, I have come to appreciate the city for nurturing the senses. Certainly my naive childhood presumption that my experience reflected the way all things are has been dispelled. I understand that consuming the world is not generally considered an appropriate way to live. What a pity. I don't want us to move into and out of the information age and discover that we have lost an appreciation of the subtle layerings of taste, having homogenized the world in our quest for security, speed and cost efficiency. I want everyone to be fortunate enough to be allowed to be open to the subtleties of the tastes, the texture, the aromas, and the flavors of food.

This book will not be a history that tries to identify definitively the origins of this dish or that, as though there could be only one influence on each dish. There has to have been social invention involved in the development of cuisine rather than individual inventors. The invention of the cuisine of New Orleans has been a collective one. And it continues to be so. And unlike the specific dishes invented intentionally at restaurants—such as Bananas Foster—developing a cuisine is an evolving and emerging process. It is a process that is always in flux. It is complicated by the fact that sometimes similar foods or methods may spontaneously develop in different locations. Social invention results in a product that belongs to everyone. That is true of the food of New Orleans.

Instead of seeking historical ties to ethnic origins of individual foods, this book will examine the philosophical and cultural forces that made a cuisine develop in New Orleans, even when similar and abundant raw ingredients and similar waves of ethnic groups came together in other locations without resulting in a cuisine. Even if the recognition of a local cuisine was intentional marketing, there is ample basis for declaring that the cuisine existed to be recognized. If there is myth involved, which there surely is, what are the basis of and the purpose of the myth?

I hope to convey to the reader the degree to which food permeates the culture and the thinking of the city. Food unites all of the people of New Orleans. Each New Orleanian respects the culinary opinion of every other New Orleanian, regardless of class, education, or status. We may argue about the fine points of a dish, but it is with respect. We talk about lunch when we are eating breakfast. We know that people of all classes and positions in society all can and do cook. Food is that basic and ubiquitous.

In writing this book I have relied on the expertise and insights of numerous people who have written many books and articles. These are people whom I deeply respect for their ability to discover and dig deeply into original documents in different languages and report and interpret those materials for us. I prefer to cook and eat my way to enlightenment. But I believe that I have legitimately used their research to explore the factors that have created this cuisine. In his memoir, *Hungry Town*, Tom Fitzmorris, a local food commentator, says with no irony that this is a "city where food is almost everything." In a city where food means so much, where it is part of every element of life, a mere exploration of dishes and their recipes would not scratch the surface of meaning. It is with an attempt to capture and share that real meaning—the almost everything—that this book is written.

~

Timeline

1727	Ursuline nuns arrive as colonists
1728–1751	Casket girls, called such because they carried their belongings in wooden boxes, arrive from France to become brides
1731	Abbé Prévost writes *L'histoire du chevalier des Grieux et de Manon Lescaut*
1743	Last slave ship arrives directly from Africa before a thirty-year hiatus
1755–1763	*Le Grand Dérangement*: the ousting of the French Acadians from Canada
1762	Treaty of Fontainebleau, a secret treaty by which France cedes Louisiana to Spain
1763	Treaty of Paris in which France cedes lands east of the Mississippi to England and New Orleans to Spain
1768	Antonio d'Ulloa, Spanish governor, is repelled by the colonists at New Orleans
1769	Alejandro O'Reilly, the Spanish governor, arrives in New Orleans
1778	Isleños from the Canary Islands begin arriving in Louisiana
1780	First covered market is built by Spanish
1791	Slave uprising in Saint-Domingue
1794	Building of the Carondelet Canal
1800	Treaty of San Ildefonso, a secret treaty in which Louisiana is ceded to France by Spain
1803	The Louisiana Purchase
1807	Passage of the Embargo Act
1808–1809	Construction of Halles Des Boucherie as a part of the city market system
1812	Louisiana statehood
1814	Federal forces capture most of pirate Jean Lafitte's ships
1815	Lafitte assists in the Battle of New Orleans and the British are defeated
1820–1840	Wave of Irish immigration due to famine
1836	Construction of the St. Mary Market
1838	Building of the New Basin Canal
1840	Opening of Antoine's Restaurant
1850s	Georg Merz produces lager in New Orleans
1856	Tujague's Restaurant opens
1859	Opening of Bruning's Restaurant
1861	Solari's market opens

1862	Café du Monde opens
1863	Precursor to Madame Begue's, Louis Dutrey's coffeehouse opens
1868	Beginning of the grocery that grew to be Schwegmann Brothers Giant Supermarkets
1874	Martin Wilkes Heron invents Southern Comfort
1876	P & J Oyster Company is founded
1881	Publication of *What Mrs. Fisher Knows about Old Southern Cooking* by Abby Fisher
1885	Publication of *La Cuisine Creole* by journalist Lafcadio Hearn; Publication of *The Creole Cookery Book* by the Christian Woman's Exchange
1885–1915	Many Sicilian immigrants come to New Orleans
1889	Emile J. Zatarain Sr. begins his business by trademarking his root beer
1890	Barq's Brother Bottling Company opens, making Barq's root beer
1891	Jackson Brewery is opened by the Fabacher family
1893	First production of Giacomo Puccini's opera, *Manon Lescaut*
1894	World Cotton Exposition at what is now Audubon Park
1899	Kolb's Restaurant opens
1902	Wm. B. Reily & Company Inc. opens a roasting business in New Orleans
1905	Jean Galatoire purchases Victor's, to be renamed Galatoire's
1906	Lupo family claims the invention of the muffuletta
1907	Dixie Brewery is opened by Valentine Merz
1910	*Naughty Marietta* by Victor Herbert is first performed
1918	Arnaud's Restaurant is opened by Arnaud Cazenave
1919	Passage of the Eighteenth Amendment to the US Constitution; Passage of the Volstead Act establishing the era of Prohibition
1922	John Mandich opens Mandich Restaurant on St. Claude Avenue
1923	Building of the Industrial Canal; Baumer Foods (Crystal Hot Sauce) is founded
1927	Progresso Italian Food Corporation is opened
1929	Streetcar strike results in the creation of the poboy
1933	Passage of the Twenty-first Amendment to the US Constitution; Repealing the Eighteenth Amendment, ending Prohibition

1939	Publication of the WPA *Guide to New Orleans*
1940s	German POWs are sent to Louisiana
1946	Opening of the first Schwegmann Brothers Giant Supermarket on St. Claude Avenue
1947	Francis Parkinson Keyes publishes *Dinner at Antoine's*
1949	Beginning of the broadcasts of Lena Richard's Creole Cookbook
1951	Invention of Bananas Foster by Chef Paul Blangé
1960	Building of the Mississippi River-Gulf Outlet Canal (MR-GO)
1965	LeRuth's opens in Gretna, Louisiana
1970	Publication of *Revised New Orleans Underground Gourmet*
1970s	Wave of Vietnamese immigration after the Vietnam War
1972	Al Copeland opens Chicken on the Run
1975	Tom Fitzmorris begins radio show
1979	Paul and Kay Prudhomme open K-Paul's Louisiana Kitchen
1987	*Frank's Place* premiers on television
1994	Louisiana World Exposition
1996	Establishment of the Crescent City Farmer's Market
2005	Hurricane Katrina
2008	Publication of *Cooking Up a Storm*
2010	Deepwater Horizon oil spill

CHAPTER ONE

~

Introduction: A Real Cuisine

Çà qui dourmi na pas pensé manze. (He who sleeps doesn't think about eating.)—Old Creole proverb

Eating in New Orleans: The Sense of Identity

It has been said that the food of New Orleans is the only true cuisine that was developed in the United States of America. Certainly in New Orleans that is a dearly held belief. Clementine Paddleford, the mid-twentieth century food writer, says that Creole cookery was the nation's most recognizable type of cooking. The cuisine of the city is a web that embraces and connects all of the inhabitants. Regardless of class or education or income or race or any other category that might be proposed as a way to separate and define people, anyone and everyone in the city is likely to cook, have a culinary opinion, and be respected for it. Talking about food, both its preparation and its taste, is the greatest equalizing factor in the city.

In his book, *Tasting Food, Tasting Freedom: Excursions into Eating, Culture, and the Past*, anthropologist Sidney Mintz distinguishes a cuisine from a group of accumulated recipes. He says that to be a cuisine, a way of eating must be so ingrained in the people who eat it that they all "consider themselves experts on it." He describes them collectively as true believers in the cuisine. He recognizes that these true believers care passionately for their cuisine and that they all know its ingredients, its techniques, and its tastes and subtleties. Applying that definition, there is no doubt that the people of New Orleans

1

Bird's-eye view of New Orleans. Drawn from nature on stone by J. Bachman, c. 1851. Courtesy of Library of Congress, LC-USZ62-16407.

have a cuisine. This definition could have been written specifically for New Orleans and its people.

Food as a basis for identity in New Orleans is not a new idea. It can clearly be traced to the late nineteenth century when the people of the city were recognized as eating differently than the rest of the country. But the city had strong and somewhat insular eating habits even before then. Those habits were mentioned in diaries of travelers and in official reports. The stories about eating in New Orleans both reflected the internal attitudes of the people and the perception of visitors. Today a website called "We Live to Eat" is supported by the Louisiana Restaurant Association and is about the food of New Orleans.

All of the peoples who lived or settled in New Orleans, whether free or enslaved, brought with them their sense of identity as defined by food. Clinging to old foodways is a common experience of immigrants everywhere. And all of the peoples contributed to what has become the cuisine of the city. The city was the crucible filled with all those component cuisines and with raw ingredients. The mixture was transformed into a unique cuisine, connected to its component parts, but distinctly different from them. This phenomenon—the merging of cuisines and transformation into a new one—is unusual in the history of the United States. In many great culinary cities, like New York or San Francisco, the food of the various ethnic groups that make up the city has remained identifiable. You can find Korean food, Thai food, Italian food, Mexican food, or Moroccan food, not New York cuisine or San Francisco cuisine. Yet the food of New Orleans is New Orleans cuisine. It is only in recent years that the city supports a few ethnic restaurants. Considering the number of restaurants that the city patronizes, the percentage of ethnic restaurants is small. In its quest for taste the city Creolizes the food of immigrants instead of allowing it to remain separate.

In many other colonies in America the dominant group of immigrants wanted to continue to eat in the way of home, for example, to eat like an Englishman, even in this strange land. The founders of the city of New Orleans, Bienville and his band, however, were actually born in the New World. They were trappers, French descendants, from French colonies in what is now Canada. These first settlers in New Orleans both from Canada and France took native slaves and ate like natives. They even moved in with and lived with the Native Americans when times were particularly tough. These early New Orleanians were eating from New Orleans and its surrounding area from the beginning.

It is said that for years the restaurants of New Orleans all served the same menu. If one were inclined to dispute this accusation, it would be hard to do so. Those who visited were bored by the sameness, food critics in particular, especially since they were used to the variety of choices of cuisine that other big cities provided. The food might have been all the same within the city, but it was remarkably different from the food of the rest of the United States. Consider the firestorm that was unleashed after Alan Richman, writing in GQ magazine in 2006, criticized the food of post–Katrina New Orleans. He claims that Creoles were fairy folk, implying that the concept of Creole doesn't exist. He treats the word "Creole" as an ethnic group or country modifier like Italian or Thai. The fact that "Creole" actually describes the merger of ethnic groups, of cultures that were born in New Orleans went completely unnoticed and unappreciated by him. But he also criticizes the cuisine as being tired and repetitive. The same food is available at each restaurant, just as it is with every cohesive cuisine. Criticizing the restaurants of New Orleans for serving New Orleans food is like criticizing Italian restaurants for serving pasta or going to China and looking for Argentinean restaurants. That is not to say that there is no bad food, even bad Creole food. There is poorly prepared, mediocre food to be found. Alan Richmond doesn't have to like it. But criticizing it because it is actually a cuisine demonstrates a woeful lack of understanding of the food.

The people of New Orleans—starting with the Native Americans—were blessed with the bounty of sea and the land. The Gulf of Mexico and Lake Pontchartrain were teeming with fish of many varieties and several types of shrimp, crabs, oysters, clams, and more. The land yielded bear, deer, bison, duck, turkey, rabbit, crawfish, frogs, and so much more. And there were nuts, fruits, and vegetables. Each wave of explorers and immigrants brought new items that were often left in the new land, with the result that the region was constantly absorbing the bounty—peaches, for example—left by others. After the Europeans first came and added new plants and animals which became assimilated, there was even more bounty in the New World. After the Africans came there was even more food representing at least three continents. If the foods from Asia that were brought by the Europeans are counted, the food of four continents was found in what was to become New Orleans.

There is much food literature written about the influences of one ethnic group or another in shaping the cuisine of New Orleans. Groups compete over the source of influences. For example, there are those who argue that jambalaya is derived from the Spanish dish paella. Others argue that it is derived from traditional African rice dishes. Even others claim that it sprang up spontaneously from rice available in the New World. What is most interesting is not which ethnic groups contributed to this dish or that.

Is this need to establish an influence on a dish a form of culinary imperialism—imposing hegemony over a dish to establish influence and power? It certainly may have been if early cookbooks are defining origins. The early cookbooks clearly try to claim mostly French influence and techniques at the expense of all other influences. Is it now a need to have the influence of your ethnic group recognized? African and Native American influences have long been minimized when first Native Americans and later Africans were primary cooks in the city. What is fascinating is that in New Orleans a new cuisine was born. In other cities where there was bounty, where there were many ethnic groups living together, and where there was time for a mingling of the peoples new dishes developed. But in most cases the food of US cities clearly retains an ethnic identity. Why did a cuisine develop in la Nouvelle-Orléans where the origins of the dishes is debated rather than merely identified? How did all of that ethnic identity become merged, really submerged, into the identity of the city? It happened to the highest degree in New Orleans, where there was access to a constant array of new people and ideas. Cuisine and identity occurred to a lesser degree in other places, often in places where people were isolated, like Gullah cuisine. Exploring the reasons for the formation of a distinct cuisine becomes an exploration of the history of the food of the city and the history of the city itself.

Given the rich culinary life of the city of New Orleans, which continues to exist and develop both within and without the culture of the United States, the question of why a culinary culture developed in New Orleans that is so saturated with its own design and tastes and that it is distinct and identifiable from all other cuisines has remained largely unexplored. That it has developed is well documented. Not only are books and magazine articles written about it, but several magazines are based upon it, and culinary careers of chefs such as Leah Chase and Paul Prudhomme and Emeril Lagasse are based upon it. Dishes that represent the culture can be identified as deriving from New Orleans—sometimes from Louisiana—by most people in the United States.

There have been attempts to describe and explore the origins of many dishes. Often the social invention that is cuisine defies a simple linear explanation of derivation. Too often the place where the origin discussion takes place is in a cookbook, which may only repeat a story that has great cultural value, but limited historical value. The amateur etymology of the names of dishes is often used as a clue to its origin, which cannot only be confusing, but totally without accuracy.

Richard Campanella describes this confusion in the meaning of the word *sagamité*. This word, found in letters, journals, and reports from many parts of the New World, is often used to describe a form of cornmeal mush that was eaten by various Amerindians. The word itself comes from the Algonquin or Cree (*kisâgamitew*)—language and means "served in hot water." It was used by native speakers to describe any sort of stew or soupy preparation. The word itself did not refer to corn or cornmeal. Yet the word was used by the French to describe a preparation that included corn or cornmeal. This word was also used by other Europeans to describe various preparations by different Amerindians in different parts of America, often when corn or cornmeal was included regardless of the name of the dish that the Amerindians might have used. The connection to hot water was seemingly lost and a new connection to corn was created, because the European users of the term identified the corn component as the most important. Consequently Amerindian preparations all over the Eastern seaboard and the south and Gulf regions were called *sagamité*, regardless of their actual names, when they included corn. This tells us something about the ubiquity of corn, but little else about *sagamité*. It also tells us much about transference of words through writing, and how those words are given interpretation.

When we use the name of a dish to try to identify its origins, we have to be careful to use other clues to origin to build a complete case. Names alone, etymology alone, are not enough. For example, the origins of the words gumbo and filé are sometimes given various attributions. The name of the dish we now call Jambalaya has been given various creative origins, often depending upon the ethnic camp in which the origin story sits. Without actually tracing the components of a dish through time and accounting for spelling variations, names alone can be deceptive.

Many techniques and methodologies are very basic and have independently been found in various places. Finding similar basic techniques in two places may not be sufficient to establish influence, let alone a definitive origin. Rendering fat, boiling in oil (frying), cooking in a vessel of water, and cooking over coals are techniques that can be found in many locations. Identifying why and whether a particular technique was the origin of a particular dish or preparation is very difficult. There is often very little evidence to explore other than the technique itself. But similarity alone is not synonymous with origin. When several ethnic groups all use a technique, like boiling, and when those ethnic groups converge, separating one boiling from another makes for treacherous historical territory.

Beyond identifying origins of dishes, an important part in the recording and documenting of a cuisine, is answering the question of why a cuisine. A cuisine requires a certain state of mind in a culture to allow the cuisine to develop; the will to carry it out, that is, to cook and prepare it; and the documentation of it. Some colonists in early Virginia are said to have starved to death rather than eat strange and unusual foods. Much was said about continuing to be English and eating in an English manner. This was not a mind-set that would allow for the development of a cuisine. These three necessary elements existed in New Orleans: state of mind, the cooks, and the documenters.

State of Mind

The city of New Orleans was founded by the French, who established themselves firmly in this place between the Mississippi River, Lake Pontchartrain, and Bayou St. John, without asking the Native Americans for permission. In the early eighteenth century the French who came to settle New Orleans, albeit originally vagabonds, had grown up in the France that thought that French food was the best food in the world. They thought that France and the French were in the vanguard of the arts, including the culinary arts, and they brought these attitudes to the New World.

In 1651 François Pierre, cuisinier to a French nobleman, published a cookbook which revolutionized the way the French thought about food. It had been more than a century since a cookbook had been published in France. He was writing under the nom de plume, La Varenne. La Varenne was the celebrated chef to Henri IV. Pierre's book was *Le Cuisinier français*, that is, *The French Chef*. It was not unusual at this time to write a book adopting a pen name. If there can be said to be an inciting incident in the establishment of French haute cuisine and the art of gastronomy, the publication of this book was that. As people began to worry about their intellectual and artistic lives, their physical delicacy was reflected in foods that were equally delicate and refined. This refinement was a new way to think about and to explain food.

The French Chef also included other innovations besides its references to the refinement of food and the raising of cooking and eating to the same level of French arts, French refinement, and French luxury as other aspects of the reign of Louis XIV. He described the food of France as a cuisine, and he referred to it as the greatest cuisine—a part of the great French lifestyle of art. The book was so influential that the people of France began to refer to their cuisine as the greatest cuisine.

The book was influential for many reasons, one of which was the way in which the recipes were presented. By the beginning of the eighteenth century, chefs in France were considered performance artists. The attitude that chefs were artists and that gastronomy was an art was something that was well accepted in France. The people who came from France to the New World to establish New Orleans carried that belief with them. The cookbook had been republished over forty times and translated into many languages by the time the colonists, whether beggar or soldier, came to New Orleans.

Cookbooks published throughout Europe also reflected this new attitude. Even in Italy, which had been the most prominent source of cookbooks at the time, and in various other countries, after *The French Chef*, new publications reflected the belief that French cuisine was the superior cuisine. The special cooking of France began to be called *la cuisine français*. *Le Cuisinier français* was translated into English and published in England (1653) as *The French Cook*. The translation and republication of a cookbook was a first. Because it was available in English it not only had a greater influence as a cookbook, but its attitudes became even more pervasive. In France many other cookbooks began to be published, which reflected a new attitude about cooking and eating.

Le Cuisinier français presented a radical change in the cookbook. This book organized the foods and their recipes into a way of thinking about them as a cuisine. It was more than a listing of ingredients. It reflected a philosophy of cooking, which the author described as French. Even in some editions the recipes are presented in alphabetical order, which makes referencing them easy and direct. Whether for economic reasons or philosophical ones, *Le Cuisinier français* eschewed the spices that had become popular in cooking. Using spices made the chef dependent on the Dutch and English traders in particular to provide the supply. It also meant that cooking was expensive. By saying that spices, except pepper, were not French, and that by using parsley, thyme, and other seasonings that could be grown in France, the food reflected the essence of France. (This idea of reflecting France would become important in New Orleans.) Even more important was the explanation of techniques like the creation and use of stocks, the basic sauces and the use of local foods in a simple presentation, all of which are largely unchanged in the current French canon. A part of the presentation was that the food be arranged artfully on the plate.

After the publication of *Le Cuisinier français* a second cookbook was published, called *Le Pâtisier français* (*The French Pastry Chef*). This book took the cuisine to yet another level of artistry. The book provided recipes that were given with a precision that had been unheard of previously. This book proved that the cuisine of France was superior, by providing detailed recipes containing unprecedented specificity, innovation, luxury, delicacy, and taste. *The French Pastry Chef* showed that the techniques of the French were without equal in the world. This author published his work anonymously as was the practice at the time. He also made assertions about the French nature of his art and the superiority of French cuisine.

The French Pastry Chef and *The French Chef* helped to make the changes that separated salt from sweet, moving the sweet dishes to the last course—*le dessert*. It was a total transformation of eating. There was also the increase in the use of butter in French cuisine. *Le Pâtisier français* describes the method for making puff pastry, which is still in use today. These two books opened the floodgates of publication in the field of gardening, simple food preparation and freshness, and the making of *potagers* (kitchen gardens). Those who could afford it planted gardens to have better fresh food, as well as fruit trees and nuts. There was even a *potager du roi* at Versailles.

By the time that the French colonists began to build the city of New Orleans they believed in the superiority of French cuisine, even if they could not cook it. They believed in simple preparations and eating what was available. They believed that good cooking and good eating were an art.

Approximately 250 years later in 1885, when *La Cuisine Creole* was published by a Creole Gentleman in the same tradition of anonymous publication as had been adopted by *The French Chef* and *The French Pastry Chef*, journalist Lafcadio Hearn announced that a new way of cooking was happening in New Orleans and used the same word, as had been used by La Varenne and Pierre in publishing his cookbook. That word was "cuisine." Between 1718 and 1885 the people of New Orleans had created a cuisine in New Orleans based on the food traditions of the Amerindians; the expectations of the French in particular, but in general the Europeans; and the culinary talents of the Africans. All three components were necessary to create a cuisine that became a part of the identity of the people, pervaded every level of society, was different enough from other eating habits to be remarkable to all outsiders, and which has a refined restaurant side, a home cooking aspect and a street food component. In other words it was a cuisine that had invaded every aspect of eating in the city.

The Amerindians

When the French began to colonize what was to become New Orleans, they found the raw materials of a cuisine. The foods that were available in New Orleans were already identified. This is an extraordinary advantage in the process of developing a cuisine. Although the journals and records of the French who were the first settlers indicated a wilderness, the assessment did not recognize the pantry that had been created by the Amerindians.

What the French found was not the look of organization with which they were familiar. But in spite of the wildness that the French found, the raw materials were available, not hidden. The French did not have to develop the food that was there. They could trade for fish, shrimp, and oysters. Game, fowl, and meats were readily available, either to be hunted or traded. Greens, fruits, squash, nuts, filé, and corn could be grown, picked, or traded.

Enslaved Indian women cooked and gathered food for the French. They shared their knowledge of what was available and how it could be obtained. It was the Native Americans who introduced the French to the foods that would sustain the new colonists. A reliable source of food from Europe that allowed them to live day to day didn't exist. The Indian women could slaughter game, clean fish, boil dishes, and preserve food. They did so for the benefit of the early colonists.

The French

France had been under the throes of the development of haute cuisine. The people of France, even those not able to eat the food, were aware of the art form that was being recognized by everyone in Europe as the great French art. Even in simple ways the development of this art was felt by all of society.

Those early colonists considered themselves in a fashion to be in France. Thus whatever they ate was French food. They also were protected by the Native Americans who allowed them to join their camps during harsh times, saving the French from starvation. Therefore the early colonists were indoctrinated into the native foods of the New Orleans area. They had no illusions about foods arriving from France, so they embraced the local foods—which were now French—out of necessity. They in turn could continue this indoctrination as new colonists arrived.

The French sent to New Orleans were a motley crew. These were debtors, vagabonds, and adventure seekers. Those sent to govern and were soldiers were ill equipped to farm and create an agricultural society. They relied on the Native Americans in the beginning of the colony and then increasingly on the enslaved Africans and the enslaved people brought in from the Caribbean.

The fact that the French had the expectation that their food was an art was not enough. They had to have the philosophical tools to allow them to reorganize the raw materials in a way that was acceptable to them, familiar enough, and presented in a sufficiently French manner to be considered French. They had to want to do more than eat well. They had to want to eat in accordance with their tradition.

Jean-Jacques Rousseau was writing with great sentimentality about simplicity and the innate knowledge of the peasants. His attitudes and philosophical beliefs affected the beliefs of both the radicals in France and the nobility. The early colonists in New Orleans came with the belief that the native people lived a life of equality and dignity. The lack of amenities and luxuries was less important than their simple pleasures in authentic experiences. Native food was authentic, plain, healthy, and from the land. This philosophy could easily be adopted in a place where all that was available was the plain, healthy food from the land in New Orleans. In France, as in New Orleans, the fresh and locally available food was appreciated and elevated. In emulating what was happening in France, the colonists set about being French.

The Africans

The Africans were brought to the New World from Senegambia and other areas with technical agricultural skills and knowledge of how to cook. They were sophisticated. They had been part of the trade cycle of Arabia for many years, exposing them to Near Eastern and European foodstuffs and goods. They were producing agricultural products for trade and had developed high-level agricultural techniques.

Although Timbuktu, the great trade city of what is now Mali, was in decline at the time of the establishment of New Orleans, the centuries of trade and culture that had been centered there still informed the people. Some of those people became slaves in the new city of New Orleans. Besides their agricultural prowess, they cooked for the colonists and for themselves. Their numbers quickly overtook the Europeans who were establishing the city for France and then Spain. As the cooks, they had control over what was eaten and how it was prepared. That is not to say that there was no influence from the people who were eating the food. But when choices could be made, it was the African and the person of African descent who was making the choice.

Because of the Code Noir (Black Code, a series of laws governing African slaves and later the Free People of Color, imposed by French King Louis XIV), Africans sold food in the street. That food could be bought by French people who did not have slaves or who did not have kitchens, thus introducing the foods of Africa to the European inhabitants. In their sophistication the cooks were able to produce rich and sumptuous and delicious foods that satisfied even the French rulers and the pretend aristocracy of the city. These three ethnic contributions are discussed in more detail in the chapters that follow.

The Mythology of Creole Food

For food to represent a city's identity, that food must be embraced by all of the citizenry, making each resident and visitor eaters of the same symbolic meals at the same symbolic table. This has happened in the cuisine of New Orleans. Somehow all of the ethnic groups, all of the classes, all of the historical twists and turns, all of the geographic opportunities and limitations have coalesced through the food and the art of eating into a cuisine that is embraced by everyone. That New Orleanians still argue among themselves about the origins of a particular dish—many groups laying claim to owning a predecessor dish, to having contributed to the invention of one of the iconic dishes, or having contributed to the transformation or adoption of an iconic dish, or having lent a method or technique—is akin to the arguing and juggling for position by siblings. The people all still know that they are connected by the food. It is this very familiarity, and their security in the connection that it gives them, which allows for endless intense discussion over minute shades of difference.

Whether a dish arose spontaneously or traces its origins to a particular ethnic group may be important in establishing bragging rights for a particular group or to establish a claim of historical accuracy. But in the end, the food that the city eats today is changing all the time. It does not matter that people in the city resist change and embrace tradition and collectively think that the food is immutable. The truth is that the food is different from what it used to be.

The food of New Orleans is probably more documented than the foods of many other American cities. Given that it was considered exotic and unusual, it was remarked upon and reviewed. The relative hedonism of enjoying food instead of just fueling ourselves was also sometimes remarked upon in more Puritan America. Regardless of the reason, the food of New Orleans was written about and discussed. But in America food would not be documented to the same decree as was art; it could not be recorded like music; and it was and is dependent on so many factors for its reproduction that it is hard to be sure that the same words today refer to the words of yesterday.

In spite of all of the emphasis on the special nature of New Orleans—the most European of American cities, the most Caribbean of American cities, the City That Care Forgot, the Big Easy—New Orleans is today an American city with grocery stores selling the same things sold in grocery stores all over the United States. New Orleanians eat frozen pizza, boxed macaroni and cheese, and canned tuna. New Orleans residents eat at fast food and chain restaurants. The city with drive-through cocktail windows also has McDonald's drive-through windows. What some people see as a unique cuisine, others have seen as limited choices, because the same dishes are so often found on the menus of different restaurants. So if there are many paths of Truth when telling a story depending on the tastes of the teller—and that includes past tellers and present tellers—that makes it difficult to intelligently compare the present and the past.

There are no cookbooks from the founding of the city to almost the twentieth century. We are left to examine the written myth, probably an inaccurate story, that we have created about the cuisine of New Orleans from its founding to 1885. The myth expresses the optimism of the people of the city that the cuisine represents our melded identity. The fact that the city needs a myth to explain the origins and the development of its cuisine attests to the fundamental importance of the cuisine to the city's identity. Recognizing that the people are an amalgam, the cuisine must be the perfect unique amalgam.

According to the myth, the cuisine is the embodiment of the harmony and acceptance that has formed among the various ethnic groups. There are no conflicts in the myth; there is only a community of people and flavors. The story of the cuisine is that it represents a melding, a oneness formed by the various influences that have been felt here. The assimilation of the food of each new wave of immigrants is an analogy for the welcoming nature of the city. The finely honed historic dishes have been burnished over time by the various descendants of the groups that contributed them—their joint efforts creating the new dishes of New Orleans. The food of New Orleans is no doubt a melding, but that melding was not intentionally created to establish a unity of the peoples. Ironically all share the food so deeply, it may be that today it does unite the peoples as a consequence, unintentionally giving some truth to the mythos.

One creation myth is the undocumented but certainly widely repeated story known by the popular name, the Petticoat Rebellion or Petticoat Insurrection. According to the story, once upon a time, during the earliest days of the colony, the French housewives of New Orleans were unhappy. These women were said to be accustomed to the varied and presumably wonderful food of France. They were dissatisfied with the food of colonial New Orleans. They stormed the home of Governor Bienville while loudly banging pots with spoons in complaint. They declared that there had to be more to eat than corn mush. Mrs. Langlois, the cook (or housekeeper, depending on the version) of Governor Bienville, was enlisted to teach the women how to cook. She is said to have initiated the women into the secrets that she had learned from the Native Americans, usually identified as the Choctaw. (It is not clear how she learned these secrets.) She taught them about corn, filé, shrimp, crabs, game, and other foods, as though fish and shrimp were unknown in France. This schooling transformed the cooking of these colonial women, who spontaneously created Creole food, and everyone lived happily ever after. In another version the "casket girls," brought from France to marry, are housed with Bienville, and he arranges cooking instructions with Mrs. Langlois as a kind of first New World cooking school. This is a lovely story, which presents Madame Langlois as the foundation of Creole food. But it is only one of the myths about a single source of the cuisine.

That a creation myth was even thought necessary says a lot about the importance of the cuisine to the population. It means that the food is considered a special and unique entity which did not exist before a certain point even if that point cannot be identified. Like all things that did not always exist, but are important today, there needs to be an explanation for its existence. Since there is no more scientific or historical account of its origin, a myth will do. The explanation holds some kernels of truth and the rest is the romantic story that the group would like to be true. Perhaps the mythmakers need it to be true as it reduces the contributions of Africans, for example, to magic, and makes Africans happy participants in its development.

Another myth that seeks to explain the importance of okra, while also explaining its presence here, holds that Africans being kidnapped into slavery loved okra so much that they carried okra seeds in their hair with them to the New World. (The alternate story is that the seeds were sewn into their clothing.) The illogic of the assumption that someone kidnapped would even have the opportunity to obtain okra seeds to then hide them in his hair or clothing is irrelevant to the story. The story implies that the Africans were going on an adventure to the New World. The pretty story glosses past the horrors of slavery, although it does acknowledge that okra came from Africa, and that it had become a precious and important food in New Orleans. It is evidence that the mythmakers want the cuisine to be a uniting and prettifying force that bypasses any unpleasantness or hard truths.

The cookbooks about New Orleans food have been written both by outsiders, those who have observed with fresh eyes, and by insiders who have brought a personal perspective to the writing. The prejudices of both points of view have contributed to the mythology. The outsiders like Lafcadio Hearn were writing partly about what they observed, and partly to sell a cookbook. Hearn was using the story for immediate marketing. He has been exposed by historian Rien Fertel as a person who has not only documented Creole cuisine and proposed the term Creole Cuisine, but who included in his book many other recipes which were lifted verbatim from other published cookbooks. Because Hearn did not comment on the inclusion of these "borrowed" recipes, it is impossible for one to know today whether these "borrowed" recipes were included because they were recipes of American food actually eaten regularly in New Orleans or simply included as filler. This unanswered question is one of the dangers of reading cookbooks as historical documents. We can only speculate about the answers to the questions. In a similar fashion, the Christian Woman's Exchange cookbook also contained additional recipes that are clearly not Creole, but American. The city had been American for almost three-quarters of a century at the time that these cookbooks were published, making it very hard to interpret their presence in Creole cookbooks.

The various versions of *The Picayune Creole Cook Book*, which was first published in 1901, reflect the racism of the day, while acknowledging just how much of the daily food preparation was done by African Americans. *The Picayune Creole Cook Book* was first written in the old style of very short and often unmeasured lists of ingredients with a brief description of the instructions. It is sometimes difficult to know when reading the recipes whether the expectation that the reader will know certain universal basics mean that they are not included (because mentioning them is unnecessary) or are not applicable. Roux, for example, is not included as an element of each gumbo recipe. But it is included in some. This leads to the conclusion that because it was sometimes mentioned, not mentioning it was intentional. Assuming that this conclusion is true a reading of *The Picayune Creole Cook Book* makes it clear that roux, as the fundamental building block of early Creole food, is one of the precepts that is unsupported by a reading of the early *Picayune Cook Books*. But that does not mean that it is not fundamental today.

An interesting example of how cookbooks create myth—as opposed to disprove them as in the roux example—is the statement in a version of the *Picayune Cook Book*, pointed out by historian, Ashley Young, in which the book asserts that it was the Spanish aristocracy who brought certain practices to the Creole table 150 years prior to the publication of the cookbook. That was also prior to the arrival of the Spanish in New Orleans. But historical accuracy is of no matter in mythmaking.

Later cookbooks written by insiders, meaning people from New Orleans, often contain expository material about the history of the cuisine or of the author's sources of recipes. The cookbooks of Natalie Scott, written in the late 1920s to 1930s, credit African Americans with being the real Creole cooks. White women had black cooks. She implies that black women learned to cook from the French and Spanish and now cooked with a kind of magical talent. There does not seem to be much explanation about what aspects of the food might be French or Spanish. A cookbook, after all, does not purport to be an accurate descriptive recorder of history. Its accuracy may be found in the recipes themselves, although even that may be questionable. Rather the descriptions of history may reflect the author's beliefs about the subject or be part of the creation of the story that the author wishes to promulgate.

In the middle of the twentieth century the cookbooks wove the tale of the French influence over the development of the cuisine of the city. This influence was not described as an attitude toward the table, but an actual reshaping of familiar French dishes into Creole dishes by the simple substitution of ingredients. The stories also romanticize the French—and sometimes the Spanish—aristocracy that in the cookbook version of history supposedly came to settle in New Orleans. They are said to have brought with them high taste and generally influenced society, including the cuisine. These cookbooks also romanticize happy slaves who added magical touches to the aristocratic dishes. The Native Americans are only recognized for contributing filé. It is interesting that the Madame Langlois creation story credits the

Native Americans for contributing raw ingredients and techniques as inter-preted through a French woman. Later stories talk about high taste that was established by aristocrats and take the raw ingredients and the preparation of the dishes for granted.

The updated versions of this tale of aristocracy are found in the documen-tation of African American recipes by white cookbook authors. Here the writers of the cookbook version of the history of New Orleans cuisine can tell the story that they wish to be true, where the descendants of the white French aristocrats have taught their African American cooks how to make the appropriate dishes, and then the authors are presenting the recipes that were invented by the white women and prepared by their black cooks. This mythmaking is built on an even more revisionist version of the history of New Orleans than the story of Madame Langlois. But it takes the story to a new level of romance. Although there was clearly French influence in the city, the bevy of French aristocrats who are referenced did not exist in the city. All of this myth building was also influenced by more general mythology about New Orleans, which has an international romantic reputation.

Giacomo Puccini's opera, *Manon Lescaut*, was also based on the mystery and fascination with New Orleans. The opera was taken from the novel by Abbé Prévost, *L'histoire du chevalier des Grieux et de Manon Lescaut*, written in 1731, when New Orleans was only recently established. Prévost's story is based on the practice of forced deportation of disreputable men and women to the French colony of Louisiana. The first production of Puccini's *Manon* was in 1893. The story, which was based on the lawless and wild place that was New Orleans, was also made into an opera by Jules Massenet and yet another opera was written by Daniel Auber. Clearly there was a European fascination with the city, however misinformed. The climax of the story has Manon and her lover die of thirst in the Louisiana desert. *Manon* certainly underscores the ignorance and fascination of the French of the real New Orleans—it was just a foreign land where bad girls could be sent.

Although not about food, *Naughty Marietta*, by Victor Herbert (first per-formed in 1910), reflected some of the romantic American rewriting of the history of New Orleans. It was revived several times in New York. The story, set in 1780, is based on a princess (Marietta) who travels to New Orleans as a casket girl and falls in love with a ship's captain. The operetta was produced as a movie that was released in 1935. The operetta was produced on televi-sion in 1955. This Marietta was clearly not one of the casket girls who was instructed by Madame Langlois. Although a state for almost one hundred years when the operetta was first performed, New Orleans was obviously still seen as an exotic location in America.

The culinary myths reveal the desire of the people of the city to recognize the transition of the colonists from their old ways of cooking using their old world ingredients to the new foods and dishes of New Orleans causing their transformation into New Orleanians. The myths also reflect a desire to derive a special transformative power from the production of, or control of, food. That power could reflect the Catholic city's belief in the transformative power of the host bread, which unites Catholics and Creole food, which creates and unites New Orleanians. Or perhaps it is the power to obtain freedom. For example, much has been made of the stories of Africans who bought their freedom from having saved enough money from the sale of calas or other foods. It is likely that some people were able to use this entrepreneurial method to obtain freedom. But it is certainly an exaggeration to expect that every slave who sold calas was able to obtain her own freedom and that of her family. The story does give comfort and hope that there was a way out of enslavement and a path of self-determination, however. It is also an indication of the belief in the strength of food.

The existence of the mythology about the origin and the power of the food of New Orleans does reflect two truths—that the people of the city believe that a cuisine exists and that it has real power. The reality of the cuisine as a body of dishes and techniques and tastes that unites the city begs the question of why it developed. It can be argued that it was the continued relationship between New Orleans and Paris until the twentieth century that allowed this cuisine to evolve. Although there was a time lag, New Orleans evolved a cuisine and a restaurant culture that paralleled those developments in Paris. The attitudes of the French Enlightenment that made eating and cooking important art forms, that took exquisite eating out of the exclusive realms of the nobility and allowed restaurants and the commerce of cooking to develop, and that allowed New Orleanians to let the food of New Orleans evolve into what it could and can become all made the development of a cuisine possible.

This statement does not overlook the real contributions of the enslaved Africans and Native Americans, and later the African Americans who cooked in homes and in restaurants, putting their food on the tables of the entire city. Regardless of who prepared the food it was interpreted through French eyes and stomachs, and after the French, through white American eyes and stomachs. It was the white American, for the most part, writing the cookbooks and the history—white Americans often with French heritage and sensibilities. They owned the restaurants and wrote the food columns, maintained the written records about parties, and recognized and took credit for the excellence of their cooks. The interpretation that they gave to the food and the expectations that they had at the table, were fundamental to how we see the cuisine of New Orleans today. They did not invent the dishes, but they did interpret them.

It was the white Americans, especially those of French descent, who in the mid-twentieth century told yet another story of the development of Creole cuisine. In this version and its variations French aristocrats and their chefs fled France during the French Revolution and came to New Orleans where they invented Creole cuisine. It is an example of mythmaking that describes a situation that flatters the tellers. The real story of the development of the cuisine of New Orleans is much more complex and interesting than this particular myth. Not being able to leave out the obvious contributions of African Americans, a variation of the cooks of the French Revolution myth usually includes the magical or voodoo powers of African American cooks to add that certain something to the food. The city continues for use many French names for its dishes and has many continuing ties to France.

Unlike other places in the Americas that also had Europeans, including French, African, and Native Americans present during the colonial period, the very French ties of the colony allowed the colonists to not only substitute ingredients from the Old World with New World ingredients, but to let them evolve into a New World food. Being a part of the Republic of Letters meant that French Enlightenment approaches to living were adopted in New Orleans. New Orleans remained a part of France in the minds of the citizenry regardless of Spanish governance or of American statehood.

That means that what happened in New Orleans was different enough from the rest of the colonies that had French inhabitants to have made a huge cultural difference. For example, a simple transference, the praline, which began as a sugar-covered almond in Paris, could become a sugar-covered pecan to the French in the New World. This is what happened in Charleston where almonds were not easy to find. There the evolution stopped. The sweetmeat remained as close to the motherland praline as the conditions allowed. In New Orleans the praline continued to evolve into a caramelized sugar candy with pecans. It is said that the New Orleans praline is really a completely new invention and not an evolution. The people of power in Charleston stopped the evolution by demanding the same dish, time after time. Today a praline in Charleston is still a sugar-covered pecan. These people were primarily of English descent and even the French were influenced by the desire to emulate the food of the homeland. The people who held power in New Orleans allowed the candy to change. Allowing the continuing change represents the French influence and attitude. It is this French attitude born in the French Enlightenment that set the stage for the development of the cuisine. The transformation of the food into a cuisine was allowed to happen.

The attitudes taken originally from the French Enlightenment continued beyond the ties to Paris and became part of the cultural mores of the city. These cultural mores allowed the food of New Orleans to keep changing, while allowing the changes to continue to represent the Frenchness, now the New Orleanian-ness of the cuisine. Thus the influx of Italians around the turn of the twentieth century, the Vietnamese in the 1970s, and the Cajun food expansion of the 1980s also continued naturally and organically to influence the food of New Orleans. Although beyond the Creole period it is part of the evolving Creole cuisine.

In spite of all of the looking backward for explanations, the food of the city of New Orleans is essentially a forward-looking thing. That ability to keep changing is what has kept the cuisine a living cuisine, not an ossified one. Tourists today can eat Creole cuisine that reflects the modern world, but that recognizes the traditional world. By looking forward the cuisine remains authentic and exciting even as it evolves.

A Living Cuisine

The food of New Orleans has grown into a source of cultural identity and pride. Regardless of when that started and how it started, by the twentieth century such an identity was firmly in place. The cuisine was not static. As concentrated waves of immigrants moved into the city, the citizens slowly made a place at the table for the new culinary influences. That meant that the basic cuisine had to be flexible, assimilating the new foods. That also meant that the cuisine was vibrant and strong enough to simply expand and change. This ability to absorb new flavor ideas is a sign of a vigorous living cuisine.

The Sicilian immigrants who came to New Orleans at the end of the nineteenth century and into the beginning of the twentieth century brought an influx of people who possessed Old World skills—they were butchers, farmers, and grocers. Besides moving to the land around New Orleans to begin growing produce, they moved into French Quarter and Tremé; they began to work at the French Market and the other municipal markets; and they opened groceries, fruit and vegetable stands, and restaurants. In other words it was another group of people for whom food was central to identity. The Sicilians expanded the use of the tomato, especially canned tomatoes, in Creole cuisine. The muffaletta heavy with olive salad, snoballs, and red gravy made their way into the cuisine of the city. As years go by the separate identity of the contributions of the Sicilians are blurred as have been the past separate contributions of other groups—all part of creating a seamless cuisine.

In 1939 the *WPA Guide to New Orleans* was published. It was a part of the WPA series of guides published to encourage travel and to put writers to work after the Great Depression. The book, published just a shade more than fifty years after the publication of Hearn's *La Cuisine Creole* and half way between the two World's Fairs, refers to the cuisine of the city, explaining typical dishes that tourists might expect. The chapter refers to the food as Creole cuisine. By then the word Creole applied as a modifier of cuisine to describe the food of New Orleans was firmly established. Yet a reading of this chapter of the guide reveals that the writers believed that most tourists would be unprepared for the cuisine and might find it unusual. The food was not typical American fare. It was considered so distinct that there were recipes included in the guidebook. The food was described as an attraction equivalent to the other attractions of the city like architecture and music. This book reflected the recognition that people who traveled to New Orleans did so in part to experience the city's unique food.

In 1984, just one hundred years after the World Cotton Exposition (1884) which brought with it the recognition of Creole cuisine, there was another World's Fair in New Orleans, the Louisiana World Exposition. Besides all of the usual international and scientific exhibitions, there was a large Louisiana pavilion. In the Louisiana Pavilion were many booths of food vendors from around the state. The vendors from Cajun country serving crawfish bisque and boudin were mixed in with vendors selling Creole food like red beans and rice or pralines and those vendors from north Louisiana selling meat pies and also border barbeque. Travel and food writers from around the country who attended the fair knew that they were eating food from Louisiana in the Pavilion. And they were eating it in New Orleans. They didn't know the differences between Cajun and Creole food, and they were in town for too short of a stay to really learn the differences. Without a firm grasp of the state's geography and with too little time spent tasting and discerning, they saw all of the food as Cajun/Creole or Creole/Cajun. They were likely unaware of the differences in the history of Cajuns and Creoles. The names of the foods were all vaguely French. Some names, like gumbo and jambalaya, were the same. They wrote about the food that they had eaten when they were in New Orleans. They called it Cajun/Creole or Creole/Cajun food. To them it was the food of New Orleans. Those magazines disseminated this new labeling of the food of New Orleans.

Not too long before the 1984 World's Fair crawfish farming as a commercial enterprise had developed to the point where there was a reliable source of crawfish for restaurants in New Orleans. From the late 1970s not only in Cajun country, that is, western Louisiana, but also in New Orleans, crawfish could be found on restaurant menus on a regular basis. Previously crawfish were associated with Cajun food and when eaten in New Orleans it was usually in someone's home or only seasonally and rarely in restaurants. By the time the journalists arrived for the 1984 Fair, crawfish were readily available. Shortly before the fair, Paul Prudhomme, the Cajun chef, was transforming the menu at that very Creole restaurant, Commander's Palace. His tenure at Commander's and his transformation of its menu was well covered in the food press. His talent and charisma caused Cajun food to explode upon the consciousness of the country. In the 1980s he and his wife, Kay, opened K-Paul's on Chartres Street in the French Quarter, serving his brand of Louisiana cuisine—which caused a further conflation of Creole and Cajun. Actually his approach to food, while informed by both his Cajun roots and his experience in Creole kitchens, is entirely his own. He was perceived as a Cajun phenomenon. This confluence of events, the commercialization of crawfish farming and the rise of Paul Prudhomme, coupled with the co-located vendors in the Louisiana Pavilion made the confusion of Creole and Cajun almost inevitable.

In any event the expectations of tourists really changed after the World's Fair. They began to look for Cajun food in New Orleans. Restaurateurs were happy to accommodate them. Today Cajun-inspired food and Creole food are both available in New Orleans. Cajuns might argue that Cajun food is hardly available in the city at restaurants. Today the most prominent Cajun restaurant in New Orleans is Cochon, a James Beard award-winning restaurant. Donald Link and Stephen Stryjewski operate Cochon and sell Cajun charcuterie and small batch pickles in Cochon Butcher. (Cajuns would have difficulty saying that the food is not authentic, but they might complain that the setting is too fancy for real Cajun food.) Vacherie is a newcomer to the Cajun claim. The tourist can find many restaurants whose signage offers Cajun food within. In addition crawfish are widely available at many restaurants. But Cajuns would dispute an assertion that New Orleans is a Cajun food town. And Cajuns would assert that the so-called Cajun food served in New Orleans is served in a manner that is fussy and distinctly un-Cajun. Rather it is Cajun becoming Creolized.

The most recent waves of immigrants, the Vietnamese in the 1970s and the Latinos in late 2005 and 2006 after Hurricane Katrina, have made further inroads into the cuisine. Vietnamese poboys stand beside meatball poboys, roast beef poboys, and peacemakers, a poboy that is half fried oysters and half fried shrimp, in the poboy roster. Crawfish tacos and other

Mexican-inspired delights accompanied by Tony Chachere's seasoning and Crystal hot sauce are making their way onto Creole menus. Soon enough even these dishes will just become part of the canon, unrecognized as new and distinct elements.

New Orleanians still believe that their food is unique and important. They want the food to remain the same: unchanging. That is, unchanging from their nostalgic recollection of it. Each person considers his mother's gumbo or red beans or jambalaya to be the quintessential dish. Although not as extreme as other parts of the United States, the city is experiencing the same move toward everyday eating out in restaurants, eating take out, and using frozen and other convenience foods as the rest of the country. Although there was always a big restaurant culture for celebration, today even daily meals are eaten in restaurants. While certainly good for the restaurants, eating at restaurants instead of at home is making the tradition of home cooking fade. Although home cooking still happens, more and more it is restaurants that are the standard bearers of the tradition of Creole cuisine. There are restaurants that take this seriously, but it is a very limited bastion. The variety of the cuisine and the practices from high to low are just not all suitable for a restaurant menu. Some people worry that the decline in home cooking will mean the decline of Creole cuisine, specifically those dishes that are lowly or seasonal and not necessarily found on restaurant menus.

It is in Creole convenience foods and manufactured foods that rests hope for Creole cuisine. Just because people have less time to cook and use prepared foods and canned and packaged foods more than in the past, doesn't mean that they will choose pizza or a can of mushroom soup. Zatarain's, Blue Runner, Camellia, Bruce, Mam Papaul's, and Trappey's are some of the boxed and canned foods that reflect Creole tastes. Jars of ready-made roux are available in different degrees of darkness, making gumbos less time-consuming. Frozen okra makes gumbo available all year. Some chefs, notably Chef John Folse, make frozen Creole and Cajun entrees which can be prepared in the microwave. Blue Runner advertises that the home cooks can sauté their own onions and celery and green peppers, add that to the creamy-style cooked red beans they offer, and make the dish both personal and quick and convenient. The proliferation of these convenience foods is a good indication that the local taste for Creole food still persists despite the pervasive problem of the twenty-first century lack of time and the general American trend away from home cooking.

CHAPTER TWO

~

The Material Resources

The environment in which New Orleans sits is very wet: the city is surrounded by a river and by a brackish estuary. The city is located at a semitropical latitude. There is heat during much of the year, but there is also rain and sun and serious humidity. The vegetation is lush. The insects, the animals, the fish are abundant. The ground is soggy. Rock and stone are scarce. Storms and flooding are a constant threat as seen throughout its past and still exists in the present. All of these elements affect not only the food that is available locally, but also what can be brought to the city from the rest of the world. The food of New Orleans is both local and international.

The city of New Orleans is almost completely surrounded by water. The original city was built on a ridge that was created over the millennia as the Mississippi flooded its banks and deposited silt that gradually raised the level of the land. The city has flooded many times over the nearly three hundred years since it was founded. The food supply is profoundly influenced by the various types of bodies of water that surround the city: river, estuary, marsh, sea.

Even more than the everyday topography, the city is catastrophically influenced by the weather. The atmosphere is damp and humid, made even more oppressive by the heat. There is rain, sometimes gentle afternoon rains and sometimes torrential downpours causing street flooding. And, of course, there are hurricanes, where wind and rain and sea combine to destroy as well as renew.

Steamboat on the Mississippi River. Lithograph, 1895. Courtesy of Library of Congress, LC-USZC4-9893.

The Mississippi River

The river begins in Minnesota and grows as it approaches the Gulf of Mexico through more than 2,500 miles gathering the watershed of thirty-one states and part of Canada. The early native peoples who lived in this watershed were the Mound Builders. Not much is known about them. They built a complex society with their own unique social system not founded upon traditional European agricultural models. A mound in Louisiana at Poverty Point is considered one of the earliest mound sites. It is a reflection of the work of a civilization that is dated from approximately 2200 BCE to 700 BCE. The presence of this mound and many others shows how widely spread the mound builders were and how complex the civilization was. Such earthworks would only be possible to build in a complex, hierarchical society. Archeologists have suggested that the villages extended for miles on either side of the Mississippi River. Archeological excavation has revealed stone vessels, pottery, and cooking balls of clay. Heated cooking balls of various sizes could be placed into pits with food to provide the heat for cooking. The temperature could be controlled by the number and size of the balls used.

The waters of the Mississippi River have formed a meandering path south toward the Gulf of Mexico. The river, which regularly overflowed its banks, deposited silt that made the floodplains intensely fertile agricultural lands. In a pattern which is typical of alluvial accretion, the largest particles of silt were first deposited close to the banks when the river overflowed. The smaller particles of silt were carried farther during the regular spring floods. Because of the herbaceous growth along the river, silt was caught in the weeds. This silting activity left the area along the river at a higher elevation than the land farther from the water. If a fissure occurred in the natural levees that formed, the rivulet that made its way through this fissure during flooding would create its own mini-levees. As the river changed its course these mini-levees became high ground. These areas are now called River Ridge, Gentilly Ridge, Metairie Ridge, and Esplanade Ridge. The portage between Bayou St. John and the river was along the Esplanade Ridge. Farms established under the French system of *métairie* were located along and near the Metairie Ridge, another Native American trail. The system of *métairie* was a form of tenancy in which the tenant shared a portion of the crop with the landlord. (Some form of sharecropping continued in this area until a streetcar was established along Metairie Road in the early twentieth century, encouraging urbanization.)

When the Europeans began to colonize the area, they found a rich agricultural land. The river formed a highway for the early trappers and the Native Americans to trade with the city, to bring the ducks and venison and other game to market for sale to Europeans. The river was a source of fresh water fish and shrimp. The early Native American market was located at the curve of the river near where the current French Market stands.

As the United States developed and the settlement both upriver and to the west of the river increased, the river became an even more important highway. Before the invention of the reliable steam engine by James Watt, and the creation of the Mississippi steamboats by Robert Fulton, barges made their way down the river, transporting the bounty of the agricultural lands of the Midwest to the port. This made the foodstuffs grown to the north readily available in New Orleans, for example, grains like wheat or dairy products or fruits and vegetables. Considering the wide basin drained by the river, during the nineteenth century the foods from all over the country were available in New Orleans, not just the foods locally grown or collected. This increased the sophistication of the table of those in New Orleans. Those tables were already full of the local cuisine. The Americans began to trade with New Orleans, especially after Louisiana statehood in 1812, coinciding with the appearance of the steamboats.

In the beginning of the city's history, although the port was apparent, it was not always an easy place to which to sail. Because of the winds' directions and the currents, the trip from the Caribbean to New Orleans was a long one. But the port must be credited for the import of early foodstuffs to New Orleans including wine, Madeira, flour, and also books, tracts, and newspapers reflecting the thinking of the French as the food of France, especially Paris, began to develop into the internationally famous cuisine that certainly did not exist when the city of New Orleans was established. The tracts of the French Enlightenment—also brought by these same vessels—influenced the people of New Orleans and the people in the French Caribbean, not only as the French approached their own revolutions, but as they approached the arts. The arts included the art of gastronomy. The table was a stage.

The river was a two-way street. Not only was food sent down the river, but the river became a way for the food of New Orleans to spread. This was especially true after the introduction of the steam engine. By the early nineteenth century there were steamboats steaming up and down the river, using the port. Before the steamboats, flatboats were used to carry cargo down the river.

Steamboats could travel easily upriver, carrying not only travelers and gamblers, but also the food of New Orleans. The traveler came in several forms. The food of the city was directly served to those who boarded in New Orleans and ate on the boats after the boats were outfitted in New Orleans by ship's chandlers, making their way up the river. But those who traveled downriver to New Orleans ate in the city, returned home, and brought home stories about and a taste for the food back to the Midwest.

To facilitate shipping on the river there was dredging. Various canals to enhance navigation have been built ever since the settlement of the city. The Carondelet Canal was built in 1794 and the New Basin Canal in 1838. These two early canals were later filled, although their names still serve as geographic references in the city in the form of street names. About a century later the still functioning Industrial Canal was built in 1923 and during the 1960s the Mississippi River-Gulf Outlet Canal, or MR-GO. MR-GO figured large in the flooding after Hurricane Katrina. After a great deal of political discussion MR-GO is being allowed to silt itself in.

The canals represent the conflict of living in a city surrounded by water. The man-made waterways create a way for the economy to be efficiently benefitted, but they also create a mechanism for the unwanted incursion of water from storm surges. Sometimes one form of flooding is traded for another. The very same levees which can keep out water can also keep it in. Mark Twain wrote about the food of New Orleans, letting even more people know about the connection between the river and the city. In 1884 he stated, "New Orleans food is as delicious as the less criminal forms of sin." It was Twain who documented the wild Mississippi River, so full of adventure and danger. He described it as a book that changed its story daily. By the 1880s the US River Commission had changed the river. It was becoming mastered for navigation. The river was controlled by dams and levees and much of the shore was defined by pilings and stones. The hazardous turns were lighted and some of the danger was removed from the journey.

The work of the commission has been taken over by the US Army Corps of Engineers, which continues to control the river with locks, with canals, with dredging, and miles of docks. This activity, beginning with the commission's work, began to affect the accrual of land in the wetlands. Intentionally or not, the work of the commission and its successor, the Corps, began to change the geography of the wetlands and thereby changed the environment that had nurtured the seafood of the Gulf of Mexico for millennia. The changes were small at first, but over the years so many square miles have been lost that not only has the spawning habitat for many species been diminished, but the protection against hurricanes has also been diminished. The environment for oysters has been negatively impacted, with the level of salinity making life for oysters less supportable. Shrimp that need brackish and fresh water at different times in their life cycles are finding the window of each type of water to be less reliable. The small islands, the marsh grasses and the shallows are greatly affected by changes in the river and in turn those changes in the environment threaten the food that grows there. This in turn affects turtles, waterfowl, aquatic mammals, and the entire food chain and ecosystem.

The river traffic also created the increased importance of the Port of New Orleans as a gateway to and from America, especially Latin America, across the Gulf of Mexico. Early in its history the port was an entry point for the coffee that began in the Caribbean and spread to Brazil and Central America. After entering the port, coffee was sent upriver and across the continent. With the increase in the port's activity and the spread of American business came the increase in the importance of the port for the importation of the fruit grown on the plantations of the United Fruit Company and the other companies of the twentieth century. The United Fruit Company meant the importation of bananas through New Orleans. Although they were distributed throughout the United States, many of them were eaten in

New Orleans. One of the recipes that spread around the country and which has become synonymous with the city is Bananas Foster.

The recipe for Bananas Foster was created at Brennan's Restaurant. In 1951 noted Chef Paul Blangé created the dish, and restaurateur Owen Brennan named it for Richard Foster. Foster was the owner of Foster Awning Company, as well as a civic leader and friend of Brennan and regular patron of the restaurant. The dish represents New Orleans in that it uses bananas brought in from the port, rum made from sugar cane, Louisiana citrus, and it is flamed. That French tradition of flaming is echoed in other dishes like Café Brûlot. This self-conscious use of Louisiana ingredients, reflecting the culinary assets of the city, is not unusual. It reflects the pride of the city in is gastronomic heritage.

The river was a sugar highway. In the beginning of the twentieth century with the establishment of the sugar refinery at Arabi, Louisiana, on the river just a few miles south of New Orleans, the river carried the newly made white granulated sugar. After the North American Free Trade Agreement (NAFTA) the port also received raw sugar from Mexico for refining.

After the port of New Orleans welcomed coffee to the city, New Orleans became a major roasting city, a site for major grinding and packaging and final distribution around the country. Eventually New Orleans became the second largest coffee port, after New York. It became known as the "logical port" because, given that so much coffee came from South America and Central America, it was geographically logical to use the port of New Orleans. Even today people passing through certain parts of the city are engulfed with the aroma of tons of roasting coffee and major companies like Folgers, Reily Foods (distributors of Luzianne, CDM, and French Market brand), and many smaller roasters.

Lake Pontchartrain

Lake Pontchartrain lies north of New Orleans. After the Great Salt Lake, it is the largest body of salt or brackish water in the United States. It is an estuary of over 600 square miles and is relatively shallow, averaging under 15 feet. It is fed by a fresh water lake, Lake Maurepas, and by salt water from the Gulf of Mexico through the Rigolets. It also receives fresh water from a number of rivers, namely the Amite, the Tickfaw, the Tangipahoa, and the Tchefuncte. Although the estuary—Lake Pontchartrain—is not a true lake, it is called a lake by residents. The waters are a source of crabs, shrimp, clams, and finfish. Pelicans, gulls, and other birds abound.

Depending on one's destination, Lake Pontchartrain, the great tidal basin, was a relatively safe route between the Gulf of Mexico and the Mississippi

River. Today it is connected to the river by the Industrial Canal. There is also a spillway, the Bonnet Carré Spillway, controlled by locks that allow the Mississippi River water level to be controlled during high periods, diverting water to the lake and the spillway.

Bayou St. John

Bayou Saint-Jean was once a body of water into which much of the swampy sections surrounding New Orleans drained. The bayou further drained into Lake Pontchartrain. At the time of the founding of the city the bayou was a large body with tributaries throughout what is now the city. Depending on the season and the rainfall the bayou was larger or smaller, being smaller in the drier parts of the year. The bayou served as a part of the Native American connection between Lake Pontchartrain and the Mississippi River. The connection continued as a land portage from the bayou to the river, where the city was founded. The portage followed along the ridge of what is now Esplanade Avenue.

At one time the bayou attracted wild fowl and was a source of otters and other water mammals, catfish, and alligators. It was a source of reeds for

Bayou Saint John at Lake Pontchartrain, c. 1934. Courtesy of Library of Congress.

baskets and tubers. It was important in the portage trail, but also a source of food.

Gradually the tributaries of the bayou were filled in as the city grew and the navigational use of the bayou declined. Drawings of the bayou from the time of the early city show a huge navigable waterway. In the mid-nineteenth century the bayou was drained and turned into a decorative water feature in the city adjacent to the City Park, but without even recreational purpose. During the Works Progress Administration in the 1930s, the bayou, greatly reduced in size by this time, was cleaned up. Currently ducks and geese can be seen floating on the bayou in the same way that they float on the shallow lagoons in City Park. The bayou no longer contributes to the foodways of the city.

The Gulf of Mexico

The Gulf of Mexico is an extremely important body of water. It defines the coastal areas of Louisiana, the fishing way of life, and the access to shipping from the Mississippi River. Just as a matter of supporting shipping was a method of bringing foodstuffs from Europe and Africa to New Orleans, it also allowed food from New Orleans to travel to Europe and Africa. The Gulf of Mexico is much more than just water to support shipping.

The Gulf receives water from more than thirty states and more than thirty major rivers. The rocks and silt from much of the country make their way into the Gulf. This dumps nutrients into the water attracting plankton. The area close to the shore is relatively shallow because of the continental shelf. This shallow water over the continental shelf is enriched by cool water from the deeper portions of the Gulf. This cooler water encourages the growth of plankton, which in turn attracts fish and shrimp.

The Gulf Stream, a strong warm Atlantic current, begins in the Gulf. With the current, it brings fish from the Gulf into the Atlantic making the Gulf an important spawning ground for Atlantic fish. Besides these fish, the Gulf is a source of redfish, tuna, amberjack, and many other finfish. In addition the marshes along the shore of parts of the Gulf provide the haven of brackish water and the Gulf salt water, which are conditions necessary for certain types of shrimp. Several species of shrimp can be found in the Gulf, spawning at different times of the year depending on salinity conditions. The Gulf also is a source of crabs, clams, squid, and oysters. The Gulf teems with animals such as several species of sea turtles, several species of whales, more than one hundred species of coastal birds, dolphins, manatees, sharks, and swordfish.

The Basin and the Swamps

It was the special environment that was created by the combination of the Gulf of Mexico, the swamps, and the basins and bays along the coast that allowed the smuggling and piracy to thrive. The smuggling began as a way to survive in the early French colony. The practice of smuggling was well established by the time the Spanish took over the colony of New Orleans. The first Spanish governor was ousted in part because he would not turn a blind eye to the smuggling. The first successful Spanish governor, Alejandro O'Reilly, was one who did countenance the smuggling. By the time that Jean Lafitte and his older brother Pierre came on the scene, smuggling and piracy were recognized forms of commerce.

These activities were nominally illegal. Those who conducted these activities were rogues and criminals. But they provided a vital service for New Orleans, ensuring that necessary goods made their way to the city. Their work was supported by and welcomed by the citizens of the city. The Lafittes (alternately spelled Laffite) operated a complete operation, smuggling and distributing what was smuggled. Jean Lafitte maintained a warehouse in New Orleans where the booty was stored. They were in operation at the end of the eighteenth century and into the nineteenth, seeing the Louisiana Purchase and statehood. Ever the Puritans, the Americans tried to gain control over the smuggling business and enacted the Embargo Act of 1807.

The Lafittes moved to Barataria Bay to circumvent the scrutiny of the American federal government after the passage of the act, which did not allow American ships to dock in foreign ports. Looking at a map the small island in the Barataria was partially hidden by the barrier islands, Grand Isle, and Grande Terre. The ships could dock at the Lafitte island, the goods transferred to pirogues (shallow draft boats that could be navigated through the bayous and swamps), and the goods distributed through channels to New Orleans. The operation continued to grow in infrastructure so that a serious port developed on the island. It became more and more open and notorious as sailors made their way to the port. Eventually merchants themselves traveled from New Orleans to Barataria for the regular auction held there.

The Lafittes expanded their operation to unlicensed piracy, which was initially lucrative, but which eventually caused the government to pursue the lawbreakers. The people of New Orleans, however, were happy to have the goods. The Lafittes were clever and had a reputation for fairness among thieves. The unmarqued privateers however were not paying customs duties to the American government, which caused the eventual downfall of the

Lafittes. It was ultimately a matter of money. Finally in 1814 the federal forces captured the majority of Lafitte's ships. In 1815 Jean Lafitte assisted in the defeat of the British at the Battle of New Orleans. He received a full pardon for this assistance. After receiving the pardon the Lafittes moved out of Louisiana into Texas. They colonized what is now the island of Galveston. It was these very waterways that were well traveled by smugglers that provided the entryway for the smuggling of rum into New Orleans from the Caribbean during the period of Prohibition. The lingering of Lafitte's exciting and swashbuckling reputation made the smuggling during Prohibition seem as necessary for the good order and identity of the people of New Orleans as had the previous activities of the pirate.

Climate

The hot and humid atmosphere of the area that became New Orleans contributed to the abundance of vegetation and wildlife, making food available. These conditions are not the most comfortable for people who arrive from other climates, but they do provide for bounty. New Orleans experiences much rain, but also adequate sunshine. Its latitude places it at a subtropical position, which means that many flora can thrive, even non-native species.

The water that surrounds the city makes the subtropical temperatures particularly humid. The water reflects the sun and warms the air above it, which contains water molecules. The water and the sun warm the air, and the humidity makes the temperature feel warmer than it is.

The city is also subject to west to east prevailing winds. This means that during winter the temperature constantly warms with a regularity of about every two weeks. Warm air from the Gulf of Mexico and continental cool air from the west compete to dominate the weather in New Orleans. All of this results in an approximately 280-day growing season. The temperature allows the city to support bananas and other tropical plantings, figs, and citrus trees. Even when it freezes, the roots of the vegetation are usually protected by warm earth, allowing the vegetation to recover after the cold season.

Rainfall in the city averages over sixty inches per year. Rainfall is heavier in the summer, with July as the month of average heaviest rainfall. The driest season is the fall. About 60 percent of the time there is sunshine in the fall. Most of the time the city is characterized as partly cloudy. The average number of sunny days in the year is a bit over 25 percent.

Because of the climate the city has had a difficult time with sanitation, drainage, and with certain mosquito-borne diseases. The climate has had a big effect on the architecture and the pace of the city. The uncomfortable summers, especially with the danger of yellow fever, caused those who could afford it to leave the city each summer. That meant that left in the city were those of lesser means and the enslaved. During this time the food of the city was prepared in the resettled locations, such as the areas north of Lake Pontchartrain and the Mississippi Gulf Coast, influencing those places and spreading the gospel of the food of New Orleans. Those who were temporarily resettled for the season were also influenced by the food of their temporary homes, which furthered the sophistication of the city's food.

Hurricane Katrina

The effects of the flooding that occurred in New Orleans after Hurricane Katrina must be mentioned in a discussion of the environment. Years of controls on the Mississippi River, the barrier islands, the prevention or control of the flooding of the Mississippi River, and larger and more numerous canals have created changes in the way that the land can absorb and reduce the intensity of hurricanes as they approach and pass over New Orleans. But Hurricane Katrina did not directly cause the flooding that inundated New Orleans and St. Bernard Parish, creating serious destruction and havoc in the area. The flooding was caused by the collapse of the walls of canals which had not been adequately maintained. (These canal walls are called levees, which can be confusing. This levee system is maintained by the US Army Corps of Engineers.) The levee system that surrounds and protects the city of New Orleans is managed by levee districts which are not federally governed. It was this local levee system which acted as the sides of a bowl, holding the floodwaters in the city. Those levees did not collapse. The result of the water, which remained in some parts of the city for up to three weeks before being completely pumped out of the city into Lake Pontchartrain, was that citrus groves outside of the city were ruined, grocery stores and houses were flooded, and the city was largely evacuated for at least six weeks.

The hurricane passed over New Orleans on August 29, 2005. (It was followed very quickly by Hurricane Rita on September 23, 2005.) The flooding that began after the hurricane had passed covered about 80 percent of the city and large parts of St. Bernard and Plaquemines parishes. The city was without power. There were more than a thousand deaths and unevacuated residents suffered severely from the flooding. Power was not restored until after the floodwaters were drained and then the power, water system, and gas lines were checked and repaired. When people returned to the city, even those whose homes had escaped the floodwaters, they found that their closed refrigerators, which had been full of food, were full of decomposed food. In many cases, seafood, meat, fruits, and vegetables had been left behind during evacuation with the expectation that people would return in a few days. Instead there was no electricity for weeks. The heat was the heat of a late New Orleans summer. The uncooled food simply deteriorated and liquefied. The seams of the walls of refrigerators were not designed for sitting liquid. In so many cases the putrefied liquid seeped into the walls of the refrigerators and was absorbed by the insulation. No amount of cleaning could remove the smell. The liquid in some cases corroded the gaskets and plastics in the refrigerators.

As people returned the accumulated wisdom from the first returnees spread to the new returnees. People eschewed the task of cleaning their refrigerators and merely duct taped them shut upon their return. These abandoned refrigerators were placed at the sidewalk in front of the house. While they sat there, the refrigerators became billboards for taggers who contributed colorful commentary about the refrigerators, as well as the attitudes of the returnees. There was a lot of anger against all levels of government expressed on these refrigerators. Eventually these refrigerators became a singular art form that included Christmas decorations and decals. In a place where food is so important, the sacrifice of the refrigerator and their transformation into a symbol of protest and anger is quite fitting. As a part of the overall cleanup, the refrigerators were picked up by hazmat-clad and -trained disposers and staged on a large neutral ground (a median) near Lake Pontchartrain. The refrigerators were treated as dangerous contaminants. After the disposal of the Freon in the appliances, they were ultimately removed and disposed of.

Before that happened the acres of refrigerators looked like a parody of the city's cemeteries. The citizenry began to call the area the refrigerator cemetery. Many photographers captured the tags and folk art decorations on these refrigerators on the street as well as in the cemetery. In the same vein of parody and satire, many people masqueraded as refrigerators during the Mardi Gras of 2006, the first opportunity to wear a costume publicly and poke fun at the same time. One group of maskers created the "Katrina Deli." This group, dressed as chefs, walked around the city pushing a moveable "deli" whose wares included a replica spoiled refrigerator, as well as such delicacies as "Bush baloney sandwiches" and "Pigs in a Blanco," all references to politicians who had disappointed the group in the post-flood environment. The "Katrina Deli" is now a part of the Hurricane Katrina exhibit at the Southern Food and Beverage Museum.

The flooding also had another personal effect on the food of the city, that is, it engendered in returning citizens a renewed sense of importance of food as a source of identity. The people from New Orleans and the surrounding area dispersed around the country during their evacuation were deprived of their food during that time. It was hard to find coffee and chicory, except in specialty stores. Filé was not available on every grocery store shelf. Camellia red beans were not available, only generic red kidney beans. When those hungry people returned to the city to reclaim their homes, they craved their food. It was basic to reestablishing their identity as New Orleanians. Many restaurateurs, whose own homes had flooded, re-opened their restaurants before even tackling their homes. Those cleaning out flood debris and ripping out drywall without a functioning kitchen were grateful to go to a restaurant after a day of work to eat familiar food and talk to others who had suffered a shared fate. Restaurants became beacons of culture and identity for returnees. The role of restaurants was recognized by the James Beard Foundation, which awarded its Humanitarian Award to the collective restaurants of New Orleans at its award ceremony in New York in 2006. Not only had the restaurants raised the flag for culture, but many restaurateurs stayed in the city and fed first responders. This was very important during the very first few days after the flood, before government was able to bring in supplies and potable water. Chefs on a national basis held fundraisers for the displaced restaurant workers all over the country. Many restaurants made it a policy to hire refugee wait staff and kitchen workers from New Orleans and the Gulf coast as their way to contribute.

The returnees to New Orleans and the surrounding area wanted traditional foods. Many of the national chain fast food restaurants that had dotted corners in the city did not return, because the demographics of the city no longer warranted such a large number of these restaurants. However, that void had the fortunate effect of allowing small family-owned restaurants to become established and in some cases reestablished without the competition of the national chains. These small family-owned restaurants mostly serve Creole food. This familiar food satisfied the needs and desires of locals. Locals flocked to the newly opened local restaurants, which have thrived since the city has begun to recover.

With 80 percent of the city under water, most inundated homes lost first floor kitchens and the cookbooks and recipe collections kept there. Judy Walker, food editor of the *Times Picayune*, the city's daily newspaper, was herself flooded with requests for recipes previously published in the food section of the paper. Walker, who is not from New Orleans, learned just how important specific recipes were to the cooking and eating population of the city. She has explained how many requests she received for recipes sought out to replace missing favorite recipes that had been part of the requestors' lost collections. People wanted to recreate their collections with now out-of-print books and recipes previously clipped from the newspaper. They were not content to merely buy new cookbooks. They wanted to resume cooking their favorites. This led Walker to write, with Marcelle Bienvenu, the James Beard Foundation–nominated cookbook, *Cooking Up a Storm*. It represents the collection of most often requested recipes that returning people had lost.

The Deepwater Horizon Oil Spill

Besides being a source of excellent fishing, the Gulf of Mexico is a body of water that is important in that it covers a seabed containing oil and gas. Some crude oil leaks naturally into the water from fissures in the floor of the Gulf. In 2010 there was a serious crude oil leak in the Gulf of Mexico that continued for approximately three months. It was caused by an accidental deadly explosion on the Deepwater Horizon oil rig which in turn caused a gusher on the Gulf floor. Eleven people were killed by the explosion. The wellhead was ultimately capped after several unsuccessful attempts. Before it was capped almost 5 million barrels of crude oil were released directly into the Gulf. Although British Petroleum, the primary operator of the Deepwater Horizon, attempted to clean up the Gulf and to prevent the oil from reaching the shore by using skimmers and containment booms, the amount of oil was overwhelming. There was serious immediate damage done to wildlife and fishing habitats, and the spill adversely affected tourism. In New Orleans the most direct effect of the oil spill was the immediate national concern about the safety of the seafood.

Although fishing and shrimping continued, there was a lack of confidence in the quality of the seafood. There were signs in seafood markets that popped up around the United States that proclaimed that the market's seafood was not from the Gulf of Mexico. The New Orleans restaurants and chefs, as well as the Louisiana Seafood Promotion and Marketing Board and the Commissioner of the Food and Drug Administration (FDA), tried to convince the public that the seafood was safe to eat. The people of New Orleans continued to eat seafood, but others in the country were afraid that the seafood was contaminated by petroleum. This drop in demand adversely affected the price of seafood, as well as made fishermen fear a permanent change in their way of life. While the scarcity of seafood after the spill had an inflationary effect on the price, there was also a fear that the scarcity might presage a serious long-term impact on seafood in the Gulf. Adult fish and shellfish were able to swim away from and under petroleum floating on the water, but it was unknown what sort of long-term effect there might be to developing fish and other seafood and how the entire food chain might be affected.

In an attempt to control the damage that could be done by the oil, chemical dispersants were used directly in the water, causing the oil to clump and sink. The long-term effect of the use of dispersants is another unknown element of uncertainty to the aftermath of the spill. It remains to be seen what the seafood supply will be like in the future. There has been speculation ranging from little or no effect to a catastrophic reduction in the ability of seafood to reproduce. Given that the Gulf of Mexico is the spawning ground for some Atlantic seafood, the damage is potentially very far-reaching.

One well-documented result of the oil spill is the damage to the coastal oyster beds. Unlike more mobile species, oysters cannot move to escape oil or to seek a more hospitable environment. The bayou and estuaries that are home to oyster beds are also home to other wildlife and important flora. To protect these bodies of water and the flora and fauna the state of Louisiana chose to divert fresh water from the Mississippi River into the bayous in an attempt to use the currents and force of the water to prevent the oil from making its way into the bayous and estuaries from the Gulf. This action caused the salinity level of the bayous to drop too low to support the oysters. They died. This has greatly affected the oyster industry in New Orleans. P & J Oysters, a company over a century old, had to lay off its cadre of shuckers. There were no oysters to shuck. Although Gulf oysters were still available from the far western Gulf—mainly off the Texas coast—many of the prime oyster beds were closed.

To deal with the tourists' lack of confidence, restaurant chefs, many of whom had lived through the flooding following Hurricane Katrina, began to search for substitute dishes for their menus. Many chefs were still very proud of Creole cuisine and were reluctant to import other fish, such as salmon, to serve on their menus. Chefs explored non-seafood traditional Creole dishes that had been off menus for years. Chicken livers, snails, and newly rediscovered beef preparations were at least temporarily offered instead of Gulf seafood. Today seafood has returned to restaurant menus. The long-term effect of the oil spill still remains to reveal itself in terms of the quantity of seafood available, taste, and general viability. At least local restaurants are obtaining a reliable supply of seafood.

CHAPTER THREE

~

The First Inhabitants and Their Foodways

The native people have lived in the area of the Mississippi Delta exploiting the land and the waters since prehistoric times. There is no written record, and what is known about them stems from a combination of oral histories and tales from modern Native Americans and the archeological record. The Europeans who explored and then colonized the area made observations about the native peoples and their habits. We do have that record.

The first wave of European documenters came with and shortly after Columbus in the late fifteenth century. Their journals and reports indicate that there were hundreds of thousands of inhabitants throughout the Mississippi Basin, who were both highly organized and lived in a hierarchical society. The second wave of Europeans, considered colonists, some two hundred years later in the case of New Orleans, found a decimated population with fewer and smaller organized villages. This difference in observation caused many historians to discount the early observations as either inaccurate observation or fantasy. However, this discrepancy has since been explained by the massive losses of lives caused by the diseases that were introduced to the New World by the European explorers. The reduced and scattered population of survivors in the New World did not have the numbers to maintain the previous complex and sophisticated societies. The two-hundred-year interim was not long enough to completely renew the population.

The study of the agricultural practices of the early Native Americans has established that certain foods, such as the sunflower, were definitely sown. This practice produced eligible seeds and roots, as well as attracted fowl and

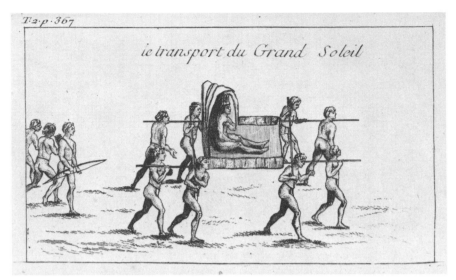

ie transport du Grand Soleil

Natchez porters transporting the tribal leader whom they worshipped as the sun. Etching from LePage, 1758. Courtesy of Library of Congress, LC-USZ62-115625.

other animals which could be captured. Later the more southern practices from what is now Mexico spread northward and the planting of the three sisters, squash, corn, and beans, was observed by the Europeans when they explored the southern part of North America, including the area that became New Orleans. They cooked food over fire and on hot rocks. They used filé (a powder made from ground sassafras leaves) as well as dried ground peppers, cooked cushaw (a squash), ate the young shoots of the sassafras tree, and ground squash seeds and nuts in their sauces and seasonings.

In addition to what could be directly cultivated, the Native Americans also manipulated the landscape to encourage the growth of native plants, which they harvested without the use of traditional European agriculture. Plantings were not carried out in straight rows and several plants were planted together, sometimes with the taller plants sheltering the shorter ones. Native Americans often hunted by using fire to create circles around their prey which trapped them. They could trap bears as well as alligators in this manner. They also managed the environment in such a way as to attract and hunt animals that they ate for meat, such as deer and bear. When the Spanish explored the region in 1519, they noted many settlements in the area around the Mobile River, as well as what they described, as towns. They recorded that the native peoples planted and cleared and moved plants and animals from one location to another. Cornfields in the forests were recorded in the journals. The three sisters of corn, squash, and beans were planted in clusters so that the vines of the beans could be supported by the corn and the squash could be shaded by the corn.

The environment in which the Amerindians lived in the area that was to become New Orleans was covered by more water and swampy area than we see today. The Native Americans lived around what is now New Orleans. Today's landscape has been filled in to create more land and less swamp. The Native American agricultural practices were well adapted to the swampy environment, but they were not the simple hunter gatherers that have been traditionally defined by history. They actively planted dewberry patches and groves of pecan trees. They harvested sassafras trees for leaves and roots. The variety of foods of the New World that were available for harvest in and around what is now New Orleans indicates how native peoples were actively managing the land. They were eating a varied and healthful diet. Because the European observers failed to see agriculture as they practiced it, they did not recognize an agricultural plan that took advantage of nature, making the gathering (really harvesting) purposeful and not randomly dependent on luck. Besides the seafood, fowl, and wild animals harvested here, there were various greens, tubers, berries, persimmons, and other fruits, nuts, legumes, mushrooms, and roots.

French-Canadian explorer Pierre Le Moyne d'Iberville noted, when observing the location for the new city in the early 1700s, that bison grazed in what is now Jackson Square. The land was burned, and the grasses that grew up on the burned open field attracted the bison. There were also domesticated chickens being tended in the settlements and towns. The chickens, not native to the New World, had been left by the Spanish two hundred years earlier and had been incorporated into the agricultural practices and foodways of the native peoples.

The Native Americans dealt with the landscape's most dangerous threat and the one with the most potential to be life threatening—flooding—by creating mounds of dirt and clam shells. These mounds created protected areas which did not flood. In addition the mounds became areas of looser, more aerated soil, sometimes amended with shells, which supported the growth of vegetation, including certain trees, which were intentionally placed there and that could not thrive in the denser wetter soil of the region.

Mounds as a form of public works had another purpose which anthropologists are still debating. What the mound culture of the first Americans does tell us is that they possessed a degree of organization and permanent settlement that is not generally associated with hunter-gatherers. As writer Charles C. Mann points out in *1491*, the organization necessary to create the mounds required that those building the mounds must be fed by others.

Obviously the food must come from somewhere, even in those areas which had not adopted traditional agriculture. It required a level of planning for those who toiled for the common cause—mound building—in which obtaining food was organized for the common good and an intentional division of labor. It also required management of food sources that would result in a food supply which would provide sufficient food for all, not just the harvesters and hunters. All of this required planning and storage, methods of record keeping, and methods of distribution.

Mounds found at Poverty Point, Louisiana, are a part of the ancient mound culture. The archeological record from this period contains many clay cooking balls. These balls were heated and could be used in several ways. They came in several sizes. By heating these balls and placing them into liquid, the liquid could be heated. The number and size of the heated balls could be used to control temperature. Additionally, food could be buried in leaf-lined pits, covered with hot rocks, with the effect of a slow-cooking oven.

The Choctaw, Chickasaw, Natchez, Chitimacha, and other tribes populated the area by the middle of the last millennium. They collected and dried fruit and made hominy and grits from corn, processing the corn with lye formed from ashes. Like other New World natives, they grew, along with corn, the other two sisters—beans and squash. Their palates were quite varied and sophisticated. Their diets were dependent on the season, but they did preserve food. They dried meat (usually bison), like early tasso, to preserve it. Salt was manufactured for preserving and seasoning by evaporating sea water. Corn, tubers, and nuts could be stockpiled to be eaten in other seasons. They ate turkey and other wild birds. The French in first exploring and settling even noted figs and peaches in Native American settlements, indicating that they had adopted and naturalized these plants from the earlier Spanish explorers from a century and a half before.

The native peoples traded on a very widespread basis. This caused the movement of species from place to place, not just as goods already harvested, but as agricultural species. The Spanish also caused foods to be transported from other New World locations to the Gulf. Another consequence of the sixteenth-century Spanish contact was the importation of diseases. The number of native peoples was greatly reduced. This reduction in human population caused the bison to roam without control. It also allowed clearings to regrow. The landscape that the French colonists experienced in the early eighteenth century was not pristine, but to some degree it had reverted back to a natural state with the decrease in human population.

The often-repeated story, recorded by Antoine Le Page du Pratz, ethnographer and naturalist, in his journals in the eighteenth century, indicates the complete manner with which the Amerindians had mastered their environment. It is remarkable to the Europeans that they had done so, in part because the Europeans were having such difficulty adapting to the new environment. The female Native American slave that was taken by Le Page to prepare his food captured an alligator, laughing at Le Page's alarm and fear. The alligator formed a part of the diet of the Native Americans.

The native people tended and encouraged the oyster beds and roasted the harvested oysters, as well as ate them raw. Not only are they tasty, but the steam that is trapped in roasted oysters makes the shells pop open, making them easy to eat. Native Americans were cultivating, harvesting, and eating oysters when Europeans arrived. They harvested oysters using forked branches. Eventually forked branches were replaced with oyster rakes. Later European oyster fishermen harvested oysters to make a living. They took as many oysters as they could carry on their boats and sold them onshore to restaurants and markets. As did the Native Americans, early European, especially Basque and Croatian, oystermen protected the harvest from the sun under canopies of wet sacks or palmetto branches.

When the first French settlement was established in 1718 the people abandoned the settlement occasionally to go live with the Native Americans, when life in the settlement was unsupportable. The Native Americans were also generous in sharing their understanding of the landscape with the new and relatively helpless settlers. Because of the waterways, which were myriad, knowledge of the landscape shared by the Native Americans greatly helped the settlers safely find and exploit the resources that they needed.

The interplay between the French settlers and the Native Americans was crucial to the establishment of a cuisine in New Orleans. The French ate and eventually learned about the native foods, which had long been identified by the Native Americans, thereby not only keeping the early settlers alive, but also introducing the Europeans to foods without the long process of discovery. Thus even the earliest dishes discussed in journals and reports mention corn, oysters, and crawfish. The Native American practices and their knowledge of the available foods gave a kick-start to the cuisine and their hands touched much of the food of New Orleans.

CHAPTER FOUR

~

The Old World in the New

The first Old World inhabitants who settled in the area that became New Orleans were the French, the Spanish, the Germans, and the Africans. They were the people who established the foundation of a cuisine, along with the native peoples, which began the journey toward Creole cuisine. It is the children of these early immigrants who were the first Creoles, being born in la Nouvelle-Orleans. The food grew and changed with them. The practicality of the Germans in growing food, the intellectual explorations of the French, and the Spanish sense of order and control, which took the native ingredients and the assistance of the native peoples, established a unique staple of dishes. With time came increased trade—both legal and extra legal—and an expansion of the foods which were available, allowing the staple of dishes to evolve into a cuisine. Then later, as future chapters will explore, more waves of immigration brought additional creativity and flavors to the table.

The French

The area around the Mississippi River was explored by René-Robert Cavelier, sieur de La Salle. This expedition completed the explorations that had been undertaken by French explorers Jacques Marquette and Louis Jolliet in 1678, connecting the waters of the Great Lakes area to the Gulf of Mexico by way of the Mississippi River. Marquette and Jolliet traveled down the river, but not knowing how far it would go, turned back many miles before they reached the delta. La Salle completed this earlier exploration and claimed the area for France in 1682 naming the river St. Louis for Louis XIV. He named the entire area La Louisiane.

As the century began to turn Pierre La Moyne, Sieur d'Iberville, a fur trader born in Nouvelle-France (Canada), was sent to establish a colony at the mouth of the Mississippi River to protect the interests of France from the British. D'Iberville had become a wealthy man from his trading and from his exploits in Canada against the British. He was not financially sponsored by the French and the colony had to be funded by his own wealth. That left him free to establish his own means of profiting from the new colony under color of French law.

On March 3, 1699, d'Iberville camped east of the Mississippi River at what is now Bay St. Louis. He shared an evening with the Houma, who welcomed him to their village. This area was not an ideal location to establish a city. With d'Iberville's ease with Native Americans he learned much about the area, determining that the place where he established La Nouvelle-Orléans (New Orleans) contained a portage from a large estuary (Lake Pontchartrain) through a bayou (Bayou St. John) to the Mississippi River.

It was d'Iberville's younger brother, Bienville, who actually established the city in 1708. The area about Bayou St. John formed the earliest part of the city; the area which is now the French Quarter was established later. Having been established by Canadian fur traders, the settlements created by the Le Moyne brothers were populated by Canadian fur traders who trapped and sold their furs to make a living. They were a wild and unruly bunch who sought out the freedom that the free-wheeling village, independently colonized, offered. Shortly thereafter there were soldiers sent by France in the colony. The traders settled with the Native Americans. They also offered captured Native American women as slaves to the soldiers.

There was great poverty in France at this time, thus supply ships were not plentiful—coming to New Orleans less than once a year. Without supplies the people in the settlement relied upon Native Americans for survival, sometimes abandoning the settlement and later reassembling. This core group was greatly influenced by their contact with the Native Americans, including their culinary practices.

To populate the new colony, already a wild and libertine place without governmental support, the French government enlisted John Law. John Law, a Scotsman son of a goldsmith, took the private investment methods of the Le Moynes to a new level. Essentially John Law, with the blessings of the French government, turned the colony into a private corporation. Money was invested based on the predicted and promised return, rather than on measureable value of goods. The investment was secured by the value of the land of France, but purely on the speculation that income could be successfully generated. There was no accurate method established for actually valuing the land. In 1717 Law's Company of the West began to establish New Orleans at what is now the French Quarter. Traditional governmental functions were taken over by Law, who had the power to tax. Unfortunately there were no precious metals to be mined, so to make the investment profitable, Law understood that agriculture would have to make his fortune. Agriculture would require people.

At this time there were fewer than 250 people in New Orleans who were French speakers. Some were Canadians born in the New World. More than half of the French speakers were soldiers. Law was desperate to populate the area. A first group of colonists arrived in New Orleans in 1718. Many had made the trip, but few survived. A solution that was adopted was to send criminals, debtors, and other undesirables to the colony. Already a wild place, sending more people who already lived outside of the bounds of order only increased the wildness without creating wealth. Whether French vagabond or French Canadian trapper, the early settlers were ill equipped to care for themselves, let alone create a city in the swampy area where they settled.

When they first arrived, the French enslaved the native people, mostly women, who served as sex slaves and cooked food for the men. Both native slaves and the occasional Frenchman maintained gardens. The French also imported slaves from Africa, bringing in almost 6,000 people. The French men who arrived were generally from the city and were not acquainted with agricultural practices—European or otherwise. Nor were they practiced hunters, as the trappers from Canada were. The few French women in the colony were more likely to have been shanghaied from the street, than from a kitchen, and they were unskilled in domestic matters.

By the next decade there was a different story being told. Sister Marie Madeleine Hachard, an Ursuline nun, wrote a letter to her family in 1727. She had been sent to New Orleans to establish a girls' school. She wrote that she found delicacies of game and all manner of water birds. She ate seasonal fish, oysters, melons, watermelons, sweet potatoes, peaches, and figs. There were sufficient quantities for preserving. Citrus was abundant.

During this early time much contact with France was made through Saint-Domingue rather than directly with France. The Caribbean colony was becoming a successful commercial sugar producer, which meant that it was economically important. Influence from France was filtered through Saint-Domingue whose town Cap Français was the closest thing to a sophisticated French town that existed in the New World. France was not wealthy, but during this time it was still the foremost place of artistic imagination and philosophic exploration in Europe during the eighteenth century.

This was the formative period of the grand cuisine in France. La Varenne authored a book considered to be the first cookbook of modern French cuisine, *Le Cuisinier français*. So many recipes in New Orleans are roux-based that the phrase, "First you make a roux," is as meaningful in writing of recipes as "once upon a time" is in the telling of fairy tales. *Cuisinier François* contains a reference to roux, a cooked mixture of flour and fat. In 1667 la Varenne published *Le Parfait confiturier* (later issued as *Le Confiturier françois*), a book of pastries. Pastries were in smaller portions and even in single portion sizes. While this was happening, attitudes were permeating the people coming to New Orleans as well as those living in New Orleans.

Later in the century another chef, François Massiolot, wrote a cookbook, *Le Cuisinier roïal et bourgeois*, which was written with greater detail and its definitions are still considered as modern French dishes emerge. By the eighteenth century cuisine was considered one of the arts in France. It was talked about, discussed, and debated with the same degree of intensity and importance as what are considered the traditional arts of music, painting, sculpture, theater, and literature. Although the degree of artistic care being accorded to eating in Paris was probably much higher than could possibly be achieved by the small number of people in Saint-Domingue who continued to identify themselves as French, this colony was aware of French attitudes toward dining, as well as the other arts. There were newspapers and regular exchanges with France.

The French and people of French descent in both the Caribbean and New Orleans formed a part of the Republic of Letters that established a conduit for intellectual exchange between Europe and America, and for purposes of this discussion especially New Orleans and Paris, during the late seventeenth and eighteenth centuries. This was just the time of the formation of the city of New Orleans, and its internal moves toward civilizing itself, and the development of the cuisine of Paris. At a time when distant communication was conducted by letters, elaborated writings were exchanged between those who could read. They discussed the ideas of the day, new essays that had been published, and examined how those ideas could be put into practice. They copied and shared writings and ideas without ever meeting.

Part of the exchanges surely related to the essays of Jean-Jacques Rousseau, one of the *philosophes* of the French Enlightenment, who contributed to the philosophy of simplicity of the new French cuisine. During the revolutionary period the massive common table of the tavern where people ate whatever was set upon the table was being replaced by the restaurant. The restaurant was related to the café, but different. The restaurant allowed for individuality of choice—choice of both when and what was to be eaten. The restaurant allowed the diner to select only the amount desired instead of sharing in a groaning board and paying one fixed price. Eating something simple, like a perfect poached egg, allowed the delicate sensibilities to be satisfied and the spirit to appreciate simple perfection.

Two Frenchmen are credited with inventing culinary literature that is written in narrative form, as opposed to cookbooks. They explored taste, philosophy of eating as well as cooking, and created an atmosphere among readers that allowed for an appreciation of the work of chefs and cooks, both at home and in the developing restaurants. One of these writers, Jean Anthelme Brillat-Savarin, born in the mid-eighteenth century and a lawyer, penned *Physiologie du goût* (*The Physiology of Taste*) which was published in 1825. Although it was published in the nineteenth century, it was a culmination and a restatement of ideas that were fomenting in the previous century. His ideas and the expression of the art of eating and dining in prose made it possible for these ideas to spread from France to other French-speaking areas, even though he did not visit those French-speaking areas.

The Physiology of Taste has been compared with Montaigne's *Essays* and reflects the principles of the Enlightenment as they were understood in France. Despite the overblown style of the essays, Brillat-Savarin's work has been in print since it was first published. An English translation was undertaken by M. F. K. Fisher, the twentieth-century food writer. Brillat-Savarin's philosophy reflected his belief in refinement. Tasting and appreciating food was an art, as was cooking. He had no patience with those who overindulged, because their excess was not a reflection of refinement. He appreciated the simplest meal when it was well presented and excellently prepared.

The other influential voice was that of Alexandre Balthazar Laurent Grimod de La Reynière, also born in the mid-eighteenth century and also a lawyer. He was an essayist and explored the good life with gusto. He became a restaurant critic, inventing the genre, as restaurants developed in France into the modern institutions that we recognize today. He wrote *L'Almanach des gourmands* each year. There are eight volumes. These were published over several years in the early nineteenth century. He is credited with establishing the art of the table. Any exchanges of letters and journals between Saint-Domingue and France would surely have included some of these works, or at least the attitudes that these works reflected, as the plantation owners attempted to remain French in thought despite their remoteness.

Thus the two attitudes of the Enlightenment, simplicity and excess, Montaigne and Voltaire, Brillat-Savarin and Grimod, were communicated to

New Orleans at a time that New Orleans was establishing itself. All colonists in every location must eat. But the French were learning to eat as a form of art. This required that cooking also be an art. It meant that appreciating the simple and available foods, well presented by Native Americans and Africans, could and should be presented with refinement. The people should appreciate the food of the street and the food set upon china on a tablecloth. The city of New Orleans was still a rough place in the eighteenth century, with poor sanitation and muddy streets. It was also a place that erected the first opera house in America in 1796 on those muddy streets. The arts and the art of living were more worthy of effort than sanitation, certainly reflecting the influence of the French Enlightenment more than the English.

The Spanish

If we credit Spain with the discovery of the New World in 1492 by Christopher Columbus, we can credit Spain with the initiation of the Columbian Exchange—the world exchange of peoples, animals, and plants. This exchange brought destruction to the peoples of the Americas through diseases which their immune systems could not fight. It also had a more positive effect of establishing diversity of plants, animals, technology and thought. It is true that many New World products were brought back to Europe, and through European trade, found their way around the world—foods such as peppers, chocolate, tomatoes, and potatoes have had a major impact on the food and culture of the world. But for purposes of the explorations of this book, it is the food brought from the Old World to the New World, specifically to the area that is now New Orleans—whether European, Asian, or African—and food from within the New World introduced to different areas of the New World, in our case New Orleans, by European (mostly Spanish) exploration, that concern us. The Spanish explorers who explored the area of New Orleans and the Mississippi River were very early. In 1519 there was the explorer Alvarez de Pineda. Pánfilo de Narváez and Cabeza de Vaca and Luis de Moscoso followed. Hernando de Soto explored the Mississippi River in 1540.

The foods of the Columbian Exchange that came from Europe include pigs, chickens, figs, honey bees, and beef cattle. The Spanish were sure of their continued explorations, intentionally leaving pigs and chickens in the New World to feed subsequent visitors. Potatoes were brought north to North America by the Spanish from the area of what is now Peru by way of the Scotch-Irish from Europe. Coffee and okra came from Africa. Citrus, peaches, rice, and sugar cane came from Asia. Not all of the plants brought to the New World were successful in the beginning. For example, the conditions necessary to grow wheat were notably absent from the Caribbean Islands. By the time that la Nouvelle-Orléans was established in the early eighteenth century, pigs from earlier Spanish explorations were found feral in the woods around the settlement. Peach trees had become established and were being eaten by the Native Americans. It is speculated that as the number of people in the Americas decreased, the animals brought by the Spanish were able to flourish. They were not being hunted by the weakened population.

The Spanish brought plants to the New World for economic reasons. They desired to make their travels worthwhile by establishing plantations of monoculture which could supply them with desired crops. This monoculture approach to growing was also adopted by the French in both Saint-Domingue and New Orleans. Sugar was one of the first food crops grown in this manner. The resulting wealth that grew from the sale of sugar in Europe encouraged the monoculture practice by other colonizers. Laborers did not become wealthy from these practices. Thus these practices alone did not encourage colonists to resettle in the New World without other incentives including force.

While this exchange continues today—insects, invasive species, and germs still make their way around the world—the dramatic exchange which exploded on the world ecosystem in the aftermath of the discovery of America changed the world's eating habits forever.

Los Isleños

In the early fourteenth century what became the Canary Islands were explored and settled by the people of Iberia. In the fifteenth century the Canaries were the logical last point of land that those leaving Europe or Africa saw before arriving in the New World, being located at about one-third of the distance between Africa and the New World. The Spanish, as colonizers of the islands, used them as the door to introduce sugar cane and slavery to the Americas. The Spanish were ceded New Orleans and territories west of the Mississippi River by France in 1766 which made New Orleans a part of the larger New Spain. New Spain had been established by Pope Alexander VI, a Spanish pope, who issued papal bulls dividing the New World between Spain and Portugal.

The Spanish governed Louisiana, but had little interest in it. The first governor of the new Spanish colony of Nueva Orleans, Antonio de Ulloa, did not arrive until 1768, and he had with him only seventy-five soldiers. He was not accepted by the French and German colonists who did not welcome

Spanish rule. Ulloa was forced to leave the city during what was called the Louisiana Rebellion. The lack of support that accompanied Ulloa in his attempt to establish New Spain in New Orleans reflected the lack of interest in the city. Ulloa did not speak French, and he did not even have permission from the Spanish government to substitute the peso for the franc. More importantly Ulloa announced that he would not tolerate the smuggling in the city, which had become an important element in the previously rogue economy, nor would he allow continued trade with France. The colonists, who strongly identified themselves as French, could tolerate neither the termination of ties with France nor the imposition of order.

Those who read of the revolution and the works of the Enlightenment could appreciate the simplicity and individuality of life in the colony. In New Orleans eating was controlled by slaves, either the Native Americans or Africans. Although some food from France was available from infrequent ships, local ingredients and "foreign" techniques of the cooks became accepted as local food. To the colonists the local food became food and was not exotic or strange.

In 1769 the new governor, Alejandro O'Reilly, returned to the city with 2,000 troops. He crushed the rebellion by executing its leaders and thus established the Spanish takeover of New Orleans. Although he was successful in establishing Spanish rule, O'Reilly took a practical approach to governance. He allowed continuing trade, he did not impose the Spanish language on the people, and he permitted smuggling to continue. The Spanish had important colonies in the New World although New Orleans was not one of them. Puerto Rico established an important strategic position in the Caribbean which protected and controlled access to the Gulf of Mexico and the Spanish holdings in Mexico. New Orleans was not perceived as important in itself, and it was occupied by colonists who were not happy to be governed by the Spanish. But New Orleans gave the Spanish a buffer against the English to the east and north, protecting Mexico.

Although they did not send great numbers of colonists, mostly soldiers and members of the government, the Spanish imposed an order on the colony that allowed it to make small advances. In 1778 colonists began to arrive from the Canary Islands and continued to be sent to New Orleans until 1783. They did not settle in the city, but around the city to protect it from various points of invasion by the English. The settlement of San Bernardo, now located in the Parish of Saint Bernard, was a farming settlement. That group of farmers produced garlic, onions, potatoes, and poultry for sale in the city. The settlements in St. Bernard were located in an area which supported the growing of sugar cane. Plantations were amassed by growers who bought the land from the Isleños. Today the Domino Chalmette Sugar Refinery is located in St. Bernard Parish, right on the Mississippi River. It is the largest sugar refinery in the Western hemisphere and the second largest in the world. Currently the refinery receives raw sugar from Louisiana, Florida, Texas, and Mexico. Some of the Isleños population settled along the coast and fished. They are credited with fishing in deeper waters than had previously been the practice, thereby increasing the types of seafood that could be regularly obtained.

The Spanish established many important legal structures in the colony, while allowing the French culture of the city to continue. The Spanish amended the *Code Noir* (Black Code), for example, expanding opportunities for manumission, and brought other legal concepts. One important legal action of the Spanish was the creation of the public market. This public works project established a covered structure for the sale of food. The market was located close to the bend of the river where the French and Native Americans had traded. The law established prices and placed like foods together so that the comparison of goods was facilitated. The laws were intended to ensure that the food was wholesome and sanitary and to decrease the risk of fraud. The original building did not last and was rebuilt more than once during the years. This led to the eventual establishment of the market system throughout the New Orleans area.

The Canadian French and the Difference between Creole and Cajun

For a person who first visits New Orleans an important question about the food that is usually addressed early on is "What is the difference between Creole food and Cajun food?" The second question is how and why did Creole and Cajun become confused in the collective minds of the country. Finally, does this confusion really make a difference?

For people from the city, especially people born before 1970, the first question is a very important one; and it does make a difference. Creole food has a history that distinguishes it from Cajun food. The most important distinguishing feature is geography. Creole food developed and was eaten in and around New Orleans. The raw materials of Creole food are the foods that are found in and around New Orleans. Similarly Cajun food was the food from the area settled by the Acadians. "Cajun" is a corruption of the word Acadian. Of course it isn't that simple. It is not just a matter of geography. The people of New Orleans are proud of their cuisine, and they can recognize the differences between Creole and Cajun even when they cannot articulate the differences. They are quick to correct the confusion of the outsider who comes to New Orleans looking for Cajun food. New Orleans is the home of Creole food, not Cajun food. But today Cajun food can be found in New Orleans. There is no doubt that in this century and the end of the twentieth century, Cajun food has influenced what we think of and serve as Creole food. Most notable is the enormous increase in the eating of crawfish in New Orleans, both in the shell at informal meals, and fried and sauced. This influence has worked in the other direction also (Creole food having influenced Cajun food), although that is not the subject for this book. The mutual influences on these two types of food does make it harder to identify the differences, especially for the uninitiated.

To distinguish between Creole and Cajun food, it helps to define Cajun food—the better to see what Creole food is not. Cajun food arose in a more isolated area and in a more limited time span. It spilled into New Orleans, and Cajun cuisine influenced Creole cuisine in a major way in the late twentieth century.

To determine what Cajun food is a bit of history is in order. In 1710 the French lost control of Acadia—or what is now Prince Edward Island, New Brunswick, and Nova Scotia, Canada—to the British. The French who lived in this area adamantly resisted British rule through such methods as simple refusal to take oaths of allegiance to actual military action. To eliminate this dissident problem, especially the military threat, between 1755 and 1763 the British deported the Acadians. Many Acadians immigrated to Louisiana through Saint-Domingue and settled in what was called the Atakapa area of Louisiana, after the Atakapa Amerindians in an area west of New Orleans. The city of New Orleans was already almost forty years old when this process began. The first Acadian settlers came to the region and settled what is now St. Martinville. The new settlers learned that they were settling in a Spanish colony sometime after their arrival—France having ceded Louisiana to Spain. This eviction of the Acadians and their subsequent diaspora has become known as the Great Upheaval, or Le Grand Dérangement.

Despite the tale of the Acadians and the strength of the culture, Cajun food is not purely French. Many non-French settlers were absorbed into the culture with Gallicized names and the assimilation of their foodways, thus their influence is masked. The German, British, Italian, African, Greek, and Spanish colonists who moved to Acadiana contributed to the development of the food, but often lost their own ethnic identity in subsequent generations as the culture homogenized. The German Weiss became Le Blanc; the Italian Cimino became Simoneaux; and Melanson was once the English name Mallinson. Many people from this region are not aware that although their names are French, their heritage is not.

The Acadians proceeded to settle. Those on the plains of Louisiana were trappers. Those who settled in the estuaries became fishermen. The food of the Acadians, which is now called Cajun food, derived from the cooking of these people. These were folk who came from a rugged place in Nova Scotia, they lived off the land and the water, and they did not have regular access to or a taste for seasonings that they could not grow themselves. Although they considered themselves French, most of them were only descendants of French ancestors. They had never eaten in France. They ate foods that were cooked in one pot, and they ate what they had. It was tasty food and Cajun food still is, but it was food that was developed in isolation by people who worked and cooked without leisure or waste. Although on some plantations located in these areas there were slaves, most Cajuns did not have slaves, and they raised food, fished and hunted, slaughtered and cooked their own meals.

At one time the word Cajun was considered an ethnic slur. In proper books it was considered a rude word that was avoided and finding early cookbooks that reference "Cajun" cooking is difficult. They persisted in speaking French long after Louisiana statehood and were punished and derided in the twentieth century for being backward French speakers who only spoke English with a heavy accent, if at all. It was Louisiana governor, Edwin Edwards, himself a Cajun, who embraced his ethnicity and made the use of the term Cajun not only acceptable, but a source of pride.

Creole Food

In contrast to the Cajun food of western Louisiana, there is Creole food or the food of New Orleans. The word Creole has had various meanings depending on the time that it has been used, the place that it has been used, and the subject that it has modified. There are many excellent discussions of the meaning of the word depending on these variables. Jessica Harris has written much about the meaning of the word, including the etymology and various racial and geographical uses of the word. The word derives from either the Spanish or the Portuguese *criollo*, meaning "born in the colonies." It referred to any persons, not Native American, born in the colonies. It was a way to distinguish those superior people, born in the mother country from those born in the colonies. It was not originally a word that denoted racial origins, merely place of birth. The word began to take on different meanings in the Caribbean Islands and in mainland America. Today in New Orleans it can have several meanings. Some people use it to denote people of mixed race. Others use it to mean descendants of the French or Spanish.

For the most part this book will use the modifier "Creole" to describe the food that was developed in New Orleans or that has come to be identified as the food of New Orleans (although the food of the Caribbean can also be referred to as Creole; except as the Caribbean has influenced New Orleans, this book does not attempt to cover the food of the Caribbean). This is not limited to foods developed before the Americanization of New Orleans caused by the Louisiana Purchase. It includes foods that were introduced after Americanization both by Americans and subsequent immigrants. For the reader and the eater this is most important in the distinction between Creole and Cajun food. Creole food is the food of New Orleans.

Like all native cuisines, the food of New Orleans—Creole food—was dependent on what was here. Fortunately there was abundance. The variety of seafood, fowl, meats, fruits, and vegetables was notable. The cuisine was greatly influenced by techniques and practices of the Senegambian region and other regions of Africa, the raw materials and practices of the Native Americans, and the cultural expectations of the Europeans who, as the documenters of the development of the cuisine, saw and reported it through their own cultural filters. If the food of the Cajuns tends to be largely one pot dinners cooked while other work was done, the food of the Creoles tends to be prepared more individually with meat or fish cooked separately from a vegetable dish. The starches of the Creole table are more varied than the Cajun table, including potatoes and grits, as well as rice. In addition the Creole dishes were often sauced. Sauces include Creole sauce, made with fresh tomatoes, served as a part of shrimp creole, for example. Remoulade sauce, a cold sauce named for but different from the French sauce, is also served with shrimp or seafood. There are many fried dishes.

There was certainly some cross-pollination between Cajun and Creole foods. Both foods list jambalaya and gumbo in their canons, for example, which adds to the confusion of the uninitiated. The similarities of the dishes also serve as evidence of the mutual influence. For native eaters of either variety of food the distinction is immediately obvious, though ephemeral and very difficult to articulate, whenever a dish is placed in front of them. The distinction between the two cuisines is important to the respective cultures. The failure of tourists and the uninitiated to distinguish between the two is a regular source of annoyance for both Cajun and Creole eaters. The failure to care about or recognize the difference is considered an insult, as well as a sign of a lack of discernment.

For modern amateur explorers of the historical origins and development of the cuisine there is a tendency to see what is observable today as a sort of benchmark for historical reference. For example the assumption that what is currently called gumbo is the same as what was meant by gumbo 150 to 200 years ago. When reading in a journal or travel article from the nineteenth century a reference to gumbo does not necessarily mean that the earlier gumbo is the same as our gumbo today. There is a commonly repeated modern refrain, "First you make a roux," which is supposed to be ubiquitous, because it is so universal and eternal. But that refrain is not universal and eternal. And it reflects what is considered fundamental today. It is not documented that there was always roux used in gumbo. Assuming that what is done today was always done is dangerous in historical research.

A check of the earliest available New Orleans cookbooks, *La Cuisine Creole* by Lafcadio Hearn and *The Creole Cookery Book* edited by the board members of Christian Woman's Exchange, both published in 1885, show that both books contain recipes for "Gombo" and "Gumbo" which do not begin with a roux. Both books contain other variations in spelling of words like "Jambolaya" and "Jumbalaya." The differences in spelling in two books that were published in the same year point out the dangers in trying to determine the origins of dishes from the names and standardized spellings of dishes that we use today. Similarly even earlier references to gumbo describe a dish that is more akin to okra soup or just boiled okra. We cannot be sure that the gumbo of the modern table, well developed and enriched with seafood or fowl, was the gumbo of the early nineteenth century or earlier. Looking at modern dishes we cannot make direct interpretations of the origin simply by making analogies to other modern dishes. When using cookbooks as sources of information, there is no guarantee of scientific accuracy of the history found in introductions or even of the explanations of the origins of the recipes of the food of New Orleans or of the supposed ancestor dish. Mythmaking, myth-repeating, and pure fabrication make cookbook reading a dicey historical romp.

These cookbooks, which refer to the cuisine as Creole, establish both the sameness of the cuisine as American and the otherness of the cuisine as Creole. It was not New Orleanians who called the cuisine Creole. To those born in New Orleans it was just food. It was Hearn, the journalist who told the rest of America about New Orleans, and the Protestant women—in a Catholic city—from the Christian Woman's Exchange who also recognized the difference in the food. Hearn wrote *La Cuisine Creole*, published in 1885, as a way to capitalize on the tourism of the World Cotton Exposition which opened in New Orleans in late December 1884. He certainly captured many of the dishes found on the tables in the city and named the cuisine Creole. But, as noted by historian Rien Fertel, Hearn also copied many American recipes verbatim from other published cookbooks. This practice makes it almost impossible to determine whether those copied recipes were popularly eaten in New Orleans or just filler that would appeal to tourists looking for something familiar within the book that also included exotic recipes.

Over forty years before Hearn's book appeared in 1840, Antoine Alciatore, a Frenchman, opened the doors of his eponymous restaurant. Antoine's was a French restaurant, reflecting the continuing French connection of the city, even after statehood, and even as the cuisine of Paris was being established. But it also served the food of the region. The shrimp and crabs and local meats were found on the menu. Besides the *pommes de terre soufflés*, a decidedly French dish, were foods prepared *á la* Nouvelle-Orléans. These dishes were a self-conscious reflection of the food of the city. Certainly even before Hearn's use of the word "Creole" to describe the collective cuisine, others had recognized the distinctive nature of the dishes without reference to the term Creole. There is a menu from Florida dated 1882 in the collection of the New York Public Library which lists "Chicken Saute, á la Creole" as a selection. Obviously this term already had a meaning in the mind of the public (although whether this was a reference to New Orleans or the Caribbean is hard to discern, especially in a restaurant located in Florida; it could even mean in the manner of the New World). This also suggests that Hearn did not pluck the term—as it applies to cuisine—out of thin air. By using it in the title of his book, he did establish the word Creole as a good description of the cuisine. It was a name that traveled back home with the book as tourists to the World's Fair returned home after their visit.

Another outsider, Sara Roahen, also explored Creole cuisine and reminded New Orleanians how special their cuisine is. In her book, *Gumbo Tales*, this native of Wisconsin cooks and eats her way around mostly Creole food. As she describes this journey, it becomes clear that Creole food is different from other American food. She defines that difference in a way that can never be captured by someone who ate it as a native, because to a native it is just food. When trying to define Creole food to a non-New Orleanian American, being informed about American eating habits is important. Roahen bridges the gap for natives by explaining how Creole food is different from what she had known before her introduction to New Orleans.

As important as the distinction between Cajun and Creole food is in understanding the history of the food of New Orleans, it must be admitted that young people whose food memories are subsequent to several events—the advent of regular supplies of crawfish, the rise of Chef Paul Prudhomme, the

1984 World's Fair—do not make as much of the distinction between Cajun and Creole. Into the restaurants of New Orleans have been welcomed crawfish, boudin, and smoked meats. Although the old Creoles might be scandalized the young are merely happy that the food tastes good as the Cajun is being absorbed into the Creole.

The Germans

When John Law began advertising for colonists in his attempt to make New Orleans a financial success, he was able to attract a few Germans from the Alsace-Lorraine area. This area, which is now part of France, had a long history of being caught in a tug-of-war between the two countries. This history could explain the easy blending of the early German immigrants into the French culture of the city. Seventeen-seventy-two is the year of the first record of the arrival of Germans to New Orleans and the surrounding area. These people were industrious and knowledgeable farmers. They settled in an area which has become known as La Côte des Allemands (The German Coast). This area runs along the Mississippi River on both sides from the town of Gretna, which is part of the greater metropolitan area until the Bonne Carre Spillway. It was they, whose early contribution to the health of the colony was their ability to successfully grow food, who may have kept the colony alive. They did not merely engage in monoculture, as did those growing rice for sale and later those growing sugar commercially, rather they grew a variety of products that could be sold at market. They had the early technical skill to actually grow food, unlike so many of the early urban French vagabonds who populated the early city. It is their engineering skill which contributed to the series of dykes and canals to irrigate the rice fields leading to the ability to grow rice reliably without only depending upon sufficiency of rain to cause the flooding of the paddies.

Even after the French were selling the city and all of Louisiana to the Americans, there were Germans coming to the city and surrounding areas to work the land. They were recognized as industrious and knowledgeable farmers contributing much to the food supply of the city. Many of the Germans who settled in New Orleans were Jewish and records show regular intermarriage with the Roman Catholic French in the city. The speaking of German was discouraged, and this, coupled with the practice of Gallicizing German names (as well as the names of other immigrants), has made it difficult for many people of German heritage to even be aware of it. This was a time during which the Alsace Lorraine region of what is now France was German, but the history of the region was one of transfer between France and Germany.

It was in many ways a separate region that shared cultural traits with both France and Germany. From the early 1800s to about 1850 more than 50,000 Germans were documented through immigration at the port of New Orleans.

During the mid-nineteenth century there was another wave of German immigration into New Orleans. This immigration continued until the Civil War and made moving to America both difficult and less desirable. It greatly added to the mix of ethnic groups and the sophisticated cultural milieu of the city. There were enough people of German heritage at the turn of the twentieth century to support more than 250 German-American societies. Many lived in the Faubourg Marigny, which was informally known as Little Saxony. It is said that as much as 12 percent of the population of the city was German. Thousands of people spoke German as a first language. The Grunewald Hotel, whose catering business contributed much to the development of the cuisine of the city in the early 1900s, was established by this group. The Cave, the nightclub at the Grunewald, has been said to be the first nightclub in America. It was one of the nightlife innovations of the city, which contributed to the establishment of the cocktail culture. The hotel was the site of the Sazerac Bar, which, although not the original home of the drink, enshrined the Sazerac cocktail in the hearts and minds of the people of the city. The two world wars of the twentieth century made it difficult to exalt in the influence of the German people in New Orleans. The Grunewald Hotel, for example, changed its name to the Roosevelt Hotel during this time, both to obscure the Germanic origins of the name and to show its patriotism.

The Germans also contributed to the beer culture of the city. In the mid-nineteenth century there were more than thirty breweries with beer gardens in New Orleans. Many were lost due to the restrictions of Prohibition. Jax Brewery, owned by the Fabacher family, continued to brew until 1974. A part of the brewery complex, still standing near the Mississippi River, has been converted into a shopping mall. The Dixie Brewery building is being considered for development. Today Germans are still brewmasters at several area breweries. Crescent City Brewhouse, a microbrewery which is located in the French Quarter, is owned by German brewmaster Wolfram Koehler.

Finding industry again in yeast and grain the Germans were also the early bakers in the city. At first when there was no flour available in this New World, because wheat was not grown here, bakers had to make do with corn flour. Even when wheat began to be grown in the English colonies in America, it was not readily available in New Orleans. In the beginning flour was only available when it was brought in from Europe. Being less refined than the flour with which we are familiar today, it did not travel well across the ocean. It arrived infested with weevils and mold. By necessity and with ingenuity the early bakers devised bread that used less flour per loaf, creating the airy, crunchy bread that New Orleanians call French bread. German descendants in New Orleans today at Leidenheimer's Bakery and Alois Binder's Bakery continue to make French bread. Klotzbach's Bakery was once a rival of Leidenheimer's. Haydel's Bakery is one of the premiere king cake bakeries in the city. It is Haydel's which has adopted the tradition of including a porcelain *feve* (cake trinket) in the cake. Hubig Pies, an individual fruit hand pie which can be found everywhere in New Orleans from gas stations to the restaurant at the cinema at Canal Place, was started by a German baker. John Schwegmann, the grocer, who at one time built in New Orleans what was the largest supermarket in the United States, was of German descent.

Finding workers to perform the backbreaking and dangerous work in the sugar cane fields was a continuously difficult one. In the early 1940s German prisoners of war were sent to Louisiana, and they worked in the cane fields and also worked in other agricultural jobs. It was ironic that they were sent to work on the German Coast. Many of these Germans remained in the area, and after World War II many Germans immigrated to the area looking for opportunity and escape from their war-torn country. They found the area to be a place of sympathetic welcome.

A number of significant restaurants were founded by Germans. Kolb's Restaurant on St. Charles Street was an unabashedly German restaurant complete with kitsch and with *gemütlich* touches like a large collection of beer steins and a fascinating ceiling fan system. It was founded in 1899 and operated for almost a hundred years until 1995. Jaeger's Restaurant is another example of German influence. Broussard's Restaurant is owned by Marc Preuss, of German heritage, whose Creole restaurant now celebrates Oktoberfest. Oktoberfest is a growing celebration in the city, where people are happy to incorporate yet another holiday—especially one so redolent of food and drink—into the calendar.

The Enslaved Africans and Their Descendants

Before La Salle's claim in New Orleans the French had established a colony in Saint-Domingue, which roughly comprised the western half of the island of Hispaniola. The people of this colony, which was populated by scoundrels and thieves as would be la Nouvelle-Orléans, finally tamed the land, the native people, and themselves, and began to grow tobacco. It was a profitable endeavor establishing French interests in the region. The fact that some profit could grow from colonies abroad was a continuing promise that encouraged the rash and the independent to try to make their fortunes in the New World.

When the French ruled New Orleans almost 6,000 Africans were brought to the city on twenty-three slave ships, according to the records reported by historian Gwendolyn Midlo Hall. After the ship of 1743 there was a hiatus of thirty years before slave ships brought more people from Africa. Instead during that interval slave ships brought Africans to the more lucrative market of Saint-Domingue. Most of the Africans brought to New Orleans were from Senegal. The people of Senegambian region were sophisticated. They lived along established trade routes, both African and Arab, and were exposed to many cultures. They had great agricultural technical skills, far superior to the skills of the Europeans. The Africans were familiar with the cultivation of indigo and rice, both of which became important crops in Louisiana, sold through New Orleans. The numbers of Africans brought to New Orleans made the Africans greatly outnumber the Europeans.

In 1685 the Code Noir (Black Code) was imposed by the French king, Louis XIV. By this time there were many enslaved Africans working in Saint-Domingue, and establishing rules of conduct with regard to the slaves was deemed necessary. The Code contained wildly disparate elements, including banning Jews from the colony, requiring the baptism of slaves, and the approval of harsh and cruel punishments against errant slaves. Most of the Africans brought to the Caribbean were from Dahomey, which is now Benin, and also from Nigeria.

When d'Iberville was establishing New Orleans there were already people of African descent living near what was to become New Orleans. D'Iberville, who was in communication with the Native Americans in the area, was informed by them that free or escaped blacks, the maroons, had formed a village northwest. These people were Spanish speakers. They were determined to be separate from any Spanish-speaking white people, whom they would run off from the area. This village would become a haven for escaped slaves.

Having already developed the *Code Noir*, the French imposed it on the new city, although originally there were few African slaves. The founders of the city enslaved Native Americans for their own convenience initially so that they would have food and provisions. Gradually, however, the slave trade began in earnest, and Africans were brought to the city to clear land, build the city, and serve as domestic servants. The population of blacks in the city grew to outnumber the whites. This disproportionate number of blacks makes it clear that food was being prepared by people of color. Because the city folk of France who were rounded up to be sent to this colony are unlikely to have had occasion to become familiar with agricultural practices, it is even more likely that urban gardening and cooking came to be performed by African slaves and their descendants. The food that was prepared for the white colonists in New Orleans must have been prepared by Africans at this time, contributing their practice of eating beans and rice and eating okra stewed with meat or fish.

When the Spanish took over the city they amended the *Code Noir*. The Spanish left in most of the requirements related to the Catholic religion, such as the mandate that all slaves be baptized and that they have a day of rest to attend church, but they eliminated some of the more gruesome punishments and importantly added the provisions of the code that provided for manumission or the freeing of a slave from slave status. These provisions not only form an important part of the mythic aura surrounding certain individual dishes, such as calas, but also illustrate how food was so important to the society that it could be used to buy freedom. These new provisions of the *Code Noir* also allowed for the development of cultural practices among the slave population that involved food, like entrepreneurship and social gatherings.

Manumission, whether granted by the slave-owner or purchased by the former slave, allowed for the development of the practice of plaçage. This recognized form of concubinage generally involved a white man who took a (usually) free black concubine and supported her and the family that developed from the relationship. This relationship could be a second family for the white man, who might have a legal white wife and children on a farm or plantation outside of the city and who preferred to have a second family in the city, where he would come for business. Or both families might live in the city.

The mixed race children of these relationships were often educated, the girls being groomed for octoroon or quadroon balls where they were presented to society and selected as concubines. Sometimes the male children were sent to France to be educated or became tradesmen in New Orleans. The growing number of free people of color—either the children of the rape of a black slave by a white owner who might have been freed for sentimental reasons or the children of plaçage—required that there be laws to recognize and codify the rights of what was seen as a separate class of people. Thus there was the law of plaçage, which allowed the concubine to be taken care of in the testament of the man. There was also law that defined the rights of *les gens de couleur libres* (free people of color).

The free people of color occupied a place in society between the slaves and the white people. They were allowed to own property, they were involved in the food business, they were poets and artists, and they were part of the complex web of race that developed in New Orleans. Today it is the descendants of this system, people of mixed race, who call themselves Creoles.

Saint-Domingue

While New Orleans was growing as a city, the colonies in the Caribbean Islands were also evolving. The French Revolution and its tantalizing promise of equality was a great threat to the plantation culture of the islands, as it would destroy the possibility of maintaining slavery. The slave/plantation system was essential to support the way of life of the white plantation owners and they were threatened by the possibility that they might lose their slaves. The white plantation owners responded to this threat by becoming more cruel and controlling of their slaves, creating even more than the usual level of tension and resentment. After a thwarted uprising, the slaves, led by François Mackandal, were successful. During this period many of the inhabitants of Saint-Domingue fled to New Orleans. Toussaint L'Ouverture went on to lead the way for an independent Haiti. New Orleans was a place that was full of French speakers. Some of the fleeing plantation owners came to New Orleans with slaves, who brought another interpretation of Creole to the kitchens of the city.

Despite their artistic aspirations, the French of Saint-Domingue were decidedly not refined in their practices regarding the treatment of the enslaved people who provided their livelihood. The number of African and Saint-Domingue born slaves greatly outnumbered the French and by using this plethora of laborers the planters lived like royalty. They used the many unpaid slave laborers to satisfy their every whim, whether to fulfill a desire for a new building, for sexual indulgence, or to indulge a delight in cruelty.

The French Estates General enacted the Declaration of the Rights of Man and Citizen in 1789. This led the slaves to hope that its principles would be put into action and that they would be freed. That did not occur. Thus in 1791 the complex revolution of Saint-Domingue erupted into its most logical action, that is, a slave rebellion. The pent-up rage caused thousands of slaves to kill some of the white population of the island during what has come to be known as the Boukman Rebellion. Boukman Dutty, the leader of the revolt, was killed and the rebellion quelled for a time. A group of disaffected *petits blancs* (white people who were not landed, but workers), also angered by their lack of status, burned a large portion of the town of Port-au-Prince. In fear many whites began to leave. Some went up the Eastern Seaboard and settled in the new United States. Some traveled to New Orleans.

As much as the French of Saint-Domingue felt abused by the French government, New Orleans—then governed by the Spanish—was not immediately a compelling haven. The Spanish were hated and the journey by ship across the Gulf of Mexico was not an easy one. They had led a pampered and privileged life on Saint-Domingue, and would be starting over in la Nouvelle-Orléans. The refugees in both New Orleans and in America maintained a hope that they could return to Saint-Domingue upon the suppression of the revolt. Those in New Orleans knew that the journey back to the island from New Orleans would be much more arduous than a return trip down the Atlantic Seaboard. In addition the Spanish prohibited the refugees from entering New Orleans with their slaves, making it necessary for them to leave everything behind. Returning to Saint-Domingue would be financially difficult as well as treacherous. Most people did not return. They became a wave of French immigrants who brought the culinary experience of the Caribbean to the city. In addition to the French immigrants from Saint-Domingue, free people of color also came to the city. They also brought their culinary traditions to New Orleans, bringing a seafood-based cuisine that had strong African roots.

Except at the city's earliest time, when there was great reliance on the Native Americans for food, with the population of the city being fed by Africans, there can be no doubt that despite the influences of the Europeans—which were myriad—the food of New Orleans was created by the hands of Africans and the children of Africa. They brought the technical skill to grow the food, as well as certain techniques of cooking. In particular rice was an established grain eaten in Africa, paired with beans. The pan southern habit of eating rice and beans or peas is a direct import from Africa. In New Orleans, where Africans and people of African descent out-numbered people of European descent, the direct adoption of certain dishes, like rice and beans, is obvious evidence of their influence on the cuisine.

Unlike in the Acadian part of Louisiana where the white Acadians mostly cooked for themselves, the people of New Orleans were most likely to have slaves or servants in the kitchen, who except at the very earliest days of the settlement, were likely to be African. They had the unenviable job of cooking to the satisfaction of their slaveholder's taste, but also cooking to their own satisfaction. Other rice dishes such as calas are likely derived from African dishes.

Because the *Code Noir* required that slaves have Sunday off, there was opportunity for enterprise and entrepreneurism. At gatherings at Congo Square, located in what is now Armstrong Park, slaves and free people of color sold calas, cups of coffee, pralines and other candies, fruits, and vegetables. This established a tradition of street food which continued into the nineteenth century and even lingering into the twentieth century.

After the cuisine of New Orleans was created in the homes of the people in the colonies, the influence of Africans continued to be developed in the kitchens of restaurants. The old-line restaurant kitchens were supported by African Americans. Although during the era of segregation African Americans were not allowed to eat in them, they certainly provided the labor to fuel the restaurants. Many of the African American cooks eventually came to be recognized as great chefs of Creole cuisine.

CHAPTER FIVE

~

Immigrants: Their Neighborhoods and Contributions

The Americans

After the Louisiana Purchase in 1803, the city of New Orleans was inundated with Americans moving to the city because of the opportunities presented by the Port. The Americans were looked down upon as uncouth by the people of both French and the Spanish descent. Up river of the French Quarter the city streets were no longer called Rue and they were renamed even though they were continuations of the streets across Canal Street. The wide median that ran between the two sides of Canal Street, which headed to and from the Mississippi River, was known as the neutral ground. It separated the French and the American sectors of the city. Medians in the city are today still called the neutral grounds.

After statehood in 1812, trade with other states such as the Carolinas brought rice, which began to be cultivated commercially in the nineteenth century. There was a resumption of the slave trade after the Louisiana Purchase bringing new Africans to the city with their own foodways and tastes. New Orleans became an important center for the trade. During this century imports of coffee expanded. American mercantilism introduced New Orleans to the full development of the Port of New Orleans and with it imports and exports of agricultural commodities.

The nineteenth century brought a great increase in travel along the Mississippi River. This made the food of New Orleans available and known throughout the journey of the steamboat. Food supplies taken on board in New Orleans provided the meals for the passengers, many of whom carried a taste for the unique dishes back to their homes. The steamboats also brought grains and other products into New Orleans. The Americans brought technology to the port and the city, making advances in agriculture and manufacturing possible.

After Creole food was recognized and defined it continued to develop and evolve with the immigration of people into the city. Unlike what happened in other urban areas where large groups of immigrants entered a city, the food of immigrants became Creolized in New Orleans. In other cities large groups of immigrants have created a proliferation of ethnic restaurants. This may be partially a phenomenon related to the timing of the immigration in certain cities. But it is absolutely related to the willingness of the people of New Orleans to allow the exchange of flavors and techniques that has resulted in the ever-evolving Creole food.

The transition of flavors from the immigrant table to the tables of the Creole cooks is known as Creolization. Although the transition of flavors can actually work in both directions, the changes in the ethnic food will probably not make it beyond the homes and restaurants of immigrants and not all the way to the home country. Within New Orleans today we can find many influences and dishes that can be identified as having been Creolized from one ethnic group or another. These influences are more easily identified because they migrated into Creole food after Creole food was established and can be recognized as distinct from the baseline of 1895 when Lafacadio Hearn published *La Cuisine Creole*. These ethnic groups have clearly influenced Creole food, but they have expanded it as opposed to having been a part of creating it. And the dishes they inspired and the cultural practices that support the dishes are now eaten by everyone, regardless of heritage. In this way the dishes conform to the definition of cuisine. They are no less Creole for having clear origins.

The Italians

Although there were Italians in New Orleans throughout its colonization, most notably Henri de Tonti who was a pre-city explorer who returned to the city after it was founded, it was the major immigration from about 1885 to 1915 that had the greatest and most measurable gastronomic influence. After the Civil War the city found it necessary to recruit laborers to work in the agricultural fields, especially the sugar cane fields, to keep up production to meet demand. Among those recruited by the Louisiana Immigration League were the Italians. A large number of those who immigrated were from Sicily. The Sicilians, all arriving in such a small window, tended to live together and support each other. Often the Sicilian dialect was more prevalent than English in the neighborhoods in which they lived.

Although many people were recruited for manual work in agriculture, after accumulating enough money, most of the Sicilians left the plantations to either create their own farms or fishing businesses, or to peddle fruits and vegetables in the city, or to work as fishmongers or butchers in the city markets. Food was something that was known to the Sicilians, and it was a business that required less mastery of English than other businesses might, as well as less access to capital.

During this period and into the twentieth century, many new dishes were added to the food of New Orleans. After a short period of working in the cane fields most Sicilian workers were ready to leave this backbreaking work. Many of them were greeted with mistrust in the city of New Orleans, where they settled in large numbers in the French Quarter. The neighborhood became known as Little Italy, with Italians coming to compose almost 40 percent of the population of the state. The new immigrants found that they could most easily move into the food businesses. Some were butchers and fishmongers in the French Market, and in traditional fashion would pass on their stalls and their training to sons and nephews. Others lived outside the city and grew produce, notably in Tangipahoa Parish where strawberry farms abound, which they peddled either in the markets that were growing up throughout the city, or on carts through the streets. Until 1980, Cannoto "the fruit man" could be found in New Orleans and in Jefferson and other parishes around New Orleans. After peddling for a time, some immigrants were able to accumulate enough money to open a small grocery. Today there are still many names in the commercial produce business that reveal the family's Italian roots—Cusimano Produce, Lucas T. Cuccia & Sons, Mistretta's Produce, and Chifici Produce.

Such a large influx of people, especially a people with a deep food culture, could not help but affect the existing food culture in which they found themselves. Foods of Sicily sometimes adapted for New Orleans produce and meats and fish were eaten by Sicilians. Some of those foods were Creolized and adopted in homes and restaurants of the city. One important example is red gravy. A traditional slow-cooked tomato sauce was adapted to Creole taste. One aspect of this new dish was the use of canned tomatoes, a practice that had been adopted by Sicilians to provide tomatoes all year-round. Tomatoes were certainly already a part of Creole cuisine, but most foods were made with fresh tomatoes. The Sicilians used canned tomatoes when fresh were not available. Creole cooks adopted this practice when making red gravy. Traditional Sicilian tomato sauce thickens by cooking down the tomatoes so that the water in the tomatoes evaporates, but Creole red gravy has a brown roux. It also contains the trinity (the New Orleans mirepoix) of onions, celery, and green bell peppers. The use of green bell pepper is not traditional in Sicilian tomato sauce. This Creolized sauce is served by Creole cooks with meatballs or Italian sausage over spaghetti. It is used on meatball poboys and Italian sausage poboys. Red gravy has a smooth mellow flavor which is imparted by the roux and manages to taste distinctly Creole even when used in the same way as a traditional tomato sauce.

Another food that had become a sandwich that tourists must eat, and locals adopted, is the muffuletta. This sandwich was sold to workers in and around the French Quarter as an easy familiar lunch by the Lupo family at Central Grocery. This was one of the many similar stores that opened in the French Quarter in the early twentieth century. The Lupos claim that the muffuletta was invented by Salvatore Lupo in 1906 and to this day their sandwiches are wrapped with a paper that claims the prize of the "Original Muffuletta." The round loaf of bread covered with sesame seeds contains a filling of olive salad, sliced Italian salumi—salami, mortadella, perhaps prosciutto or ham—and slices of cheese—sometimes smoked provolone or mozzarella. The bread is similar to a round loaf called muffuletta in Sicily. The practice of stuffing a loaf of bread with these ingredients is a common one in Sicily. But the sandwich was eaten in New Orleans and was adopted for workers who were not Sicilian, simply because it tasted so good.

A street tradition which was easily absorbed into street food practices of the city with a lasting impact is the snoball—shaved ice with syrup. Snoballs are sold today at neighborhood snoball stands that operate seasonally only in the warmer months. Snoballs were a tradition brought to the city by Sicilians. It was taken from the old Italian tradition of mixing snow with flavored syrup. The Sicilians mimicked snow by shaving blocked ice with a hand shaver. Until recently, when street food has become trendy and artisanal products are valued, snoball syrup recipes had not often been written about in cookbooks. Making snoball syrup for the occasional home snoball is not a usual activity. Snoballs are almost always eaten out. They are seasonal. They are only occasionally described as part of the culinary tradition in various New Orleans travel guides, often being overlooked because the writers come to the city in the cooler months.

As snoballs became more popular, the work of shaving the ice has been taken over by machines. Originally machinists would create a single machine for a family snoball stand. The Hansen family, which is now operating Hansen's in the third generation, still operates a stand with a machine made by Mr. Hansen, who was a machinist. In 1948 George Ortolano patented a commercially produced snoball machine which allowed anyone to buy a machine and open a snoball stand. It is the quality of the shaved iced which is the measure of the snoball for connoisseurs. It must be fluffy and light and not packed. This is in contrast to crushed or ground ice which might be found in a snow cone. Other snoball fiends based their favorite snoball selection on the quality of the syrup. Today there are several companies making commercially available machines, many syrups, and fierce competition between the companies. Many snoball stands, attempting to produce the best results for their customers, provide for freshly made syrups, not prebottled syrups. Another cold treat, Italian ice cream and ices, also remain a favorite for New Orleanians, still sought after at Brocato's and well described by Richard Collin in his *New Orleans Underground Gourmet* (1970), but rarely addressed in other sources. These ices and ice creams are different from gelati that are popular in the United States today.

These foods greatly deepened and expanded the canon. For example it was the Italian acceptance of canned tomatoes that truly made the use of canned tomatoes a part of the Creole table. The use of tomatoes all year changed the way Creoles thought about tomatoes.

St. Joseph is the patron saint of Sicily, and St. Joseph altars have become a regular celebration in New Orleans, enjoyed even by those who are not Italian. St. Joseph is also the patron of travelers, immigrants, craftsmen, the working class and social justice, and fathers. Although not all of Sicily celebrates the Albanian medieval custom of St. Joseph altars—some towns celebrate other saints—the altars united the Sicilians in New Orleans and other towns in Louisiana. When a person has a favor granted by St. Joseph that petitioner promises to build an altar on March 19. Originally the altar was an individual worship built in a person's home. Word of mouth and advertisements in the newspaper let pilgrims know where they could go to visit altars. The pilgrimage would be made by those who visited multiple altars, often those of friends, but also ones with a reputation for opulence.

The altars, several tiers of offerings, almost always have a statue of St. Joseph, and in addition there are usually photos of family, flowers, and candles. In addition they are covered in breads and other pastries that are molded into special shapes that represent certain religious symbols like the sacred heart and the staff of St. Joseph, and there are candles, flowers, fruits, and vegetables. There are many other dishes made for altar like olive salad, pastas, fish, and artichokes.

The making of the altar was a group activity, often involving the extended family and friends, and a form of group worship. Even non-Sicilians and non-Catholics have become involved in cooking for the altars. Words that describe the food have made their way into the food vocabulary of the city, like *cuccidati* and *pignolatti*. On St. Joseph's Day a boy and a girl were ritually fed, representing Mary and Joseph. People were invited to admire the altar. Sometimes the altars were blessed by a priest, and people left after the visit with a lucky bean—a blessed fava bean. The excess food was given to the poor. Knowing how much food to take—not to be greedy—was as much a religious act as the prayers and the mounting of the altar. The food was to be shared with the needy.

Most altars contain a bowl or basket of lemons close to the door. It is said that a young woman who steals a lemon from a St. Joseph altar, some say you must be seen stealing it, will be married before the next year's St. Joseph altar.

Today most altars are not privately made in people's homes. They are mounted in churches, community centers, and restaurants. There are still group activities and a form of group worship. Women usually cook for weeks, sometimes freezing food prepared in advance, to assemble the altar. B. Montalbano Italian Delicatessen, operating in the French Quarter from 1930s to the 1950s, was known for its Roma Room. This room contained a permanent altar to St. Joseph as well as holy pictures and other religious artifacts. It was full of food and prayer every March 19. The deli offered a muffuletta that they marketed as a Roma sandwich.

Since the early twentieth century African American Spiritual churches have also celebrated St. Joseph's Day with altars, including many Sicilian foods. This may be because of the close relationship that arose between African Americans and Sicilians, when the large immigration of Sicilians began. The Sicilians often worked in the cane fields and at the docks side by side with the African American workers. In addition the Sicilians and African Americans shared the same neighborhoods. St. Joseph, the patron of social justice, was analogous to Black Hawk, an important saint in the Spiritual theology. This is how the tradition of Mardi Gras Indian parades on St. Joseph's Day arose.

A similar feast day is the feast of St. Rosalie, September 14, with a parade and a feast, and has remained an Italian American celebration, while the St. Joseph celebration has been embraced by the entire city and its foods, especially the cookies, are bought all year long in groceries and bakeries by all of the citizens of the city, not just those of Italian descent.

Jews

Only a few Jews were living in New Orleans in the mid-eighteenth century. Although they were prohibited from living in the colony by the *Code Noir*, this provision of the Code does not seem to have been the reason there were only a few Jews in the settlement. The Spanish were more vigilant in enforcing this aspect of the *Code* during their governance, although it seems that the expulsion by the Spanish of Isaac Monsanto and the confiscation of his wealth was as much to do with power as to anti-Semitism. The small number of Jews who settled in the first century of the colony were primarily Sephardic Jews.

During the next century, Jews arrived from France and from Eastern Europe. The French Jews fled the violence in the Alsace-Lorraine during a transition of the area from France to Germany. The Jews who arrived were not fleeing religious persecution. They were mostly cultural Jews rather than strongly religious. Since New Orleans was still a French-speaking area even after statehood, these immigrants did not have difficulty acculturating.

The Eastern European immigrants arrived about thirty years later and were more orthodox in their religious practices. They were leaving Poland and Russia because of religious persecution. They were as grounded in the beliefs as in the culture and remained somewhat distant from the small Jewish community that was already established in the city. The newer immigrants brought more orthodox religious eating habits with them, in contrast to the community of Jews who ate the myriad varieties of shellfish available in the area.

In spite of their small numbers Jews have been important in the food and culture of New Orleans. Samuel Zemurray was the president of the United Fruit Company. Edgar Stern founded WDSU-TV which did much to preserve Creole homecooking through the broadcast of cooking shows, including the shows of Lena Richard, Terry Flettrich, and Leah Chase. The Katz and Besthoff drugstore chain was famous for its brand of Creole cream cheese ice cream.

In her book *Matzoh Ball Gumbo*, Marcie Ferris describes the interrelationships between upper middle class Jewish homes in New Orleans and other parts of the South and the African American domestic servants who worked for them. She documents the subtle influences in cooking as the African American cooks learned about the religious requirements of the table and the influences in taste caused by the cooking itself. It is an important recognition of how all tastes and tables are influenced by the relationship between the cook and the eater. The tradition of kosher catering in the city was mostly carried on by African American caterers based on their experiences in keeping kosher kitchens.

For the Jews in New Orleans who keep kosher, Mildred Covert has written cookbooks and articles featuring recipes of traditional Creole foods made in compliance with kosher rules. The popularity of Covert's work indicates just how important Creole food is to New Orleans Jews. It is also an indication of how rich and varied the food is that, even without certain foods like shellfish, whole cookbooks can be written about it. Kosher Cajun New York Deli and Grocery is a kosher haven in the city since 1988. Casablanca, a Moroccan and Middle Eastern restaurant, has been operating since 1995.

Felix's Restaurant

Felix's was established in the early 1900s and has been family owned and operated for more than 70 years. It has long been a favorite of locals and visitors alike, and has been made nationally famous by guests "bellying up" to the oyster bar or dining on our delicious Creole and Cajun cuisine.

Oysters on the Half Shell - Felix's only serves LOUISIANA oysters!
Oysters Rockefeller, Bienville or Mixed
Char-grilled Oysters

Red Beans and Rice with smoked sausage
Jambalaya with shrimp, Italian sausage, chicken and smoked sausage
Crawfish Étouffée
Bayou Platter Sampler – Red Beans, Jambalaya & étouffée
½ Po-Boy & Side shrimp, catfish or oyster with side of étouffée, jambalaya, gumbo or red beans

Fried Seafood Platter – shrimp, oysters and catfish
Fried Soft-Shell Crab Platter
Fried Shrimp & Oyster Platter
Fried Shrimp Platter
Fried Oyster Platter

Fried Pickles
Catfish Nuggets
Fried Crawfish Tails
Crawfish Cakes (2)
Sweet Potato Fries

Turtle Soup
Seafood Gumbo
Shrimp Cocktail
Shrimp Remoulade

Soft-shell Po-boy
Crawfish Po-boy
Grilled shrimp Po-boy
Grilled chicken Po-boy
Hamburger Po-boy

Bread Pudding
Pegan Pie
Red Velvet Cake

Felix's menu, c. 2000.

The Croatians

The Croatians in Louisiana hailed largely from the Dalmatian coast of the Adriatic Sea, mostly coming in the nineteenth century. Most of the new settlers came to the coastal areas, where they took up fishing. A great many of them became oystermen. Often the families would live in fishing camps built on pilings in the marshes. In the early twentieth century many families would move to the cities and larger towns with schools during the school year, the men remaining at the camps to fish. That brought many families to New Orleans. The largest concentration of Croatians is found in Empire and Buras. The influence of the Croatians is felt in the food.

Oysters and seafood are the key. The families have opened restaurants, and they continue to supply oysters to the cities. Luke Jurisich, who came here in the mid-nineteenth century, is considered the initiator of the modern oyster industry in the state. With John Popich, another Croatian immigrant, Jurisich formed P & J Oyster Company. The company has been supplying oysters since 1876, making it the oldest continuously operating oyster company in the United States, although today it is owned by descendants of Italian immigrants, the Sunseris. Today the oysters of many restaurants in New Orleans are supplied by P & J. The company was stymied after the Deepwater Horizon oil spill, when it could not supply oysters and the shuckers were laid off. The industry is slowly rebuilding.

Another Croatian oyster family, Drago and Klara Cvitanovich, opened a restaurant in 1969. The centerpiece dish of the restaurant is the charbroiled oyster. The restaurant is now run by Tommy, Drago and Klara's son, who invented their signature oyster dish. The restaurant recently joined the growing list of food trucks. Their charbroiled oysters are now available on the outfitted fire truck. Other restaurants founded by Croatian families are well known in the city, having exercised a great deal of influence on the city's eating habits. Another Drago's, opened by the Batiniches, was in Lakeview. Sam's Place, which opened in 1938 and served until 1978, was founded by Sam Batinich.

John Mandich opened a restaurant in 1922 on St. Claude Avenue, an active area close to the river. Port shipping magnates, who had been riverside from the early morning, would eat around 1 or 2 o'clock. In 1939 Lloyd English purchased the restaurant. In the 1950s Lloyd Jr. took over the restaurant. He renovated and expanded it and, most importantly, had his wife Joel become the chef. Lloyd Jr. tended bar. The oysters bordelaise were one of the specialties of the house. This dish was an oyster served with the traditional meuniére sauce. The restaurant flooded after Hurricane Katrina,

French Quarter oyster bar with expert crew of "shuckers," 1946. Associated Press.

causing the Lloyds to retire, closing what Gene Bourg called the "Galatoire's of the Ninth Ward."

Other Croatian restaurants were Gentilich's and Zibilich's. Uglesich's, in Central City, enjoyed a rabid national following. The award-winning restaurant always had lines when it was open, and the family also authored several cookbooks. Chris Steak House was opened by Chris Matulich. It was the Chris Steak House that was bought by Ruth Fertel and became Ruth's Chris Steakhouse. Rival steakhouse, Crescent City Steak House was opened by the Vojkoviches, and Bozo's by the Vodonoviches.

The Irish

Irish immigration to New Orleans occurred in several waves. The first wave was toward the end of the eighteenth century, when the predominantly Roman Catholic city was a refuge to the Irish escaping the British. There was a second wave of Irish immigration, because of famine in Ireland, starting about 1820 and continuing for roughly twenty years. The Irish did not bring many traditions to the table in New Orleans. However, they did work at the port unloading ships that brought food from various places to the port of New Orleans and they dug the New Basin Canal. They also contributed to the bar scene of the city, bringing a drinking tradition that included whiskey, which supplemented the wine tradition of the French and Spanish.

Margaret Gaffney Haughery came to New Orleans from Baltimore with her husband, Charles Haughery. Her husband and infant child died within a year of the move to New Orleans. Her parents had died in Baltimore, leaving her an orphan. The entire family had immigrated to America from Ireland where Margaret had been born. Her experience of loss and her sympathy for orphaned children defined her life's work. She worked with the Female Orphan Asylum operated by the Sisters of Charity. She chose food as a method for supporting herself, to support orphans, and to support the poor. She began a dairy to support herself and the Asylum, delivering the milk herself. Later she opened a bakery that was very successful and modern. Margaret's bread was famous throughout the city, as was her work on behalf of orphans and the poor. She died in 1882.

Descendants of Irish immigrants—the Brennan family—have had a deep influence on the restaurant culture of the city, including carrying the torch of Creole cuisine to other parts of the United States. Pat O'Brien was a leader in protecting and preserving the drinking culture of the city through Prohibition and through his eponymous bar. The drinking tradition continues on St. Patrick's Day. Parade participants during the various St. Patrick's Day parades distribute carrots, cabbage, potatoes, and onions, as well as green Moon Pies. Parasol's, Fahy's, Tracey's, Kerry Pub, and Finn McCool's carry on the tradition today. Matt Murphy, an actual Irishman, serves up traditional Irish fare at Irish House.

Because the city is known for its parades and because St. Patrick's Day and St. Joseph's Day are so close, March 17 and March 19, respectively, those people belonging to the marching clubs throughout the city, which march for these occasions and always coordinate the parades, often follow each other to maximize the city's fun. For St. Patrick's Day Irish bars all serve green beer. During the parade, marchers pass out potatoes, carrots, onions, and cabbages—the ingredients of an Irish boiled dinner. The Italians, for St. Joseph's Day, do not usually pass out food. That can be found in abundance on the St. Joseph's altars.

The Chinese

At the same time that Louisiana was recruiting Sicilians to work in the cane fields, the plantations were also recruiting the Chinese who had settled in the Caribbean. After short stints in the cane fields the Chinese immigrants began fishing and developed a technique for commercially drying shrimp. Dried shrimp are still used to this day to add another level of flavor to gumbos and shrimp dishes. Still today small packages of dried fish can be found at checkout points at grocery stores all over the city. Like anchovies in Italian cuisine or Asian fish sauce, the dried shrimp in New Orleans become the unidentified undertaste of umami in many Creole dishes.

The Vietnamese

There are more than 14,000 people of Vietnamese heritage living in and around New Orleans. Most of these people are from South Vietnam. Those whose families originally came from North Vietnam mostly moved south after 1954 following the communist takeover of the North. The fall of Saigon created the circumstances that brought thousands of Vietnamese immigrants to New Orleans through the auspices of Catholic Charities. There were two aspects of life in New Orleans that made the city an enticing place—it had a strong Roman Catholic heritage and it provided for a fishing culture.

Since their immigration and settlement the Vietnamese in New Orleans have become, as many immigrants, all about food. Of course they have been involved with other things, but for purposes of this book, the exploration of their food is relevant. The Vietnamese community has elaborate community gardens where Asian vegetables are grown and sold at markets. The markets in the Viet Village sell the seafood that is caught by the fishermen. Vietnamese restaurants are popular with New Orleanians who have no trouble asking for their favorite offerings in heavily accented Vietnamese.

There is much more. The community has been developing since the 1970s so there are offspring who speak English and as first-generation Americans form a bridge between those whose English skills have not developed and the greater community. They bring banh mi, known in New Orleans as Vietnamese poboys, to compete at the annual Poboy Festival. Often banh mis are made with the bread from Dong Phuong Bakery in New Orleans East. These days even traditional New Orleans poboys are turning up with pickled vegetable options. The French connection is something that is common to the Vietnamese and the people of New Orleans. For example, some Vietnamese bakers arrived already skilled at making baguettes. That history has made the transition to making king cakes an easy one. Hi Do Bakery is famous for the seafood-shaped king cakes that it sells with a more traditional brioche dough, rather than the now prevalent Danish dough.

Cajun Crawfish is a phenomenon that exploded beyond New Orleans and spread to Vietnamese communities around the country. In fact, because spicy crawfish boils are so easy to find in New Orleans, there is little need for Asian Cajun restaurants to open. The phenomenon of eating crawfish cooked with crab boil–like spices, served in their shells for peeling at the table, and referencing Cajun food is a clear crossover of cultural practices.

A popular restaurant is Pho Tau Bay. It began on the West Bank of the Mississippi River, but had expanded with other restaurants in New Orleans proper. It closed all of its expansions and still operates in Gretna. It is one of the expansions that did not survive the changes in city demographics after Hurricane Katrina. The Vietnamese vegetable list is familiar to the South; such foods as mustard greens with hot sauce can commonly be found on menus. Nine Roses serves its mustard greens with pork and shrimp, a familiar combination of flavors in the city. Yet another restaurant with excellent banh mi is Tan Dinh.

Pho, the Vietnamese noodle soup, is served with Crystal Hot Sauce, a popular local hot sauce, in restaurants all over the city, including grocery stores like Rouses. Many restaurants offer a daily gumbo and a daily pho. Pho is reminiscent of yaka mein, also called "Old Sober," a noodle dish very popular in New Orleans and often sold as street food at second lines. It is a folk remedy for hangovers and a regular stand at the New Orleans Jazz and Heritage Festival. Perhaps the similarity makes pho all the more appealing and easy to accept.

Some traditional New Orleans restaurants serve spring rolls in Vietnamese wrappers stuffed with mirliton. In just a few more generations the Vietnamese will have become so integrated into the foodways of the city that New Orleanians will have forgotten the origins of those pickles on poboys. Those pickles have found their way to the table at Cochon, which is an undeniably Cajun eatery. More and more the restaurants of New Orleans reflect the acceptance of the Vietnamese palate as a part of the city's palate. The restaurants of Emeril Lagasse and also of John Besh have regular nods to the Vietnamese influence, for example, Miss Hay's chicken wings at NOLA.

The Latin Americans

Before Hurricane Katrina the largest group of Latin American peoples living in and around New Orleans were those from Honduras. According to the 2000 Census there were more than 11,000 people in this area who had been born in Honduras. Because of their large presence Hispanic bodegas carry

Honduran food products and Hispanic restaurants offer food in the Honduran style, for example, black beans or encurtidos (pickles). For years one of the major street vendors in the city was Manuel's Hot Tamales.

Because of the port of New Orleans and the relationships that formed in Latin America due to the commerce that developed, the city has strong ties to families there. The relationships formed because of the activity of United Fruit Company and other fruit companies made the foods of Latin America familiar to and appreciated by the people of the city. Coffee, bananas, rum, and other foods were serious imports with great impact on the food and people of the city.

After Hurricane Katrina there was a large increase in the number of Hispanic immigrants, especially those from Mexico, even while the city as a whole lost population. These were people who came to the city and its surrounding area to assist in the rebuilding of the city. Their presence led to the emergence of taco trucks all over the city to feed the workers. In the early days after Hurricane Katrina, there weren't many restaurants open and personnel necessary to enforce various health and inspection codes were not to be found. These trucks arrived with wonderful food, but without licensing.

People working on their own houses and the construction workers who were working on other houses were all happy to see the trucks, which were serving excellent food. As with many areas that had numerous taco trucks, residents began to try them all with the idea of identifying the best trucks and the best offerings of various trucks. The taco truck operators began using locally available ingredients, offering crawfish tacos and poboys stuffed with turkey mole. Eaters and truck owners were happy, but as New Orleans normalized after the Hurricane, she became more bureaucratic and regulated. The taco trucks often disappeared instead of being licensed. Today they still exist but are not as numerous.

CHAPTER SIX

~

Markets, Retailing, and "Making Groceries"

"Making groceries" is a New Orleans expression for going shopping for groceries. It is a phrase that is a direct translation of the French term for shopping, *faire marcher*. The phrase has been long used in markets of the city. The people of New Orleans have been making groceries in many ways since the beginning of the city.

Native American Trading

Before the establishment of the French Market, a covered market in the French Quarter, in 1791, buying food on a retail basis was a rather informal affair. It took place on the shore of the Mississippi River at approximately the place of the current French Market. This was a place where Native Americans traded with each other. Later they and colonists came to trade there. Fish and game could be gutted and vegetables could be cleaned on the banks of the Mississippi and the tide would clean the banks. Trading was a source of food for immediate needs. Native Americans did preserve food, but they did not practice the kind of monoculture that France, and later Spain, needed to create wealth. Food was mostly seasonal.

The French and Trade with Europe

The French used the two rivers in America, the St. Lawrence and the Mississippi, to create a trade circuit through the country. Expeditions would start up the St. Lawrence, cross to the Great Lakes, and then cross to the Mississippi, picking up goods along the way. From New Orleans they would cross the Gulf of Mexico, stop in the Caribbean Islands, and continue on to France. There were no fine metals or spices with which to finance the trip, only tobacco and other agricultural products. In the Caribbean sugar was an important economic incentive, making the stop in the Caribbean an important last stop before crossing the Atlantic. To make the expedition worthwhile financially the trafficking in human beings developed, carrying the ships across the Atlantic from Africa to America. This created the financial incentive for the trips as well as created a cheap labor force for the colonies.

The sail from the Caribbean to New Orleans was an ordeal. It took about two months to travel from France to the Caribbean. It was another three months from the islands to New Orleans. The cargo had to be worth it, and it had to be able to survive the journey.

Port of New Orleans

The port of New Orleans was always important. Even the founders of the city knew that it would represent a strategic advantage to France as it developed. With statehood the port became increasingly important as America itself developed. Goods were floated down the Mississippi River to be exported to Europe. These goods made a short stop in New Orleans, providing the city with the bounty of the middle of the continent. With the development of the steam engine goods could travel both up and down the river. Besides bringing in goods from Europe and the Caribbean, the port grew to be a point of export to northern South America and Europe. After the building of the Panama Canal, the port of New Orleans could send and receive shipments from the Pacific side of South America and from Asia.

The port made New Orleans what became known as the Paris of the Mississippi. As in Paris one thing that the moniker meant that was that foods from all over the world, as well as people from all over the world, made their way into the city. It was because of the port that the Domino Sugar Refinery was located at New Orleans in the early twentieth century. It was because of the port that today coffee entered the city from Brazil, Central America, and the Caribbean, and roasting and distribution represents a huge portion of the coffee roasting of the entire country. It was because of the port that the banana and other fruit made their way from Central and South America into the United States. The port also allowed the bounty of grain, rice, and wheat to leave the country and feed the rest of the world.

Street Food

Food was sold on the streets from the early establishment of the colony. Although the Spanish tried to limit street sales, except for farmers associated with the market, it was next to impossible to keep people from selling in the neighborhoods. The vegetable peddlers wheeled barrows. Some carried fruits and vegetables on their heads in the graceful African manner. Others carried baskets of food singing to the neighborhood to alert people of their wares, sometimes in French and sometimes in English. In a collection of Louisiana folktales, *Gumbo Ya-Ya*, Robert Tallant was able to publish cries that were still being sung in the city in the 1930s, and some street cries were recorded by the Smithsonian Institution. The fruit and vegetable vendors advanced to wagons and to trucks. Other vendors have sold prepared foods for enjoying on the street or at home.

Today the most prominent fruit and vegetable peddler is known as Mr. Okra. Mr. Okra sells his fruits and vegetables from a truck completely painted by local outsider artist, Dr. Bob (Bob Shaffer). Mr. Okra's truck is equipped with a public address system that broadcasts his presence as he slowly drives through the streets. He still sings the old street cries, but they are amplified through his speakers. He has been the subject of a documentary and numerous newspaper and magazine articles. Besides Mr. Okra, who still moves through the neighborhoods, there are a number of fruit and vegetable vendors that maintain trucks at specified corners. They can always be found at their designated sites, selling from their trucks.

The tradition of street vendors in the city is an old one. Enslaved Africans, allowed Sundays off by the *Code Noir*, sold vegetables that they had grown, as well as hot coffee, candy, and calas. Free people of color also peddled in the street. It was a method of entering the marketplace that did not require a large capital investment. It also was compatible with the street life and hustle of the growing city. It is said that *vendeuses* (women street venders) were able to buy their own freedom and that of their families through their enterprise.

The sale of pralines and other candies by African American women on the streets of the French Quarter was something that was observed into the twentieth century. Postcards depicting the vendors wearing tignons, aprons, and carrying baskets of candies abound. The women, dressed in this distinctive style which reflected African clothing customs, were so identified with the sale of pralines that stores where pralines were sold were marked with life-size dolls or cut-outs dressed like the venders. This practice was similar to the manner of using a statue of a Native American to mark a tobacco store.

Another food that is associated with African American venders is the cala. Calas are fried rice fritters. They were usually sold by women venders, sometimes in pairs, where one person fried the fritters and another person walked around with a covered basket filled with hot calas, returning to refill the basket as the fritters were sold. Cries of "*Calas, Tout chaud*" (Calas, very hot) were heard when hot calas were available. It is said that slaves bought their freedom and the freedom of family members through the sale of calas. The sale of pralines, calas, and other foods was clearly an accessible source of entrepreneurship for these women, some of whom expanded from street sales to shops. Selling prepared foods was a method of making money which was available even to the enslaved. They could resourcefully use their skills and transform inexpensive basic ingredients into a desired commodity.

Other immigrants were quick to understand the benefit of street sales, most importantly the need for minimal capital to start the business. It was especially Sicilian immigrants who were found selling fruits and vegetables around town. The need to speak English was not as important when farming and displaying vegetables as it was in other jobs, which was another aspect that made street vending an available source of revenue. Vendors could drive carts to regular locations with a mule or horse, leave the cart with a vender, and use the same mule or horse to move a second cart to a different location. This was often the same mule which had pulled the plow in the fields to grow the vegetables. There were several venders who sold waffles on the street. The hot waffles were buttered, wrapped in paper, and sprinkled with powdered sugar. L. Gandolini could be seen painted on the side of one of the carts. Another name was Sam Dekemel, known as Bugling Sam, the Waffle Man. Vendors blew horns and rang bells to get the attention of customers. The waffle men were colorful enough to inspire musicians to write songs about them. OKeh Records released a record in 1924 called "The Waffle Man's Call." The song was a foxtrot. The artist was Johnny Bayersdorffer and His Jazzola Novelty Orchestra.

The Roman Candy Man, Sam Cortese, sold taffy candy from his horse-drawn truck. His grandson now runs the business. In the beginning the taffy was made at home and simply sold from the truck. However, later the taffy was made on the truck and stretched on a wheel. Roman Candy from New Orleans has been included in the Slow Food Ark of Taste. The Roman Candy truck is still seen on the streets of the city.

Lucky Dogs are a relatively modern street food in the city. It is said that the vendors are the important characters, and much more important than the hot dogs. The carts are made in the shape of a hot dog and bun. The company was started by Stephen Loyacano. In the 1970s ownership passed to

Doug Talbot and Peter Briant after a revamping of the health code changed the requirements for the carts. It is one of the few street vendors still allowed to sell in the French Quarter. The New Orleans City Council grandfathered in Lucky Dog carts and vendors when passing an ordinance banning new street carts, which they claimed were causing congestion in the narrow streets of the French Quarter. This ordinance was upheld by the US Supreme Court. The carts were considered a part of the fabric of the French Quarter. The Lucky Dog and its quirky vendors were immortalized in the 1980 novel *The Confederacy of Dunces*, by John Kennedy O'Toole. This book is just one more work in which the food of the city is almost a character, saying more than any direct explanation can about what food means to the city and its inhabitants.

In 1932 Manuel's Hot Tamales began selling tamales on the streets of New Orleans. The founder Manuel Hernandez sold his wares from a push-cart. These tamales were in the Mexican tradition and were not similar to the tamales of the Mississippi Delta. They were cooked in tomato sauce and oil and were at one time wrapped in corn husks. They were a powerful taste memory in New Orleans. They did not return after Hurricane Katrina although family members still dream of returning to production.

Today food trucks in New Orleans are a part of the great American food truck movement. In some ways it is a return to earlier traditions of street food that were disappearing from the city. The city was losing these traditions as modern life changed the need for food sold on the street. The resurgence of street food is an example of how phenomena are cyclical. Food available from food trucks can be very trendy, as opposed to traditional. Green to Go, for example, is a vegetable-based mobile food vendor which is bike powered. La Cocinita, a food truck that sells tacos and Latino fare, is a truck that appeared after Hurricane Katrina. It is becoming chic to arrange for a food truck to park by a party that allows good food to come to the party without catering or mess. SliderShak posts its locations via Twitter and Facebook, and offers sliders and fries, as well as a Creole malted milk. Ruby Slippers Nola is try-ing to create a moving dining room in a bus that will serve traditional New Orleans cuisine. This trend is growing in the city, having already spawned its own website, nolafoodtrucks.com.

The French Market

In 1780 the Spanish, who had become alarmed at the chaotic nature of the informal market, built a covered market at the levee for the sale of food. By creating a location from which food must be sold the Spanish could impose

French Market, c. 1906. Courtesy of Library of Congress, LC-D4-34323.

control. The control allowed the Spanish to inspect the food for sanitary purposes, control prices, and control quality. It also provided a source of revenue for the government. Under this umbrella preserved meat, game, grain and all manner of fowl were sold. This took place on the levee for a prescribed period during the day.

After the end of market hours food was sold by street vendors in the neighborhoods.

In the mid-1780s the Spanish government also realized that it could tax the vendors. The local Spanish government built a larger market and controlled the days when various foods could be sold. A rental fee was charged to the vendor for the stall that was assigned. Fishermen, who had been selling in the open air were also assigned appropriate stalls and they were not allowed to dump the remains of cleaned fish in the street. Anyone who sold spoiled food, especially turned meat or fish, was fined. Selling outside of the market could result in being fined or jailed. (Slaves who sold tainted food could also be lashed.) This helped maintain public health and safety.

There were gardens associated with the market. Those gardeners were allowed to vend in the street or the market. As they often do today, those shopkeepers who were paying rent and had the expenses and limitations of real estate objected to street vendors. Wholesale marketing was still taking place on a larger scale on the levee. The Spanish interfered beyond health and safety by setting prices and controlling merchandise. The French Market was said to be officially established in 1791. Marketing under a covered structure had already been established.

The French Market, ironically established during the Spanish regime, was a place of great commerce. In its heyday it reflected the cosmopolitan nature of the city. In 1857 Mark Twain described the fruit that was piled in pyramids in the French Market. There was citrus, watermelon, various berries, bananas, figs, pineapples, and more. He also saw myriad vegetables, meats, fish, lobsters, pastries, tea and coffee, and various types of nuts, game and other meats. Even that late in the development of the city the people of the Chitimacha, the Choctaw, the Houma, and the Natchez could still be identified, as well as Africans speaking various languages, and many Europeans and Asians speaking countless languages. The French Market was talked about as a tourist destination, where the whole world met, until well into the twentieth century. It was the early dawn time when restaurants made their purchases and even retailers in groceries bought from the French Market. Finally grocery stores made the market obsolete and the attraction of the world began to wane. Today the French Market, the oldest continuously operating market in the United States, is a tourist retail spot selling prepared foods, clothing, and antiques.

The City Market System

The French Market was the original, but in the 1830s the city began to establish a series of markets around the city. There was the Poydras Market and the Dryades Market, and many more markets as the city grew. These markets sprang from the original desire to provide clean and sanitary locations for the sale of food for the protection of the citizenry. These markets were also a source of revenue for the city, which tried to limit the ability of vendors to sell food outside the markets. In the early days market farms also grew up around the markets, making the sale of fruits and vegetables fresh and convenient. The markets themselves became centers of civic and neighborhood activity. They marked each neighborhood center, they reflected the character—as well as shaped the character—of the neighborhood, and they were a source of public works. Eventually other stores opened and were allowed to sell fresh goods, as well as the canned goods that dry goods stores already sold.

Nuns in the French Market, 1936. Courtesy of Library of Congress, LC-USF33-T01-000623-M2.

It was in the twentieth century, when the markets were not well maintained by the city, that the system began to decline. By some accounts the markets were unsanitary and corrupt (charging bribes for stalls), and they served no civic purpose. When grocery stores became privately owned, well promoted and responsive to consumers, it signaled the end of the market system in the city. Corner grocery stores were easy to reach, bringing the food to the street, instead of requiring that a person walk to the central grocery. Telephones and other advances in communication made the community gathering center that the market represented less crucial. The city tried to legislate prohibitions of corner stores close to a city market in an effort to keep the market system alive. But these efforts were unsuccessful in stopping the demise of the market system. In 1911 there were more than thirty public markets in the city. But as the city continued to expand and with the spread of automobiles, the markets could not survive. Their end was due to city mismanagement as well as changes in lifestyle.

Grocery Stores

Solari's

Located in the French Quarter at the corner of Royal and Iberville Streets where Mr. B's Bistro operates now, Solari's was a specialty market that housed a soda fountain and a lunch counter. It opened in 1863, selling those products that it could outside of the French Market. Its founder was John B. Solari. It sold Italian specialties and cheeses. What made it nationally famous was its sale of specialty foods, including fruits and vegetables that were out of season at a time when that was a true luxury. Solari's sold prepared foods like roasted chickens and gumbo, making it a precursor to grocery store prepared foods and specialty delis. Solari's not only carried caviar, imported olives, and specialty cheeses, it had an entire counter of eels and perfect fruits and vegetables. Solari's also sold its specialty imported foods through a mail-order catalog, which was another innovation in the market—harbinger of other mail-order food companies and Internet sales. Like most markets of its day, Solari's delivered, but shopping inside allowed a full exploration of its treasures. The sales staff was well dressed and polite. They were able to show off the luxury goods displayed with aplomb behind glass. Goods were attractively displayed. The fruits and designs of the marzipan counter alone were worth a trip to the store.

Clementine Paddleford recognized Solari's as the most luxurious grocery store in the United States. It had been for at least twenty years when Paddleford wrote about it. The fact that the curious and the hungry could mail order these luxuries was itself an innovative luxury. Solari's sold its own brands of New Orleans products at the store, through mail order, and at specialty stores around the country. These exotic specialties available around the country spread the gospel of Creole food and underscored the special relationship between New Orleans and delicious, unique food. Solari's closed in 1961.

Schwegmann's

John G. Schwegmann was born into a grocery family in 1911. John G. was the son of a German immigrant who owned and operated Schwegmann's Grocery and Bar in the Bywater neighborhood downriver from the French Quarter. John G. finally joined the family business after having worked several other jobs. He decided to become a grocer—but on a grand scale.

Schwegmann Brothers Giant Supermarkets introduced many innovative grocery industry practices. Led by John G., the Schwegmann brothers began to open private markets designed to lure shoppers away from the city markets that dominated the shopping life of New Orleans. As the city markets deteriorated, becoming unsanitary and unappetizing places, the Schwegmann Brothers stores offered competitive prices and more pleasant conditions. At one time the largest supermarket in the United States, at 155,000 square feet on Old Gentilly Road, was a Schwegmann Brothers store.

The local chain was built up from the original grocery founded in 1868 by John G. Schwegmann's father. John G. built a grocery empire filled with an imaginative approach to the experience of making groceries. His marketing practices would spread to groceries around the country. For example, to eliminate the expense of delivery and reduce the use of assistants in the store, common practices of the time, Schwegmann's offered a discount of 10 percent for those shoppers who shopped for themselves in the store and carried their own groceries home with them. The lure of the discount eventually overcame tradition for thrifty Creole cooks, and Schwegmann's began to be the place for everyday discount shopping in the city.

A list of other Schwegmann Brothers' Giant Supermarket innovations include: Schwegmanns' packaging its own house brand of myriad products from liquor to orange juice to coffee which it branded, but did not produce; the establishment of a bar inside the stores that allowed husbands to have a beer while they waited for their wives to finish shopping; the store accepted payments for various utility charges, which allowed shoppers to pay bills while shopping; the store opened its own bank; and the store used its paper bags as propaganda and marketing tools, for instance, decorated to become trick or treat bags at Halloween, to become book covers at the beginning of the school year, and to display political campaign materials, urging shoppers to vote for Schwegmann and others in various elections. Schwegmann successfully challenged minimum pricing in the state (the case involved milk prices)—ruled a form of price fixing by the courts—and thereby won the loyalty of many New Orleans shoppers, who considered Schwegmann a consumer advocate. The ruling allowed the Schwegmann stores to charge prices less than the going rate for everyday items such as Schwegmann milk, giving Schwegmann a competitive edge.

John Schwegmann's son, John G. Schwegmann Jr., expanded the business and continued the consumer advocacy of his father. John Jr. was elected to the Public Service Commission and his wife, Melinda Schwegmann, served as the Lieutenant Governor of Louisiana. Eventually the business declared bankruptcy and closed. With its closure ended a local shopping experience that continued the tradition of the marketplace as a center of community, while at the same time introducing new ideas into that marketplace.

Other Groceries

Rouses is the largest locally owned grocery chain in the city today. Before Hurricane Katrina Rouses was not well established in New Orleans, although it was a well-established store in the Houma-Thibodeaux area, which is about sixty miles away. J. P. Rouse founded the City Produce Company in Thibodaux, Louisiana, in 1923. The company began to supply grocery stores around the United States and served as an outlet for many Louisiana-grown products. In 1960 J. P.'s son, Anthony, and cousin, Ciro DeMarco, opened a grocery store in Houma. Anthony's sons, Donald and Tommy, joined the company as it expanded in the Houma-Thibodeaux area and throughout the southern part of Louisiana. In 1995 they expanded to a suburb of New Orleans, and Rouses was on its way to becoming the largest independent grocer in the state.

After Hurricane Katrina several large chain grocery stores did not reopen in New Orleans. In 2007 Rouses took over several grocery locations that had been part of the Sav-a-Center chain owned by A&P. This allowed the company to enter the New Orleans market, as well as enter the Mississippi market. Rouses specializes in local products and attractive presentation. Today the chain operates five stores in New Orleans and other stores in the greater metro area. It is a major supplier to home kitchens in the city, selling New Orleans dishes that are prepared in its deli kitchens—everything from its own version of Creole pho to muffulettas.

There are other local grocery stores like Zara's, Matassa's, Robert's, Breaux Mart, and Langenstein's which have a long legacy in the twentieth century. These stores do not have the individual reach of the Rouses stores. The family names reflect the history of the city. These local stores each have their own specialties and personalities and loyal customer bases.

Farmer's Markets

In today's world buying from a supermarket means that most foods are available all year round regardless of the season. Because of the way food is distributed today, supermarket shopping also creates some detachment from the origin of foods, since food often comes prewashed and cut, shrink wrapped, and processed. The desire to have a closer connection to our food and more control over our food choices has spawned a resurgence of the greenmarket or farmer's market. In New Orleans that means coming full circle to an urban practice that was once an important part of New Orleans history and identity. The original market on the Mississippi River, which became the French Market, the oldest continuously operating market in the United States, expanded to the market system of the entire city. The market system gave way to private grocery stores and the city lost its greenmarkets. The new concept of the greenmarket has emerged and become a cluster of independent farmer's markets in the city.

The resurgence of local greenmarkets (part of a national trend) is a return of the city to its early market roots. The fresh fruits and vegetables that were so important to the emerging cuisine are once again available. This trend ensures that Creole cuisine can continue to be cooked at home and continue to evolve. New groceries selling local foods—Rouses—have opened and continue to open all around the city.

Today in the city, as in the rest of the United States, there can be found trendy politically correct talk about the locavore movement and the use of the entire animal when cooking. There was a time in the city when mostly only local food was available. Food preservation like drying and smoking made it possible to travel with food or to use food in trade. With the popularity of coffee and chocolate, in many cases part of the Columbian Exchange, came changes in habits of drinking and eating. The world was explored in search of spices. Fortunes were made with the importation and distribution of coffee. Those who could afford it were quite pleased to be able to purchase the new foreign products without concern of a negative impact on the world. As the city of New Orleans was first settled, the settlers were dependent on the food that was locally available. With the increase in shipping to the area, wine, coffee, flour, and many other things were shipped into the city. There were many transfers of food, drink, and food customs and technology. Even later with refrigeration and advances in ground transportation, it became possible to ship perishable food that would remain safe to eat after it had traveled long distances. It became possible to eat food that was desirable, but not local.

Despite importation, remarkably the food of New Orleans was very local, because of the bounty of the environment. The food that was desired—oysters, crabs, shrimp, crawfish, finfish, pigs, figs, citrus, tomatoes, and so much more—was locally available. The food of New Orleans was naturally local. But this is definitely changing. Various environmental factors have reduced the bounty of the Gulf of Mexico. Crawfish, although farmed and plentiful, face the competition of Asian-farmed crawfish that are less expensive than Louisiana-grown crawfish. New Orleans, being a port city, has considered the foods brought into the port to be local. This means that coffee, for example, definitely not grown in or around the city, is local. It is roasted here and distributed all over the country. There are many local brands. For New Orleanians the local brand and local processing is all it takes to make the food local. New Orleanians still eat at home in accordance with custom— red beans and rice on Mondays and seafood on Fridays (whether Roman Catholic or not). All of these factors have influenced the new greenmarkets in the city.

The mother of these modern markets is the Crescent City Farmer's Market (CCFM) operated by Market Umbrella. The CCFM was established in 1996 by a coalition that included Loyola University and Wm. B. Reily Company, which lent its parking lot for a weekly downtown market. The Saturday market still continues in the Reily parking lot. The market provides a conduit for small growers, creating a market for the sale of food directly to consumers without a distributor. The market now operates in two other locations in different parts of the city, in addition to the Reily parking lot, during the week. The current organization, Market Umbrella, has developed an expertise in organizing and establishing markets and now serves as a consultant to many communities and markets across the country. The market also holds a Tuesday market in the Uptown area and a Thursday market near Bayou St. John.

The CCFM has been innovative in several regards. It has established the use of wooden tokens for those who shop with a credit card or with a SNAP card (Supplemental Nutrition Assistance Program). At a stand at the market one can purchase tokens that are accepted by the vendors in lieu of cash, but saving each vendor from having to accept credit cards or SNAP cards. The CCFM has been on the forefront of encouraging people to eat fresh and healthy foods by doubling the purchasing power of certain categories of buyers.

The Hollygrove Market has a different mission. It operates as an urban Community Supported Agriculture (CSA) and was created in post-Katrina New Orleans to provide fresh food to a neighborhood that was considered a food desert. Hollygrove purchases fresh produce, as well as grows it, and resells the produce in a box for a fixed weekly amount.

There are other markets now throughout the city. There is the large Vietnamese market Saturday mornings in New Orleans East. There is a market, the Sankofa Market, in the Ninth Ward on St. Claude Avenue every Saturday from 10:00 a.m. to 2:00 p.m. There are also monthly markets throughout the city that are often combinations of craft fairs and markets.

After Hurricane Katrina, as people returned to the city, not all of the grocery stores returned. Some of the national chains that had been operating in the city were slow to return. They were waiting for the demographics of neighborhoods to be right for their reopening. Most of the locally owned groceries did reopen and this changed the buying patterns and habits of the city. But some areas did not bounce back as quickly as others, leaving areas where there was no fresh food sold. In some areas this caused the development of new greenmarkets and interesting ad hoc vegetable markets, which in the New Orleans tradition also sell prepared food.

National Companies and the
Packaging of New Orleans Cuisine

There are companies that offer a little bit of New Orleans outside of the city. The fact that these companies exist, some of which have been bought by national or publically traded companies, indicates that the city's reputation as a crucible of unique flavor continues to thrive. It also indicates that the people of the city, even when they want to take advantage of the convenience of prepackaged foods, still want to eat in their own style. They still want to eat Creole food, even if they get it from a can or a box. That urge was strong enough to allow Creole food to make its way into the national supermarket arena. It also means that a little bit of Creole flavor is available everywhere.

Progresso
The Italians took their cooking into the modern era. Besides local bakeries, groceries, and fruit and vegetable distribution companies, the Italians were also responsible for Progresso Foods. Since the turn of the twentieth century, Vincent Taormina, one of the Sicilian immigrants to the city, had been importing Italian products to New Orleans and redistributing them to meet the demands of the growing population of Sicilians in the city and in the surrounding parishes. The family was involved in this endeavor and in 1927 Progresso Italian Food Corporation was established. Progresso was a company that eventually developed canned prepared Italian soups and specialties, especially Italian beans. The company became large enough that it attracted the attention of national food companies wishing to grow by accretion. The family sold the company in the 1970s. Now owned by General Mills, its heritage as a New Orleans company has been lost. That a local company developed to such a large following that it was picked to become a part of a larger publicly traded company reflects both the food and business acumen of the people of the city.

Zatarain's
In 1889 Emile J. Zatarain Sr. received a trademark for his root beer. With that his company was in business. The company began to sell prepared foods for the local market, selling mustards and pickles, spice mixes, and other products that conformed to local taste. In 1963 the Zatarain family sold the business. The new owners took the manufacturing process to the West Bank of the river. Today the company is owned by McCormick & Company, Inc., and sells more than two hundred different products reflecting the flavors of New Orleans. These flavors, including boxed mixes for Jambalaya, crab boil, filé, shrimp

creole, and red beans and rice are sold in regular grocery stores all over the country. This company makes New Orleans food available around the nation.

Wm. B. Reily & Company Inc.

This business is a manufacturing and packaging company in New Orleans. It is the owner of Luzianne, a tea and coffee brand that is associated with Louisiana and New Orleans, as well as with the South in general. The Southern connection is particularly strong with regard to Luzianne tea, which claims to be specially blended to brew the best iced tea. The company was founded by William B. Reily as an outgrowth of his grocery business in Bastrop, Louisiana, in the 1870s. He continued to open grocery stores around Louisiana. In 1902 he opened a business to roast, grind, and distribute coffee. It made sense to locate in New Orleans where a large majority of the coffee that came into America was imported. Shortly after getting started the company added its special iced tea blend.

In the 1960s the company began to expand by acquiring other companies. Its brands include Blue Plate mayonnaise, CDM coffee, French Market coffee, and Swan's Down Cake Flour. The Reily products, especially its coffees and tea, represent New Orleans all over the South.

Magic Seasoning Blends

This company is the brainchild of Paul Prudhomme. His spice blends, reflecting the flavors of New Orleans and Louisiana, are packaged for distribution all over the United States and around the world. His company also makes cured meats.

Baumer Foods

Baumer Foods is the producer of Crystal Hot Sauce, which is the hot sauce of choice for many New Orleanians. The company was founded in 1923 by Alvin and Mildred Baumer. Crystal Hot Sauce is sold all over the country and in many international countries. The company also makes other sauces, but the hot sauce is at its core.

Popeye's Chicken and Biscuits

Popeye's opened originally as Chicken on the Run in 1972. Not long after that Al Copeland, who determined that the fried chicken should be spicy and delicious, the founder began selling franchises. He successfully translated the Creole flavor for national and public consumption. The company grew very quickly adding hundreds of franchises. In 1989 the company merged with Church's Fried Chicken. At that time Church's was the second largest fried chicken company, while Popeye's was the third largest. In 2004 the holding company sold Church's and kept Popeye's. Popeye's current advertising conflates Cajun and New Orleans cooking. The menu includes Cajun fries, but it also sells its New Orleans flavors. This confusion reflects the national understanding—or misunderstanding—of the food of New Orleans. Or, perhaps, more accurately, it reflects the current merging of all of these flavors in New Orleans. The company uses New Orleans musician Dr. John in its television commercials, who sings their catch phrase, "Love that chicken from Popeye's."

Barq's

Although this root beer is now owned and bottled by Coca-Cola, the company is closely identified with New Orleans. Especially in its earlier incarnations the soda had a strong sarsaparilla flavor that wasn't too sweet. The company was established in New Orleans as Barq's Brothers Bottling Company in 1890 by brothers Edward Charles Edmond Barq and Gaston Barq. Edward married, and he and his wife moved to Biloxi, Mississippi. The company bottled other drinks besides the root beer drink. That list included red drink, a New Orleans name for crème soda, soda water, and Orangine. Orangine was an award-winning soda. In 1976 two men, John Koerner and John Oudt, purchased the company. Marketing the company was difficult because various Barq's companies existed in New Orleans and Baton Rouge, creating confusion. There were oral agreements which made ownership of recipes and trade names in question. These conflicts were resolved by the Coca-Cola Company in 1995, when it purchased the company. Barq's is a root beer marketed with caffeine.

There are bakeries that ship king cakes all over the country like Randazzo's and Haydel's. There are seafood distributors who supply Louisiana crawfish and other seafood to Louisiana restaurants around the country. It is true that the appreciation for the food of New Orleans has spread around the country and the people of New Orleans are ready to satisfy the itch. Many companies have just decided that they are big enough, and don't grow because growing might mean that everything changes.

Many small local companies provide convenient packaged shortcuts to preparing a Creole meal. It is possible to find pre-browned roux, coffee and chicory, seasoned fish fry, canned red beans, seasoned rice, canned and frozen gumbo, and packaged olive salad next to national brands of American prepared foods. Most of these foods are not sold around the country but are popular enough that the companies are sustained and successful with only local distribution and purchase.

CHAPTER SEVEN

~

Restaurants

Restaurants in New Orleans, in the style that we currently recognize restaurants, really started in 1840 with the establishment of Antoine's Restaurant. Previously transient eating was accomplished by eating at a boarding house or by making purchases of street food. The practice of eating at a restaurant with family or friends, making a special order from a menu in the French manner, was new to the United States. Only Delmonico's in New York could claim to have introduced the practice into the country. Once that first restaurant opened in New Orleans, the practice of eating out, that is, eating as entertainment, became firmly established in the city, and new restaurants followed. Eating out is still entertainment in the city. It is an endless source of discussion and exploration for all of the denizens of New Orleans.

The early restaurants, Antoine's, Tujague's, and Bruning's, were all named after the proprietors, who were sometimes also the chef. These restaurants were personal expressions of the culture of restaurants that was developing. Throughout its history, the restaurants of New Orleans have continued to influence the cuisine, often with the personal stamp of the chefs and restaurateurs shaping attitudes as well as the dining and the taste experience.

One of the most interesting and important influences on New Orleans, at least when discussing cuisine, is the development of the restaurant in Paris. The restaurant was developing in Paris during the period of the development of New Orleans. As is usually true in the hinterlands, a parallel development that lagged behind in time like an echo can be traced in New Orleans. Because the city continued to identify itself as French—receiving French journals, newspapers, and books, and later as it became more established and sophisticated received all of the French arts, even though it was technically being governed by the Spanish—there is a long period to established parallelism. Even after the Louisiana Purchase and statehood, French was spoken in the city into the twentieth century. This allowed parallelism to continue. Thus from a governmental standpoint the Spanish did have influence upon the development of the cuisine, as did the United States, but France continued to be the motherland of attitudes toward eating.

The Enlightenment

Much is written in the United States about the Enlightenment in both France and England and the contributions of this philosophical period on attitudes of freedom and equality, leading to the times of the American and French Revolutions. Whether called the Age of Enlightenment or sometimes the Age of Reason, this philosophical movement took place in the eighteenth century in Europe, most notably in France and England. While both French and English philosophers often addressed the same themes, the attitudes and the thoughts considered most important in the two strains of this movement were not identical. Without the French Enlightenment the restaurant would probably not have developed. Without the restaurant in France, philosophical attitudes toward eating and cuisine would not have developed and spread to New Orleans. Without the special French approach to cuisine and the restaurant and the corresponding mid-nineteenth-century eating experience that it created, there would be no cuisine in New Orleans and there would be no special restaurants.

England had recognized a certain level of popular rights as early as the Magna Carta in 1215. The writings of the English Enlightenment were built upon the rights already assumed to be established. These writings laid the foundation for the type of thinking that led to the American Revolution. In the most simplistic interpretation, the American Revolution changed the government; it did not revolutionize the culture, because culture was not seen to be held exclusively within the province of the monarchy. Eating, as culture and as art, was not a popular notion in England or in the English-influenced colonies in the New World. Eating and cooking, as an art form, are still active values in New Orleans to this day.

The French Revolution, as reflected in the writing of the French Enlightenment, was a cultural as well as political revolution. The French Enlightenment resulted, for example, in the enshrining of the practical and industrial arts in the *Encyclopédie* that was compiled and edited by Denis Diderot. Especially as it pertained to the upper classes dining was a public artistic activity that was actually observed by the masses. The lower classes literally watched the members of the court and the nobility dine. The poor were allowed to converge on the table to take the food left on the table when it was abandoned by the diners.

During the time that New Orleans was being founded, the restaurant was being developed in France. The *table d'hôte*, or common table, was a style of eating that was similar to a public house or tavern in other cities. The diner sat at a table with strangers (although if one ate at a particular place daily or at least regularly, the group might become acquaintances) and ate what was served by the "host" that day. Sometimes that also meant that by the time a dish had been passed around, there might not be enough for everyone. Many tables had drawers for storing a napkin for use during several meals or even for cutlery (although most people carried their cutlery with them to avoid theft). Women were not allowed to attend these public meals. There was a further limitation. The food was only served during certain hours. If one was hungry at a different time, one had to wait. There were allegations that the *tables d'hôte* were not sanitary because of the practices of sharing plates and sitting with unwashed people. There was a general lack of control over the preparation and serving of the food.

The practice of the *table d'hôte* existed during a period, the eighteenth century, in which there was a belief that the body's energy was finite. The intellectuals—the artists, the poets, the thinkers—used so much energy in their intellectual pursuits that they had little energy left for digestion. To sustain their health, those whose brains were taxed needed to eat special foods, things easily digested and very nourishing, to allow their bodies to have enough energy to be able to think. Their artistic sensibilities made it unhealthy for them to digest coarse food. The alternative to the coarse food served at *traiteurs* and *tables d'hôte* was to sip a *restaurant*, or restorative. A *restaurant* was a type of bouillon made of boiled meat served in a porcelain cup. Drinking this delicate and simple food was a healthy way for intellectuals to be nourished.

Also during this time the storefront was developing. To provide people with *restaurants*, shops began to appear. These shops offered cups of *restaurant*, or restorative, on demand. The cups were served at individual tables. For the first time women were allowed to be served as this was a matter of health, not sociability. In spite of the Enlightenment's embrace of simplicity and nature, not everyone embraced the trendy *nouvelle cuisine* that was on offer. Notably that curmudgeon, Voltaire, found the simple fare offered at the restaurants to be just as contrived as the supposedly complicated food that it was replacing.

The restaurant became established as a place, named after the cup of restorative. It began to undergo gradual changes as entrepreneurship prompted improvements in the offerings. Each establishment had to find a way to distinguish itself from the others. Additional offerings were simple and health conscious, developed for the delicate eaters (and by implication, thinkers) who ate there. Such things as boiled eggs, fruit, or simply prepared fish were common. Just like the restorative, these dishes were available on demand, served at one's individual table. The customer paid only for what was ordered, not a *table d'hôte* price. (From this beginning, the menu, restaurant reviews, and restaurant promotions developed.)

Significantly with women allowed to go out and eat at a restaurant without scandal contributed to restaurants being places of fashion and cosmopolitan attitudes. Restaurant owners wanted important people seen at their restaurants. The area of Paris around the Palais Royal developed as a center of restaurants, commerce, and the planning of revolution.

It was then that restaurants came to New Orleans. Although the city was a part of the United States after the Louisiana Purchase in 1803 and then statehood in 1812, the connections to France continued. The people of the city continued to speak French at home and in certain public parts of the city. They continued to travel back and forth to France and keep up with French thought. For example, many francophone New Orleanians with family in France left the city to live in France during the Civil War. When the artist Edgar Degas came to New Orleans to visit his brother for almost six months in 1872, he was able to negotiate the city in French. Although New Orleans was provincial in size and in thought as compared to the much older and larger Paris, it still represented a bit of French attitude in the United States. The city's first restaurant, Antoine's, was established in this environment. Some of the restaurants, such as Begue's and Tujague's, opened in the older style of the *traiteur* with *table d'hôte*. The existence of both types of restaurants merely reflects the transitional nature of the period.

Antoine's

Antoine's was founded in 1840 by Antoine Alciatore. Antoine apprenticed at restaurants in Marseilles where he was born. He traveled to New York and then to New Orleans, where he worked at the St. Charles Hotel. About a

Restaurant Antoine

Fondé En 1840   Depuis Plus De 100 Ans.

Le service chez Antoine exclusivement á la carte

Avis au public: Faire de la bonne cuisine demande un certain temps. Se on vous fait attendre, c'est pour meiux vous server, et vous plaire

Nous Recommandons

Huîtres en coquille á la Rocekfeller (notre creation) 1.00   Canapé Balthazar .90

Crevettes rémoulade .90   Pâté de foie gras á la gelée 1.75

Crabes St. Pierre .90

Entrées

Pigeonneaux sauce paradis 3.50   Poulet sauce rochambeau 2.25

Entre côte marchand de vin 4.00   Filet de boeuf Robespierre en casserole 5.00

Desserts

Omelette au rhum 1.10   Gâteau moka .50   Fraises au kirsch .90

Fromage

Roquefort .50   Camembert .50

Gruyère .50

Café et Thé

Café brulôt diabolique 1.00   Demi-tasse .15   Thé glacé .20

Eaux Minerales – Bière – Cigares – Cigarettes

Vichy   Bière locale   Cliquot Club   Cigares   Cigarettes

Ω Ω Ω

Antoine's menu, c. 1945.

year later he rented a building in the Vieux Carré. The original restaurant, located in the French Quarter, maintained rooms for boarding, as was common at that time. Although the location is not original, the restaurant has been in continuous operation by the family since its opening. (The restaurant did close for remodeling and repairs after the building was damaged in Hurricane Katrina.) It is still a family-owned and operated restaurant. It has vied with Delmonico's in New York as the oldest continuously operating family-owned restaurant in the United States. Antoine's has served a combination of local fare and French offerings since it opened. Only relatively recently has its menu been offered in English.

Antoine left for France, where he died after being diagnosed with tuberculosis. His son, Jules, eventually went to France to work in restaurants there, before returning to continue the family tradition. His mother ran the restaurant in his absence, but she turned over the duties to Jules in 1887. Jules's son, Roy, took over the restaurant in 1934. It continued to be handed down in the family, so that it is, to this day, still a family operation.

The waiters at Antoine's illustrate the tradition of waiters in the older establishments in the city. The waiters have been known to work at the restaurant for fifty years or more, with sons or other relatives of the waiters

Service at Antoine's. © Bettmann/Corbis /AP Images.

also working at the restaurant. If you are a regular at the restaurant you will have your regularly assigned waiter. If you are not recognized immediately at the door you may be asked who your waiter is. When you identify your waiter he will be called to take you to your table or if that waiter is not readily available, a busboy or steward might lead you to your table, where you will be served by your waiter. Your regular waiter, a professional, will remember what you drink, what your preferences are, recommend very fresh fish, and will pick out choice morsels for you. Should you not be a regular, a recommendation from a friend who has a regular waiter will allow you to ask for a waiter by name. When you are seated you can reveal that so you can pass along the recommendation.

Antoine's has contributed the flaming Café Brûlot to the canon of Creole food. It is also famous for its very French twice-fried puffed potato, Pommes Soufflées, which is also served at several other old-line restaurants in town. Jules, Anotine's son, took over the restaurant from his father. Jules created Pompano en Papillote and Oysters Rockefeller.

Many Mardi Gras krewes celebrate at Antoine's, which maintains private rooms that sport portraits of former kings, like the Rex Room and the Proteus Room, and other krewe memorabilia. Former queens of Mardi Gras lunch at the restaurant before Mardi Gras. The restaurant was memorialized in the Frances Parkenson Keyes's book *Dinner at Antoine's*. The family also operates a less formal restaurant as part of its offerings called Antoine's Annex.

Begué's

A storied place that has become the stuff of legend was Begué's, due to the talents of Madame Begué. In 1863 Louis Dutrey opened a coffeehouse, which was located across the street from the French Market. Workers at the market ate a second breakfast at the coffeehouse prepared by Dutrey's German wife, Elisabeth Kettering. Workers at the market, butchers and vegetable vendors, enjoyed a cup of coffee and a piece of bread at dawn to prepare for the early sales that the market attracted. By eleven o'clock there was a lull in sales, which afforded them the chance to enjoy a second breakfast. Dutrey died and Elisabeth remarried. Her second husband, Hypolite Begué, was one of the butchers who had partaken of those second breakfasts. The coffeehouse was renamed Begué's in 1880. At that time Madame Begué's fame as a talented cook was spreading, attracting the upper crust of New Orleans to eat breakfast at eleven o'clock at the coffeehouse. Guidebooks listed a meal at Begué's as an important part of any visit to the city, suggesting reservations be made by telephone.

Begue's Exchange Restaurant, c. 1900. Courtesy of Library of Congress, LC-D4-16337.

Madame Begué published a Creole cookbook and was important to establishing the reputation of the city as both a bohemian (where working-class and in-the-know members of the upper class ate together) and a gourmet experience. Existing photos of the coffeehouse reveal it to be a simple place, which means that the current willingness of New Orleanians to eat anywhere that the food is good, is not a new idea. Begué's served snails, tripe, cheese, eggs, steak, brandy, and wine. Meals there were an experience. After Elisabeth died in 1906 the coffeehouse continued serving with family operating it. M. Begué died in 1914 and the coffeehouse closed. Tujague's Restaurant now operates in the same location as did Begué's. It was operated by Jean-Dominic Castet, who had worked for M. Begué.

Tujague's Restaurant

Guillaume and Marie Abadie Tujague came to New Orleans in the early 1850s from Bordeaux, France. Despite the fact that Louisiana had been a state since 1812 French was still widely spoken in New Orleans, and there was still regular movement between the city and France. Guillaume was a butcher in the French Market prior to opening the doors of Tujague's in 1856. The restaurant served market workers, dock laborers from the river, and others working in the French Quarter. Lunches were generous and large, as was the custom in working class restaurants, filled with people working very hard. Specialties included a brisket served with horseradish sauce and a cold, spicy boiled shrimp dish. Tujague's and Begué's were competitors for the same customers and served similar fare.

Guillaume died in 1912. Before he died he sold the restaurant to Philbert Guichet. Guichet and Jean-Dominc Castet decided to close the old Tujague's location and moved together to the site of Begué's which they reopened as Tujague's. Jean-Dominic's wife, Clemence, was the considerable force behind Tujague's until her death in 1969. In 1982 the Guichet family sold the restaurant to Steven Latter. Latter has maintained the restaurant's traditions—still serving coffee in shot glasses—as well as continuing to serve the brisket with horseradish sauce and the shrimp remoulade, retaining the lack of pretention of the old coffeehouse style.

Bruning's

In 1859 Theodor Bruning opened the doors to Bruning's Restaurant, built over Lake Pontchartrain in the West End of New Orleans. Theodor had immigrated from Germany in the 1840s, first opening a restaurant on Claiborne Avenue. In its early days the restaurant, far from the center of New Orleans, was located in what was a resort area. The restaurant featured gambling and cabaret-style dancing waitresses. As the city moved out toward the lake, the restaurant became more family oriented and known for its seafood, especially the stuffed flounder. The restaurant was a familiar fixture at the lake, forming one of the group of seafood restaurants that served casual family-style meals, including boiled crabs, boiled shrimp, and raw oysters. The restaurant also served many types of fried seafood. The specialty of the house was the whole flounder, usually served stuffed. Other restaurants included Fitzgerald's, also located on pilings over the water. In 1998 the restaurant was besieged by Hurricane Georges. The family had anticipated that the aging structure might not continue to survive hurricanes and had purchased a lakeside building—not over the lake. The restaurant reopened in the new location shortly after the hurricane, continuing its tradition as an informal, family friendly seafood restaurant. In the flooding of 2005 following the collapse of the canal walls after Hurricane Katrina, Bruning's was inundated for weeks. The property was used for staging by the Corps of Engineers as it worked to pump water out of the city and rebuild the canal walls. The restaurant did not reopen. The mid-nineteenth-century bar from the original restaurant was donated to the Southern Food and Beverage Museum, where it is on exhibit.

Arnaud's

Arnaud's opened its doors in 1918. Originally only occupying one building on Bienville Street in the French Quarter, it has spread through the years to occupy almost an entire block between Bourbon and Dauphine Streets. Léon Bertrand Arnaud Cazenave was from the Basque country of France. He came to Louisiana intending to study medicine, but found his English wanting. Instead he worked at the Old Absinthe House until he was able to open his own restaurant. This restaurant was in the old style with rooms for rent to people who would also eat at the restaurant.

Cazenave was known as a *bon vivant*, and his manner of dress and charm earned him the nickname "Count." Count Arnaud ran his restaurant in the manner that was common in the day, with the owner setting the tone, but not being the chef. As it was being established, the chefs at Arnaud's would take the Count's ideas and turn them into menu items. Arnaud's claims many dishes such as Oysters Bienville and Shrimp Arnaud (a variation of the shrimp remoulade). He is also credited with inventing the cocktail, French 75, for which the current bar at Arnaud's is named.

Perhaps because of her father's flair, the Count's daughter, Germaine, developed into a young woman with a desire to perform. She reigned as queen of a number of Mardi Gras krewes and won a talent contest which allowed her to perform on the RKO vaudeville circuit. Her father died in 1948 and soon thereafter Germaine took over the restaurant. In her flamboyant way Germaine continued the inventiveness of the kitchen by adding many flaming dishes to the menu, ensuring the Cornish hens and desserts arrived ablaze at the table. She also enshrined many of her ball gowns and her father's royal finery in cases that can be seen by visitors to the restaurant. Germaine began the Easter parade of New Orleans that begins at the St. Louis Cathedral and proceeds via mule-drawn carriages to Arnaud's for Easter dinner.

In 1978 Archie and Jane Casbarian acquired the restaurant, imparting the traditions of a second family to Arnaud's. The family restored the building, and the next generation of the family still operates the restaurant. It is said that Germaine saw in Archie a person who would carry on the restaurant in her father's tradition and that is why she chose Archie as her father's heir. Now, in addition to the continuing formal dining of Arnaud's, there is also a more casual component called Remoulade.

Galatoire's

There was a time when a New Orleanian could bank on no changes at Galatoire's. This Bourbon Street restaurant was adamant about no reservations. It held on to its house accounts for years, sending out monthly invoices to its regulars. The restaurant was a place where the food was consistent, the waiters unchanging, and the décor tired, but familiar. Jean Galatoire purchased the restaurant (Victor's) in 1905. In 1956 there was a fire at the restaurant. After a two-week period during which the restaurant was repaired, it reopened, having been restored to its pre-fire décor. There was no attempt to change the restaurant. Later, it was renovated to great objection in 1999. Before then it had remained a place that looked like the bistro that it was. The restaurant retains its black-and-white tile floor, mirrors, and ceiling fans. But it is air conditioned and, since its renovation, has reopened its upstairs dining area and spruced up wall-coverings.

Jean Galatoire came to New Orleans from France by way of Alabama where he found French speakers in sufficient numbers for comfort and familiarity. Originally the restaurant maintained private dining upstairs. In the main dining area there is a clock on the back wall as well as a counter and perch for watching over the entire ground floor. In true bistro style long tables were once reserved for various business people to join each other for lunch. There were white embroidered and appliquéd café curtains in the Bourbon Street windows. The white tablecloths and napkins were once embroidered in a chain stitch with a script "Galatoire's" signature in red thread. Jean retired in 1916 and Justin stepped in to take over with his brothers, Leon and Gabriel.

Many stories have been told throughout the years about the occasional dignitaries who have been forced to stand in the egalitarian line that formed for entrance into the restaurant, because there were no reservations. It was not unusual for people to pay others to stand in line for them so that they could shop or drink down the street while awaiting a table. It was not uncommon for those who wanted to avoid waiting in line to eat at 5 p.m. or some other odd time.

The restaurant was known for serving fresh local products, especially seafood. In addition the waiters mixed drinks for their customers. As at Antoine's the regulars at Galatoire's had and still have regular waiters. The waiters kept their customers happy with excellent service and strong drinks.

Galatoire's has had a loyal following for all of its existence. Each change in the restaurant—no matter how small—has caused a degree of trauma for

Galatoire's

All subject to availability

Oysters: Oyster cocktail (one dozen)
Broiled or en brochette
A la Creole
Pan roast

Soups: Turtle
Gumbo
Creole gumbo

Seafood: Trout Meuniere Amondine
Broiled pompano
Red fish Courtbouillon
Sheepshead
Shrimp Creole
Soft shell crab
Fish papillotte

Meats: Kidneys – En brochette or broiled
Veal chop
Lamb chop
Pork chop

Vegetables: Brabant
Au gratin
Boiled or mashed
Lyonnaise

Coffee: Demitasse
Café brulot

Galatoire's traditional or guest menu, c. World War II.

regular customers, some of whom have been quite vocal with their complaints. Besides the complaints when the restaurant was renovated, there were complaints about the end of the practice of embroidering the napkins and tablecloths with the name Galatoire's in bright red thread, because not only did that signal change, but it indicated that a linen service was being used instead of an in-house laundry.

By far the most vocal complaint related to change occurred when a popular waiter named Gilberto was let go. There were lawsuits filed after the termination, but the effect on the customers and their reaction was extreme. Letters to the local newspaper, the *Times Picayune*, complaining about the termination poured in. The customers used the opportunity to complain about everything that they didn't like that had changed at the restaurant, including such things as the philistine use of an ice machine instead of continuing the practice of hand-chipping ice with an ice pick from a block.

The number of letters was so large that a local pundit, Chris Rose, who was then a columnist at the *Times Picayune*, turned the letters into a play called *The Galatoire's Monologues*. The play was popular with locals, having been performed many times around the city. Often the very people who wrote the letters actually performed the reading of the letters. The play was performed in other cities and states. Somehow the play about the passion of diners in New Orleans about their favorite restaurant was not hard for others to accept.

Most recently the family has shared ownership with an investor. The restaurant, which had required men to wear a jacket to dine, has loosened its jacket policy for lunch. Those who had arrived without a jacket could borrow one from those hanging from the coat bars in the foyer. They are no longer needed at lunch. The menu has changed slightly, and there are other subtle changes that only the regulars will appreciate and complain about.

Brennan's

This restaurant opened in 1946, more than one hundred years after Antoine's. However, it has become one of the famous restaurants of the city. Owen Brennan, the founder, was of Irish descent and seemingly the perfect personality to become a restaurateur. He worked at the Court of Two Sisters in the French Quarter before buying and operating the Old Absinthe House. (The Old Absinthe House was a restaurant run by Arnaud Cazenave prior to his opening Arnaud's.) He made this bar, in a neglected old building when he acquired it, a success. He was adept at making the most of publicity, and he took advantage of every myth and superstition surrounding the Old Absinthe House to entice visitors. It was here that Owen began using his sisters as employees in his business, employing Adelaide to be a bookkeeper and at first using young Ella as her chaperone.

As the story goes, Arnaud Cazenave goaded Owen about the ignorance of the Irish in the ways of food, finally making him prove his mettle by opening his own restaurant in the location of the former Vieux Carré Restaurant. He opened Brennan's Vieux Carré. It was here that the training ground of the entire Brennan family continued and expanded. Paul Blangé became the first famous chef at Brennan's. Blangé and Brennan's sister, Ella, developed a distinctive menu and style, which included such famous dishes as Bananas Foster and Eggs Hussarde.

With the help of Lucius Beebe, Owen Brennan invented breakfast at Brennan's. After reading about the publication of Francis Parkinson Keyes's book, *Dinner at Antoine's*, and the recognition and attention that it brought to the restaurant Antoine's, the two of them decided to promote this new idea. They devised a breakfast menu to rival those of Madame Begué and a new alliterative custom was born. With it also came the stylized cock that has come to symbolize the restaurant and its morning offerings.

Because of their success the family decided to move to a larger space—to the location where the restaurant is today. While the building was renovated, Owen Brennan died. In spite of this the family opened the restaurant on time. Although the entire family—Owen's siblings and Owen's wife and sons—operated the restaurant together after Owen's untimely death, disagreements arose. Today the restaurant known as Brennan's on Royal Street is operated by Owen's three sons, Pip, Jimmy, and Ted.

The Brennans

The several generations of the Brennan family are an important and influential restaurant dynasty in New Orleans. Their holdings extend outside of the city. This makes them ambassadors of the cuisine, establishing bastions of Creole cuisine outside of the city. The restaurant dynasty began with Owen Brennan who began his career with a successful bar at the Old Absinthe House and expanded to what is now Brennan's Restaurant. He included his family in the restaurant—his siblings, who contributed their different talents to the restaurant.

As many family businesses have had difficulties with generational change, the Brennan family had two generations to deal with. After Owen's death his children were not ready to take over the restaurant, and it had been supporting all of the siblings. There was a legal settlement which divided the assets that had been developed leaving the original Brennan's Restaurant in the ownership of Owen's sons and his widow. Commander's Palace, a fairly new acquisition, went to the other siblings. The family went on to divide its assets so that Palace Café and Commander's Palace were not jointly owned by the family.

Ella Brennan
From the time she was eighteen years old, Ella Brennan, sister to Owen Brennan, worked at the Old Absinthe House for her brother. At first she acted as bookkeeper, but she graduated into writing menus, training staff, and developing concepts of service and new restaurant ideas. She became an important part of the development of the identity of Brennan's. She and her siblings, Dottie, Dick, and John, purchased Commander's Palace in the Garden District in 1974, where she served what she referred to as haute Creole cuisine. She served excellent fresh New Orleans food coupled with extraordinary service. Ella Brennan is credited with discovering, nurturing, and developing culinary talent, such as Paul Prudhomme, Emeril Lagasse, and Jamie Shannon.

Ralph Brennan
Ralph Brennan is co-owner of Mr. B's Bistro, Commander's Palace, and Brennan's of Houston. He owns Red Fish Grill, Heritage Grill, Ralph's on the Park in New Orleans, as well as Ralph Brennan's Jazz Kitchen in Downtown Disney. He is a co-owner of Commander's Palace. Not trained in culinary school, Ralph was trained in the traditional manner by working on the line at Brennan's. He studied business at Tulane University and talks of his family's emphasis on the diner and the business. He has been president of the National Restaurant Association and very active in many civic activities.

Dickie Brennan and Others Brennans
Dick's son, Dickie Brennan, trained under Paul Prudhomme at Commander's Palace, trained as a chef in France, and returned to open Palace Café in New Orleans in 1991 in a historic building on Canal Street. He served as Executive Chef at the Café. In 1998 he opened Dickie Brennan's Steakhouse with his sister, Lauren Brennan Brower, and business partner, Steve Pettus. In 2002 he opened Dickie Brennan's Bourbon House Seafood and Oyster Bar. He has also written a cookbook. Lauren Brennan Brower began her restaurant career at Mr. B's Bistro and Commander's Palace. She trained at Ville de Francais and La Varenne Cooking School. As did her brother, Dickie, she began working at Palace Café when it opened in 1991. Family investment in restaurants continues to expand with more restaurants planned.

Ti Adelaide Martin and Lally Brennan, cousins, co-own (with Ralph Brennan) and operate Commander's Palace, and they own and operate Café

Adelaide. They also wrote a cocktail book, *In the Land of Cocktails*, and call themselves the Cocktail Chicks. Ti is the daughter of Ella Brennan and is continuing in her tradition. Lally is the daughter of John Brennan. The cousins continue to expand their restaurant investments.

All Brennans have had a tremendous impact on restaurants and eating in New Orleans during the twentieth and twenty-first centuries. They have collectively recognized and promoted chefs who have become household celebrities. They also have opened restaurants that serve traditional New Orleans food around the country, thus spreading the exposure of others to Creole food. They have a reputation for high standards of service in their establishments and a commitment to community service.

Commander's Palace

Commander's Palace has a history predating the Brennan influence. It was opened in 1880 by Emile Commander as a fine dining establishment in the American section of the city not far from the Mississippi River. Such notables as Mark Twain and local writer George Washington Cable ate there. Later, under a different owner, it became a place frequented by riverboat captains and the establishment reflected the risqué side of New Orleans. In the mid-twentieth century the restaurant was purchased by the Moran family. They maintained the restaurant until its purchase by the Brennans in 1974.

Dooky Chase

Dooky Chase had its start as a sandwich shop and bar that also sold lottery tickets. The business began in a double shotgun with the family living on one side and the business operated from the other. The first Mrs. Edgar (Dooky) Chase, Emily, was an excellent cook, and she sold lunches as well as sandwiches. Gradually she expanded her business. Her son, Edgar Chase Jr., also known as Dooky, was a musician. He and Leah fell in love and married in 1945. Leah Chase had been working at a restaurant in the French Quarter. During this time of racial segregation, she could work in the restaurant that only served white patrons, but she could not eat there. Her experience of working in French Quarter restaurants gave her a view of what restaurants could be. Building on the base of the bar and sandwich shop of her in-laws, she created a fine dining restaurant.

At nineteen the new Mrs. Dooky Chase Jr. wanted to expand the business of bar and sandwich shop to a real restaurant. She wanted to create a white

---

Commander's Palace

Frank Moran, Proprietor

Luncheon Special 1.35

Choice of one: Shrimp Remoulade or Turtle Soup

******

Calf Sweet Breads Saute – Jardinere

Or

Broiled Red Snapper Steak – Aux Fines Herbes

With
Black Eye Peas, Parsely Potatoes, Salad, Dessert
Iced Tea, Coffee or Milk

Merchant's Lunch .85

Boiled Brisket with Horseradish Sauce

With

Black Eye Peas, Parsley Potatoes, Salad
Iced Tea, Coffee or Milk

Desserts

Caramel Custard .30

Commander's Parfait .60

Coup St. Jacques 1.00

Peach Flambeau Plain 1.25

Commander's Palace menu, c. 1945.

tablecloth restaurant where black people could dine. After a few false starts the idea caught on. During this time Dooky Jr. was touring as the Dooky Chase Band, which helped promote the name and the restaurant.

The restaurant boasts an enviable art collection. Many of the artists were supported in some way by Mrs. Chase. Much of the civil rights movement of New Orleans was planned at the restaurant, which was visited by Israel

Augustine, Thurgood Marshall, Dutch Morial, and many others, as well as show business celebrities and US presidents. As a supporter of civil rights, the arts, and the community in general, it is appropriate that she is the model for Tiana, the title character in the Disney movie *The Princess and the Frog*.

Mrs. Chase, an actual living legend, has created a restaurant that is a standard bearer of New Orleans cuisine. Even during the era of segregation she defied the law, and her restaurant served whites and blacks. She has written several cookbooks and hosted television cooking shows over decades that have taught many New Orleanians how to make traditional dishes and new dishes with a New Orleans twist. Her personal and delicious interpretation of Gumbo Z'Herbes draws hundreds of people to her restaurant on Holy Thursday each year. Traditionally a Lenten dish made of an odd number of greens without meat, Mrs. Chase has added lots of meat and serves the dish as Lent is about to end with Easter.

Mrs. Chase is known for wearing a colorful chef's jacket, often bright pink or green. She says that she doesn't wear a white one, because white jackets are reserved for trained chefs. Her grandson, Edgar Chase IV, Lil Dook, graduated from Le Cordon Bleu in Paris. He is currently working at the restaurant and is clearly the heir apparent to the family tradition.

Mrs. Chase has received many honors, among them a lifetime achievement award from the Southern Foodways Alliance (2000), induction into the James Beard Who's Who of Food & Beverage in America (2010), many honorary degrees, and the naming of the Leah Chase Louisiana Gallery at the Southern Food and Beverage Museum. In April 2012 an exhibit of the work of Gustave Blache, a New Orleans artist living in New York, opened a show at the New Orleans Museum of Art. The work is portraits of Leah Chase in her restaurant kitchen or speaking with patrons in the dining room. After the show one of the portraits was installed in the National Portrait Gallery in Washington, D.C., enshrining Leah Chase in the pantheon of special Americans.

LeRuth's

LeRuth's was opened by Warren Leruth in 1965 in Gretna, a town on the West Bank of the Mississippi River, part of the greater metropolitan area of New Orleans. The New Orleans Underground Gourmet proclaimed in 1973 that LeRuth's was one of the finest restaurants in the world. The restaurant was frequented by celebrities and locals. The chef-owner, Warren Leruth, started his career as an apprentice chef at Solari's making pastries. He served in the Korean War and attended army's chef training.

He was a creative chef who worked for industry, creating such products as Green Goddess salad dressing for Seven Seas, and other products for national companies such as Outback Steakhouse. He developed red beans and rice and biscuits for Popeye's Fried Chicken and Biscuits. Leruth was consulted by restaurants around the country, using his New Orleans sensibilities to put a creative stamp on his work. Some of the famous dishes at his restaurant included Oyster and Artichoke Soup, Oysters Carnival, Crabmeat St. Francis, and offering house-made bread and desserts before this was considered de rigueur. He offered a house-made vanilla ice cream made with super-fatted cream. He offered an exceptional wine list, as well as frog legs, lamb, and veal when these foods were unexpected and unusually refined.

In 1982 he sold his restaurant to his sons, who operated the restaurant until it closed in 1991. Warren Leruth continued to eat red beans and rice on Mondays, a New Orleans chef connected to his roots. Leruth was also known for giving back to the community. He was a cofounder of the Chefs Charity for Children, which raised money for St. Michael's School.

Austin Leslie

Austin Leslie was the chef-owner of Chez Helene Restaurant, open from 1964 to 1995. Chez Helene was opened by Leslie's aunt, Helen Pollock. She had had several restaurants before opening Chez Helene. It was a casual restaurant with red and white checkered tablecloths. Austin was famous for his fried chicken. He had a distinctive appearance—sporting mutton chop sideburns and a yachting cap. The television show that appeared in 1987, *Frank's Place*, was modeled after Leslie and his restaurant. The production company flew Leslie to California to train the crew and actors about running Frank's Place. The program, which only lasted one season, introduced many people to the food of New Orleans.

Leslie had a job while in high school at Portia's Place, where he learned to cook fried chicken garnished with pickles from Bill Turner. Turner was famous for his fried chicken. He also worked behind the scenes at D. H. Holmes, a department store on Canal Street with a restaurant. When his aunt Helen opened Chez Helene in 1964 he went to work there. He bought the restaurant from her in 1975.

The restaurant was a darling of food critics, like Calvin Trillin and Johnny Apple, as well as recognized by locals as a great place to eat. Richard Collin, the Underground Gourmet, wrote about Chez Helene as early as 1971. Jack Duarte from the *Times Picayune* was a fan. In 1995 Leslie closed his restaurant because of the decline of the neighborhood. He relocated the restaurant to the French Quarter, but it did not catch on in its new location. Leslie began to cook at Jacques-Imo's, bringing his signature fried chicken talents with him. In 2004 he joined the front of the house at Pampy's Restaurant. He was trapped in his attic after the flooding following Hurricane Katrina and died about a month after his rescue.

Austin Leslie was important in twentieth-century Creole cooking. Not only a talented and innovative chef, Leslie was the kind of personality who ensured that his food reached beyond his restaurant and influenced others. He was an ambassador for Creole food. Besides his fried chicken, he served a special potato salad and a remarkable trout meunière and trout Marguery, and he was famous for his stuffed peppers.

Café du Monde

Café du Monde is located on Decatur Street in the French Market of New Orleans. It is a traditional coffeehouse that serves a very limited menu of café au lait or black coffee, hot or cold chocolate milk, plain milk, orange juice, and beignets—fried dough covered in powdered sugar. The coffee shop modernized by adding iced coffee and soft drinks to the menu. The coffee is brewed with chicory. The coffee house opened in 1862. At one time it was one of two large coffeehouses that book-ended the French Market. The second coffee house, Morning Call, was opened in 1870 by Joseph Jurasich. It moved from the French Market in 1974 to its current location in Metairie.

Café du Monde operates twenty-four hours a day and is only closed on Christmas Day. Debutantes and their escorts in evening attire can be seen having a restorative cup of coffee during the wee hours of the morning in the coffeehouse, sharing space with less elegantly clad customers. The coffeehouse is owned by H. N. Fernandez, Inc.

Today there are several locations of Café du Monde throughout the city, as well as locations in Japan. The company sells a boxed beignet mix as well as other logoed memorabilia. Rabbi Uri Topolosky of Beth Israel synagogue recently ensured that the beignets sold at Café du Monde are certified kosher by the Louisiana Kashrut Committee. This means that Jews wishing to include the fried treats in their Chanukah celebration can do so with assurance that the treats are religiously correct, representing another way that New Orleans cuisine crosses ethnic boundaries.

An ongoing monologue performance piece, *Meanwhile Back at Café du Monde*, was created by Peggy Sweeney McDonald. She produces regular

Café du Monde waiter serving chicory coffee and beignets. Courtesy of Library of Congress, LC-DIG-highsm-13227.

events during which people tell a short story about food in their lives. It is about how the mood at Café du Monde encourages discourse, and that discourse over and about food can happen anywhere. Her events have taken place in cities all over the country. A book about these food monologues is in publication and is expected to be available in late 2012.

The Modern Era and Its Influence

Broussard's

Broussard's was opened by Joe Broussard, a man from the era of the restaurateur where cooks remained unsung in the kitchen. He served French food at his French Quarter restaurant and the décor reflected his personal affection for Napoleon. Upon his death in 1968 the restaurant closed. Shortly thereafter it reopened under new ownership (1974), which included Sicilian restaurateur Joe Segreto, who combined the French and Italian heritages in true Creole tradition. Nathaniel Burton, former chef at Broussard's, coauthored the 1978 book, *Creole Feast*, with Rudy Lombard. It is an important book about the cooks of African American descent who ran the old-line Creole restaurants, their influence, and their recipes. Lombard was a Freedom Rider when he was president of the student body at Xavier University. As a native New Orleanian he was very aware from his own experience how the unseen cooks in the city's great restaurants had influenced the food of the city. His book tells their stories and memorializes their recipes. Today the restaurant is owned by chef-owner Gunter Preuss and his wife, Evelyn.

K-Paul's and Paul Prudhomme

Paul Prudhomme was born in 1940 in Opelousas, Louisiana, the youngest of thirteen children. He learned to appreciate the subtleties of flavor and taste in his mother's kitchen. He traveled the United States as a young man, honing his taste buds. He grew up in Cajun country but became the executive chef at the great Creole restaurant run at that time by Ella Brennan, Commander's Palace, where he worked with her to transform the menu. While he was working at Commander's Palace, he introduced the world to his own transformation of both Creole and Cajun food. Prudhomme and Brennan are credited with pairing Gulf trout with pecans instead of almonds, for example, making the dish truly Creole.

In 1979 he opened the French Quarter restaurant K-Paul's Louisiana Kitchen with his wife, Kay. When the restaurant opened Prudhomme was in the kitchen. Seating was communal, so tourists and locals alike were seated together at common tables. The restaurant didn't take reservations when it first opened. Today the restaurant takes reservations and tables are private, but the atmosphere remains elegantly casual. Chef Prudhomme has written eleven cookbooks, appeared on many seasons of public television cooking shows, and been the subject of countless magazine and newspaper articles.

He was the force that catapulted the cuisine of Louisiana around the world. His cooking is firmly grounded in Louisiana flavors, but his dishes are innovative and contain layers of flavor. He does not merely repeat the canon of dishes. He uses the flavors and techniques to create completely new dishes. Because of his books and his restaurant and his television shows, he made the world aware of the food of Louisiana. There are Louisiana-themed restaurants in Tokyo and London which opened after Prudhomme stunningly appeared on the scene.

The popularity of his invention, blackened redfish, caused such extensive overfishing of redfish that the fish population was threatened. The technique caught on: heating a cast iron pot until it is white hot, and quickly cooking fish—or now almost any protein—dredged in spices. The technique requires great finesse to avoid overcooking or burning the spices and the protein. Too often bad and overly peppered versions of this dish are offered at restaurants. In Prudhomme's hands the dish is delicate and moist.

In 1983 he opened his company Magic Seasoning Blends, which not only produces his own line of Cajun Magic Seasonings, but also develops and packages seasoning blends for many other companies. He continues to use his ability to taste on behalf of clients. He sells his blends all over the United States and internationally. In addition there is a catering business and smoked meats and sausage. His work in developing and making spice blends for restaurants is a behind the scenes way of continuing the influence of the food of the city.

After the city of New Orleans reopened and once the water was pumped out following the flood of Hurricane Katrina, Chef Paul converted his parking lot at the spice factory into a trailer park to house employees so that they would have a place to live. He reopened his restaurant and metaphorically floated it and employees on the back of the profits of the spice factory through the long wait for the return of people to the city. He was a strong voice in the reopening of the city at that time.

Emeril's and the Collection of Restaurants of Emeril Lagasse

Emeril Lagasse cooked at Commander's Palace as Executive Chef in 1982. He was recognized for his cooking by the James Beard organization. Both a musician and a chef, he studied culinary arts at Johnson and Wales University in Rhode Island. After leaving Commander's Palace he established his own restaurant, Emeril's in New Orleans in the warehouse district. It opened in 1990 to great acclaim. It was named Restaurant of the Year by *Esquire*.

After opening his flagship restaurant, Emeril opened Emeril's Delmonico on St. Charles Avenue in New Orleans. Delmonico's was an old Creole restaurant that had been named for the much grander restaurant in New York. Lagasse reopened the restaurant and kept is name, which was familiar to New Orleanians of a certain age. Emeril's Delmonico is a steak house. Emeril also opened an informal restaurant, NOLA, in the French Quarter.

After a long relationship with the Food Network, where Emeril taught the people of America about Creole food as perhaps its most famous ambassador, he has joined Martha Stewart Living Omnimedia. Perhaps because he was not from New Orleans and only adopted it, he could better interpret the food of the city for those outside of New Orleans. His success in bringing Creole food and Creole-inspired food to the United States continues to this day. He is now associated with the Martha Stewart organization. He continues to write cookbooks, writes for Stewart's magazines, and continues to make television shows. Although it did not last very long, Lagasse starred briefly in a primetime show about a chef who was much like himself.

Today Lagasse owns and operates more than ten restaurants around the country. He maintains a home base on St. Charles Avenue from which he conducts many aspects of his business operations, although his television production is not done in New Orleans. He has developed many prepared products sold in groceries, such as tomato sauce and spice mixes. He has also endorsed a line of appliances.

He has been on the forefront of chef's charities, having established a foundation encouraging and supporting charities related to children. He has supported the culinary program at the New Orleans Center for Creative Arts, St. Michael's School, and Café Reconcile.

Bayona

Susan Spicer began as an apprentice in a French Quarter restaurant in 1979 and after gaining experience all over the world, she and her business partner opened Bayona in 1990. It has captured the national spotlight as an important New Orleans restaurant located in the French Quarter. Spicer has run a specialty food store that offered prepared foods, cooking classes, and special breads. The breads, from her Wild Flour Breads, are sold throughout the city. Spicer has touched many restaurants in New Orleans, such as Herbsaint, Cobalt, and her current casual restaurant, Mondo.

The Besh Restaurants

John Besh has become a television personality, cookbook writer, chef and restaurateur, and a proponent of eating at home, home cooking, and the family meal. His flagship restaurant, Restaurant August, which reflects a farm to table local focus, is located in the Central Business District. He also owns nine other restaurants, mostly in the New Orleans area. Besh was a finalist on the Food Network show, *Who Will Be the Next Iron Chef?* He has a cooking show on public television. He was one of the restaurateurs who worked to feed first responders in the aftermath of Hurricane Katrina.

CHAPTER EIGHT

∽

Drinking in New Orleans

The drinking culture of New Orleans is just as important as the eating culture. The two cannot be separated. The free lunch, which attracted people to bars to have lunch while they drank, was the perfect melding of the drinking and eating culture. Wine, beer, spirits are all part of the cuisine and foodways of the city. Half jokingly it is said that the people of the city are functioning alcoholics. Alcohol is everywhere. Even grammar school fairs serve alcohol, although it may be on the sidewalk outside of official school grounds. There is alcohol at funerals, at weddings, in the streets, to celebrate, to lubricate social situations, and to help deal with tragedy. There are no "ABC" (Alcoholic Beverages Control) stores in Louisiana. Alcohol can be bought in drugstores, gas stations, and corner groceries, even on Sundays. It is served at graduations, at parties, and at malls. Until recently even a person driving a car could have a drive-through daiquiri.

The wine culture of Europe, the spirits culture, the pirates, the disrespectful attitude of the vagabond toward rules conditioned New Orleans to join the sporting life that allowed the pre-Prohibition bartender to become a person to be admired and respected. In the nineteenth century the spirit of adventure and the need for independence that fueled the Manifest Destiny of western expansion also supported the sporting life. Those men of means who could live without visible means of support, without personal connections and responsibilities, found several cities particularly compatible to that life. Those cities were New York, Chicago, and New Orleans. One of the ways that support for this life manifested itself was in the number of saloons found in the city. And New Orleans had many. These bars, really supporting the social drinking of spirits by men, flourished in New Orleans until Prohibition.

The cocktail has always been prominent in the culture of the city. There would no doubt be great controversy if an attempt were made to name the most famous or the most important cocktail. Being first is not important here. The cocktail was and still is part of the identity of the cuisine of the city. Despite the tradition of wine drinking in France and Spain, spirits were important here. When cocktails took second place to wine drinking in the later part of the twentieth century in the rest of America, the people of New Orleans just drank cocktails and wine.

The apocryphal story is that the cocktail was invented in New Orleans. It has been speculated that the word "cocktail" was derived from the French word *coquetier*, which is a two-sided egg cup. Early cocktails were served in the bowl of the egg cup. Cocktail is said to be the corruption of *coquetier*. The facts do not support that story. According to David Wondrich, cocktail and spirits historian, in the early 1800s, most cocktail historians consider the first written reference to a cocktail in *The Farmer's Cabinet*. The word was surely in use before it appeared in print. But the fact that the cocktail wasn't invented in New Orleans is really not important. A cocktail culture developed out of the drinking culture of New Orleans. Even William Sydney Porter, also known as O. Henry, wrote about drinks invented by Creoles.

Prohibition (1920–1933) was an interesting time in New Orleans. Although the Louisiana legislature did ratify the Eighteenth Amendment to the US Constitution establishing the ban on alcohol, it was not an overwhelming victory for Prohibition. Much of the state of Louisiana had already banned the sale of alcohol before the passage of the amendment. But New Orleans was decidedly not dry. There were more than 5,000 saloons in New Orleans at this time, and Prohibition was not welcomed in the city. It is safer to say that it was ignored. In preparation for its time of privation the city drank through record numbers of bottles of champagne and other drinks during the last New Year's celebration before the imposition of Prohibition on January 1, 1920.

In the United States, and in New Orleans, those people who continued to drink alcohol were able to find it in speakeasies in warehouses and basements guarded by secret passwords, special knocks, and locked doors. Many of the former saloons cum speakeasies had stockpiled cases of liquor in preparation for going underground. This period allowed for the flourishing of organized crime and the concomitant rise of federal agencies to combat the crime. It has been said that the constitutional amendment made federal felons of ordinary people overnight.

Elizabeth Pearce, New Orleans cocktail historian, tells the story of a federal agent, Isadore "Izzy" Einstein, who was sent to New Orleans to assess the degree of access to alcohol in the city. His informal method of making this assessment was to enter a city and try to obtain alcohol. It took him fourteen minutes to obtain alcohol in New York City. In New Orleans it was merely a matter of seconds. The taxi driver that he asked for help offered to sell him a fifth right from the cab. The federal agents considered New Orleans its wettest city during Prohibition. Some city had to be the least compliant. Such flouting of the law was consistent with New Orleans history. Considering that Prohibition was repealed and being considered a mistake, it is understandable that New Orleanians did not consider their lack of cooperation in the support of Prohibition wrong. New Orleanians were simply ignoring Prohibition until the country came to its senses.

The people of New Orleans—including the police—did not actually take Prohibition seriously. Such an indifference toward the law reflected the city's long history of winking at if not downright ignoring the laws that were not convenient or not considered reasonable. In the beginning of the colony it was an early acceptance of pirating and smuggling as necessary for survival. There was the practice of ignoring pronouncements and regulations of distant governments with no real interest in New Orleans. Some laws were enacted for convenience. They were written to make what would have been unacceptable and illegal behavior reflect reality, especially when the behavior did not necessarily reflect established (read Puritan) norms. An example of such a law was the establishment of plaçage, which recognized that white men could legally support concubines. When the country imposed Prohibition, the mere adoption of the law did not make freewheeling New Orleanians respectfully obey. Thus restaurants began to serve alcohol in locked rooms, but before the end of the year they had abandoned the ruse and served alcohol openly. Several restaurants, Delmonico's and Commander's Palace to name two, were padlocked by federal agents enforcing the Volstead Act. "Count" Cazenave was tried for the transgressions of Arnaud's Restaurant in violation of the Volstead Act, but he was acquitted.

Ironically it was the tradition of successful smuggling and rum drinking that caused the later problem of too much rum upon the repeal of Prohibition. As a sly nod to the past, during Prohibition rum was smuggled into New Orleans from the Caribbean, reinstituting the rum running and smuggling corridors of former days. New Orleans also served as a distribution point for rum to the rest of the South, with the Mississippi River serving as a highway. Rum was shipped in various disguised containers. Upon the end of Prohibition and the return to drinking other spirits, distributors had excess rum to get rid of. Speakeasies made an easy transition to legal saloons. Places like Pat O'Brien's, for example, merely moved to more commodious and easily accessible quarters.

The rise of speakeasies also had an interesting effect on the former male-only sporting life. Since alcohol was available in restaurants and speakeasies, it was now becoming acceptable—during its Prohibition—for women to drink. The saloons, which had been primarily male bastions, did not return to exclusively male haunts after the end of Prohibition. The Sazerac Bar in the Roosevelt Hotel was a bar patronized by politicians. It was a male-only bar. Women were only allowed in the bar on Mardi Gras Day. The Sazerac Bar was "stormed" by women who wished to be served there. Seymour Weiss bought the bar and moved it to within the hotel. He opened it for men and women. On September 26, 1949, women were welcomed into the bar and staged the storming for its photographic value. The date is now commemorated annually by women who dress for the occasion, sponsored by Tales of the Cocktail.

In 1988 the Louisiana legislature raised the drinking age from eighteen to twenty-one years. New Orleans had famously continued its history of drinking and only raised the drinking age when facing the threat of losing federal highway funds. The Twenty-sixth Amendment reduced the voting age from twenty-one, long the traditional age of majority, to eighteen in 1971. In other parts of the country many states reduced the drinking age to correspond to the reduced age of majority, but in Louisiana, the drinking age was already eighteen. With an increase in teenage highway deaths, there was a political move, largely pushed by Mothers against Drunk Driving (MADD), to return the drinking age to twenty-one. The short period of eighteen-year-olds drinking in those states, which had reduced the drinking age to the voting age, did not allow for the development of a learning period for teenaged drinkers. Thus they were misusing alcohol.

New Orleans has had teenage drinking for decades, if not centuries. Drinking was something learned at home under parental supervision. Drinking was not an unusual activity. Thus a teenager accompanying a family to a restaurant in the 1960s might see the waiter pause over the teenager's glass and look for permission from the parents to pour a glass. If the parents nodded permission, wine would be served to the teenager at the parents' table. This was the era of the Shirley Temple and the Roy Rogers, nonalcoholic cocktails that children could order to emulate their parents. In the post–Prohibition era, alcoholic beverages were drunk openly.

Another modern indicator of the place that drinking has in the culture of the city and the reputation for drinking that New Orleans has is the success of Tales of the Cocktail. This is an annual gathering of bartenders and alcohol purveyors and people interested in the cocktail culture spearheaded by Ann Tuennerman and the New Orleans Culinary and Cultural Preservation Society (NOCCPS). This annual event celebrated its tenth anniversary in summer 2012. Tales brings thousands of people to the city to study mixology, to talk about liquor and its history, and to drink, eat, and enjoy themselves.

The French Tradition

The French in the eighteenth century drank wine and not water. They brought this tradition with them to New Orleans. *Vitus vinifera*, the grape that is the mother of wine in Europe, did not grow well in the climate around New Orleans. The grapes that were native to the New World, like *Cynthiana*, sometimes hybridized with European vines, were grown north of Lake Pontchartrain by the early nineteenth century. This viticulture was conducted in addition to the wines that were imported from France and Spain. Viticulture was hampered in New Orleans by Pierce's disease, which is very prevalent along the Gulf Coast, attacking bunch grapes. The glassy-winged sharpshooter, a leaf hopper, is the insect that is the carrier of the bacterium (*Xylellafastidiosa*) that causes the disease. The disease kills the vines by causing them to dry out until the death of the vine. The progress made in combating the disease was completely stopped by the coming of Prohibition in the twentieth century. Today only Pontchartrain Vineyards north of Lake Pontchartrain grows and makes wine from bunch grapes in Louisiana.

Some other fruit wine was made, in particular when such practices were part of the traditional customs of the people of their countries of origin. Orange wine and strawberry wine were made from the citrus and strawberries that became well established in and around New Orleans. The end of Prohibition wines made from these fruits and others were made openly and were commercially available. In addition *vin d'orange*, a flavored wine made with citrus peels and sugar, was produced.

From the beginning the French drank wine that was brought to New Orleans from France. The wine might have been the worse for its journey across the Atlantic, but it remained alcoholic. It could be added to foods, like sherry in turtle soup, in addition to being drunk. The Spanish and other Europeans brought their wines and wine culture to the mix. The older historic restaurants have supported traditional wine and dining clubs for many decades. Many special menus reflecting the activities of these clubs can be found in the various archives of the city.

Madeira

The people of New Orleans also drank Madeira. Madeira is a fortified wine made off the coast of Africa. Because it was considered an African wine, it was not taxed as was European wine. Unlike regular wine Madeira was improved by its sea voyage. The changes in temperature and the agitation of the voyage made the Madeira taste better. Before a genuine wine-making tradition could be established in the colonies Madeira was an untaxed drink of choice. At the Louisiana Purchase the role of Madeira was made evident by the fact that it was the wine that represented the United States in the toasts that accompanied the signing ceremony.

Rum

Rum has two stories vis-à-vis New Orleans. The first story has to do with the vagabonds and other criminal denizens of the early city. Rum made in the Caribbean was much closer geographically than wine made in France. It was cheap and readily available. When ships between Europe and the New World were not frequent, wine was not always available. Making rum was a financially sound use of sugar cane. The rum had a long shelf life and converted acres of cane into bottles could be easily transported and stored. The distillation process added value to sugar and increased the growers' profits. While wine may have been the former daily drink of the Basques, the French, the Spanish, and the others who became buccaneers of the New World, rum became what they drank in the New World. Rum had a higher alcohol content than wine, so its effects were felt after fewer glasses. Rum was made with readily available ingredients and was not adversely affected by travel.

During Prohibition New Orleans rum runners carried on the traditions of smuggling that had been well established by smugglers and privateers in the eighteenth and nineteenth centuries. The pathways through the swamps and bayous worked as well for rum as for other goods. Once in New Orleans much of the rum remained in the city, and the rest was distributed to the state and beyond. In the 1940s after the end of Prohibition, whiskey was not as available as rum. Rum had been over produced and people were tired of drinking only rum. Liquor distributors had more rum than they could get rid of, so when they sold whiskey, which was much desired, they required bars to buy large quantities of rum at the same time. It was this requirement to buy rum to get whiskey that led to the invention of the drink, the Hurricane. Pat O'Brien, owner of the eponymous bar, had been running a speakeasy. At the end of Prohibition he converted the speakeasy to a legitimate bar in 1933. He and his partner, Charlie Cantrell, mixed rum with fruit syrup, and served it in a glass shaped like a hurricane lamp. Today the hurricane is a sought-after drink in the city. It is still served in the signature glass.

New Orleans is now also home to a rum distillery, Celebration Distillation, started by artist James Michalopoulis and friends, beginning as a kitchen table operation. The artist and some friends created their own still and use it to create Old New Orleans Rum out of Louisiana sugar cane. The first rum from the distillery was marketed in 1999. After more than ten years of operation, the distillery has many awards under its belt and now produces several styles of rum. For all of the rum drunk in New Orleans and imported from the Caribbean, this is the first rum ever actually produced in the city.

Absinthe

The relationship between Paris and New Orleans, which still existed throughout the nineteenth century, meant that the licorice-flavored spirit called absinthe would make its way to New Orleans. The Old Absinthe House is a remaining remnant of absinthe-drinking in the city. Drinking

Old Absinthe House bar. Courtesy of Library of Congress, LC-D4-16335.

absinthe, with all of its ritual, was just one more component of the drinking culture of the city.

Absinthe, a distilled spirit with a high alcohol content made with various herbs, has an anise or licorice flavor that was popular in the nineteenth century. It was said to have been invented by a pharmacist in Switzerland. It was associated with the arts and with the supposed iconoclastic and Bohemian lives of artists. Baudelaire, Toulouse-Lautrec, Rimbaud, Verlaine, and Degas were French artists and writers identified as a part of the *demimonde* and associated with absinthe. The drink was often called *la fée verte* (the green fairy) and was thought to cause hallucinations and violent behavior. One of the herbs used in the flavoring of absinthe, wormword, an herb used as far back as the Egyptians as a vermicide, was blamed for the hallucinations. Although not widely popular in the rest of the United States, it was very popular in New Orleans. The drink was available in several brands. The Old Absinthe House in the French Quarter was just one place where the drink was available. It was a known drink of journalist Lafcadio Hearn.

Because of unproven scientific assertions and the political influence of the wine industry, absinthe was banned in France in the early twentieth century. Shortly after that, in 1912, the drink was banned in the United States by the Department of Agriculture and the FDA. With absinthe popular in both Paris and New Orleans it is yet another indication of the continuing ties between New Orleans and France which lasted until about World War I.

The building that became the Old Absinthe House was built in 1806 by Pedro Font and Francisco Juncadelia as their place of business. The import business, selling groceries, wines, and tobacco run by the two Spanish immigrants, continued for years. In 1846 a part of the ground floor was converted into a coffeehouse, Aleix's Coffee Shop, run by a nephew of the family, Jacinto Aleix. Absinthe was already sold at the building for twenty years before the coffee shop opened. In 1869 the bartender Cayetano Ferrér began to work at the Coffee Shop, being hired away from the French Opera House. In 1874 Ferrér rented the Coffee House and he renamed it the Absinthe Room. His place was popular because he served absinthe in the French style, meaning with a fountain, a special spoon, and with a sugar cube. During Prohibition—the doors were closed by federal officers—the bar moved to a warehouse down the street. Pierre Casebonne bought the famous fountain, the marble bar, and the wall murals and installed them in a warehouse two blocks away to the Old Absinthe House Bar. The bar and fountain were purchased in 2004 and put back into the first building. That building operates as Jean Lafitte's Old Absinthe House.

Drinking absinthe in the United States was so identified with New Orleans that the Old Absinthe House that opened in New York claimed that it served absinthe just like the Old Absinthe House in New Orleans. A marketing booklet in 1935 claimed that the fountains were the first such fountains brought to the New World. Owen Brennan bought the Old Absinthe House in 1947. He ran the bar successfully until he opened Brennan's Restaurant. Today the bar is owned by the Morans.

In 1934 the New Orleans Absinthe Manufacturers Association was formed. It is interesting that this association was formed after the FDA and the US Department of Agriculture had already banned absinthe. There were many absinthe substitutes developed in the city, such as Herbsaint. Jung & Wulff was an absinthe manufacturer called Milky-Way. This company became Solari's Green Opal. It is interesting to see how food vendors, manufacturers, and distributors cross paths in the city. Absinthe was an important drink, appealing especially to culture makers and their followers. It also was one more tie between the city and Paris. The Solari family, which had a famous and successful fine food emporium, was also connected to absinthe. Nouvelle Orleans was also manufactured as a substitute for absinthe by the J. C. Yochim Company. The anise liquor, Ojen, made in Spain, also became a popular substitute for absinthe. The Ojen cocktail is associated with Mardi Gras and the Rex organization. The last distillery which made Ojen in Spain sold its entire production to Martin Wine Cellar in New Orleans. The drink remained important to Mardi Gras, but was no longer popular enough in Spain to keep the drink in production. In 2009 the last of the stockpiled Ojen was sold. Individuals may have personal stockpiles, but there is no longer a commercially produced source.

The Old Absinthe House has been visited by the nineteenth-century American literati like Mark Twain and Walt Whitman and other members of the cultural demi-monde, just as were absinthe houses in Europe. Many bars in the city served absinthe, but not all of them had absinthe in their names. New Orleans was a city of culture and intrigue. Even without paved streets it was the home of the first opera house in the United States. Absinthe added to the cocktail culture of the city.

Ted Breaux, a New Orleanian, features in the modern history of absinthe. A biochemist, Breaux became enamored of traditional absinthe and tested it through mass spectrometry. He determined that the levels of thujone, the chemical derived from wormwood thought to make absinthe so dangerous and hallucinogenic, was present in such a small quantity that it was not dangerous. Rather, it was moralistic zeal and scapegoating which had been the cause of the banning of the drink, not chemistry. It was Breaux's scientific work and the legal advocacy of others which convinced Alcohol, Tobacco, Tax and Trade Bureau to lift the ban on absinthe in 2007, making it possible to import and sell grand wormwood absinthe in the United States again. The continuing cycle of absinthe drinking in the city has been revived by a New Orleanian.

Brothers Ray and B. J. Bordelon have amassed a collection of absinthe artifacts in New Orleans that rivals French collections. Besides the European artifacts they have collected, their documentation and collection of material culture of the absinthe drinking culture of New Orleans, centered around the Old Absinthe House, is unrivaled. Their ever-expanding collection is exhibited at la Galerie d'Absinthe at the Southern Food and Beverage Museum in New Orleans.

Napoleon House

The Napoleon House was once owned by one Nicholas Girod, mayor of the city between 1812 and 1815. He was an admirer of Napoleon Bonaparte and is said to have offered the building, a fine residence, in 1821 as a place for the former emperor to retreat upon his exile. Napoleon did not take up Girod on this offer, but the name attached itself to the house. It still is today. Since 1914 the business has been owned by the Impastato family. Until the end of Prohibition the building became a grocery, and after Prohibition became a bar. The bar is known for its Pimm's Cup. It has been a Bohemian haunt and a place where the literati could be found. The bar retains its nineteenth-century feel and, besides drinks, serves a basic Creole fare of red beans and rice, gumbo, and muffulettas. The bar plays classical music in the background.

Bitters

Bitters are a tincture of spices or herbs in alcohol. Bitters usually taste bitter, hence the name, or bittersweet, because of the addition of a sweetener. They were first made by pharmacists who would mix the bitters with spirits, water, and perhaps sugar. The medicinal qualities of the herbs in bitters made the bitters a medicine. Some bitters, especially those in an alcohol base, came to be sold as patent medicines. Some of the traditional bitters are now served as digestives. Today bitters are also used as an ingredient in some cocktails and even in cooking. Today not all bitters are water soluble.

A pharmacist in New Orleans, Antoine Amédée Peychaud created a bitters with a primary ingredient of gentian in 1830. His family had come to

New Orleans from Saint Domingue in the late eighteenth century. Peychaud Bitters are an essential component of the Sazerac, the official drink of New Orleans.

Bourbon

Bourbon traveled to New Orleans from Kentucky and Tennessee (where the same spirits are generally called Tennessee whiskey) where it has been distilled since the 1800s and where it was copiously drunk. It is said that the drink was placed in charred barrels for transport as well as for aging. Bourbon is a spirit that uses old techniques from European distilleries and aging techniques with American ingredients, namely corn. New Orleans features in the lore of bourbon. It is said that barrels of whiskey made the trip to New Orleans, where all spirits were welcome. When the bourbon arrived in New Orleans it had become amber and taken on the flavor from the barrels. Unaged bourbon was also shipped to New Orleans. To make the drink a bit more palatable, flavoring the liquor was often undertaken, contributing to the cocktail culture.

Southern Comfort

Today Brown-Forman Corporation owns the brand Southern Comfort. It is a liqueur that is currently derived from neutral spirits, thus it does not derive flavor from the underlying spirit, but from spices and flavorings. It was originally made from whiskey and flavored with vanilla bean, citrus peels, and spices. The liqueur was created by Martin Wilkes Heron, a bartender, in 1874. Eventually Heron moved from New Orleans to Memphis. He patented his drink and sold it. In 1904 the drink was awarded a gold medal at the 1904 World's Fair which was held in St. Louis, Missouri. The plantation house found on the label today is the Woodland Plantation, located just outside of New Orleans. The drink is still associated with New Orleans and uses that association in its marketing.

Recently Southern Comfort has partnered with a Louisiana product, Tabasco, and sells a version of the liqueur flavored with the pepper sauce.

Sazerac

There is no denying the importance of the Sazerac. This cocktail has been named the Official Cocktail of New Orleans by the Louisiana Legislature. It has been proffered as the first cocktail, although the drink includes Peychaud bitters and New Orleans bitters, and it originally was made with absinthe, then Herbsaint when absinthe was banned. There is a bit of simple syrup or sugar with a twist of lemon. It is like the history of New Orleans in a cocktail. It was originally made in the 1880s with cognac, the Sazerac de Forge et Fils brand. The cocktail took the name of the brand of cognac. Today the drink is usually made with rye. It has been speculated that without the Sazerac and the city of New Orleans the rye industry might not have survived after Prohibition. Today the Sazerac is memorialized as the name of a bar at the Roosevelt Hotel. The Sazerac was at one time a "gentlemen's" bar. In 1946 women stormed the bar, ready to open the bar to women. This publicity event is reenacted annually at the bar to celebrate the freedom of women to frequent the bar.

Ramos Gin Fizz

Another famous drink is the Ramos Gin Fizz. The gin fizz took advantage of the new ability to create soda water. The Ramos Gin Fizz was invented in the late 1880s or 1890s by Henry C. Ramos. He and his brother operated the bar called the Imperial Cabinet Saloon. The bar became very popular during a time of increased tourism in the city. It was profiled in travel articles. It was a very labor-intensive drink, requiring many minutes of shaking to create the proper thickness, because it contained both cream and egg whites which required a long time and much shaking to emulsify. When the drink was at its height of popularity, bars would have to bring on extra bartenders and use employees who would just shake the drink to serve its customers. Stories abound about the various Mardi Gras celebrations that took place at the Ramos establishment.

Brandy Milk Punch

This punch is associated with the city and its brunch. This is one of the nuanced day drinks of the city. Brandy, sugar, milk, and nutmeg make for a simple punch which is an old-fashioned counterpoint to the more modern brunch standbys of Bloody Mary, a screwdriver, or a mimosa.

Coffee and Chicory

Coffee was imported from the Caribbean in the eighteenth century. After being established there, coffee plantations arose in Central America and in Brazil. New Orleans became a major port of importation of coffee beans, a major center of roasting and grinding, and a significant point of distribution of coffee to the rest of America. It also developed its own coffee culture along the way. Drinking café au lait in the French manner from large bowls was a common breakfast practice. There were coffee houses around the city during the nineteenth century and early twentieth centuries. (The poboy was invented at the Martin Brothers Coffee House.) New Orleanians drank coffee all day. Parisian-style demitasses of dark black coffee were served after evening meals.

Chicory, made from the root of the Belgian endive, is roasted and ground. It was originally sold separately as a coffee substitute. It was blended at home with roasted coffee. The taste for chicory coffee developed in New Orleans and persisted even after coffee was abundant enough to be affordable. Today local coffee companies sell a coffee and chicory blend which can be up to one-third chicory.

Café Brûlot Diabolique

In the nineteenth century flaming drinks and desserts were popular when Antoine Alciatore was living in France. When he established his New Orleans restaurant, Antoine's, he created a flaming drink for the menu. That creative impulse gave rise to the particularly New Orleans drink, Café Brûlot Diabolique. Today this drink is traditionally prepared tableside at restaurants with lights dimmed just before flaming, a delicious end to a grand meal. The drink is prepared by peeling the rind from a lemon or orange or both. The peel is studded with cloves. Sugar cubes and cinnamon are added to a bowl of hot coffee or coffee and chicory. Warmed cognac is poured over the citrus peel and the rest is added to the coffee. It is lit and dramatically served in stemmed cups. At Antoine's a bowl of silver and copper decorated with jesters or devils is used. It is ladled into the cups with a special ladle that filters the cloves and spices so that they do not make it into the cup.

This flavor was duplicated in a soda that was available for a short time in the early twentieth century. The soda, called Café Nola (brulo), was made by the Gruenwald Catering Company. The red-suited devil was used in advertising of the drink. The same character, dressed as the devil in Faust, is found on the brulot cups for serving the flaming brandy drink.

Hurricane

Another famous drink is the Hurricane, invented at Pat O'Brien's. This drink, made of rum and passion fruit syrup and served in a glass shaped like a curvaceous hurricane shade, is said to pack the wallop of a hurricane. Pat O'Brien ran a speakeasy prior to the end of Prohibition. Afterward he converted his speakeasy to a legitimate bar. Later he and Charlie Cantrell expanded into a larger space in the French Quarter with a lovely patio and is still serving drinks today. As previously described, bourbon and scotch were becoming hard for bars to obtain in the mid-1940s. American distilleries were being converted to wartime uses and Scotch was scarce. Liquor distributors required bars to purchase many cases of rum for each case of whiskey, creating a real oversupply of rum. O'Brien and Cantrell invented a pretty, dark pink sweet drink.

More modern cocktails include the Creole Bloody Mary, which is laced with Louisiana Hot Sauce. Today Tabasco makes a Bloody Mary mix. The Handgrenade is another late-twentieth-century drink found in the French Quarter. The drink was actually trademarked by the Tropical Isle bar. It is served in a tall green plastic glass that has been molded into the shape of a hand grenade at its base. Drinkers walking up and down Bourbon Street can be seen carrying this large green glass go cup.

Breweries

The city was at one time a city of many breweries. Many of them were started or run by the German immigrants living in New Orleans who arrived in the later half of the nineteenth century. In the first half of the nineteenth century a mild form of beer was produced in New Orleans. This beer, city beer, was not stable and therefore not suitable for exportation outside of the city. This all changed with the influx of Germans after 1850. Before Prohibition and the changes in distribution laws that came into effect after the end of Prohibition, breweries distributed their own product through ownership of bars and taverns, or they invested in restaurants and bars. In either case their products were sold exclusively. Many German immigrants worked in the breweries, so the German beer culture not only provided beer for the city, but also employment for the members of this ethnic group.

In the 1850s Georg Merz produced real lager in New Orleans at the Old Canal Steam Brewery. Later Dixie Brewery opened in 1907 by Valentine Merz, a nephew of Georg Merz. He had been the president of the Jackson Brewing Company and others. The Merz family, of German descent, had been in brewing for several generations. The Dixie brewery was damaged by flooding and equipment was looted after Hurricane Katrina. It is currently produced by contract breweries out of Louisiana.

Jackson Brewery opened in 1891 in the French Quarter, owned by the Fabacher family. This brewery closed in the 1970s. Falstaff Beer, a product of the National Brewing Company, was not locally owned, but like the other breweries, it was a part of the culture of the city. Other local breweries were Weckerling, Columbia, and Pelican. All of the breweries sponsored softball teams and played the other breweries. Employees could take home buckets of beer and drink as much as they wanted on the job.

Today there is a microbrewery at the Crescent City Brewhouse in the French Quarter, also operated by a German. Gordon Biersch also operates a microbrewery in the city. Abita Beer, located on the north shore of Lake Pontchartrain, produces a bottled beer. Contemporary breweries such as New Orleans Lager & Ale Brewing Company operate within the city. New Orleans Lager & Ale Brewing Company, also called NOLA Brewing, was established in 2008 as a craft brewing facility by New Orleanian Kirk Coco. It produces both lagers and ale and is located on Tchoupitoulas in the Irish Channel neighborhood. NOLA Brewing is the most recent addition to the city's brewing history.

Open Container Law

It is hard to talk about drinking in New Orleans without mentioning the Open Container Law. Those who visit the city are often surprised by the ability of drinkers to ask for a "go cup" from the bartender when they are ready to leave a bar or restaurant. A person in New Orleans is allowed to walk down the street with an open plastic cup filled with an alcoholic beverage and drink while walking. In anticipation of the need to provide a portable drink at the end of the evening, the go cup is often printed with the name and logo of the bar or restaurant that provides it, giving a bit of advertising to those who see it as the drinker walks down the street. For the sake of safety walking down the street with an open container made of actual glass is prohibited.

Those from New Orleans often share their first experience of having requested a go cup from a bartender in a city outside of Louisiana and being forced to chug their remaining drink, since walking out of the establishment with a go cup is not a legal option. It is one of those moments that makes the native New Orleanian understand what a special place the city is. Sharing a drink in public is a part of the experience of drinking in New Orleans, thus sipping wine on the balcony as you watch the passing parade, having a picnic with wine on the beach, or having a beer in the park are all experiences that New Orleanians share. The inability to enjoy alcoholic beverages in open areas in other places causes many a traveling New Orleanian to appreciate the customs of home.

Tourists are often amazed by the drive-through daiquiri shops. Until recently even an open container in a car was allowed. In the 1950s and 1960s a drive-up window at a restaurant was as likely to sell a cocktail or a beer as food. Whether because of the early tradition of hedonism, the lack of Puritan roots, or because the city simply admits that drinking is one of its historically legal pleasures, drinking in public is not taboo. It sets a tone in the city. The city drinks.

During parades—whether Mardi Gras, St. Patrick's Day, St. Joseph's Day, Halloween, or any other celebration—walkers often carry their own beverages. Mardi Gras walkers often pull a wagon equipped with an ice chest full of alcoholic beverages so that there is no need to stop and purchase such sustenance along the parade route.

CHAPTER NINE

~

Cooking at Home and Cookbooks

Family and Identity

The real basis for a cuisine is the food people cook and serve at home. The food of New Orleans began to develop long before restaurants were found all over the city. In a place like New Orleans where most restaurants serve local cuisine, it is still not the restaurants that nurture the flavors, the dishes, and the cultural foodways of the city. It is the home cooks, who prepare food to share with their families and friends, who are the guardians of our food traditions and who are the transmitters of the traditions into the future.

Before the coming of the Europeans to settle in what was to become la Nouvelle-Orléans, the native peoples prepared meals reflecting the great natural bounty of the area. The native people cultivated and tended to oyster beds, gathered fish, crabs and shrimp, caught crawfish, hunted duck and turkey and deer, tended corn, pecans, tomatoes, onions, sweet potatoes, peppers, peanuts, pumpkin, and beans. This list of great variety does not reflect all that was available and exploited by native people. Through trade they had access to such things as chocolate and potatoes. This diverse natural pantry formed the basis of plentiful and generous foodways.

The Europeans established the city of la Nouvelle-Orléans in the early eighteenth century. In the earliest days the French and other Europeans were hard pressed to duplicate their traditional dishes and cultural practices. There was an abundance of local product and there were also occasional ships bringing supplies. The food that developed was home cooking and street food. It was the addition of enslaved Africans who were often employed as cooks that made the city's home kitchens the crucible for the development of what has come to be known as Creole cuisine.

In 1881 Abby Fisher wrote a cookbook in San Francisco, *What Mrs. Fisher Knows about Old Southern Cooking*, that contained recipes whose names establish that Creole was at least recognized as a reference to New Orleans cooking in recipes. This first African American cookbook, written by a former slave, contains a recipe for Creole Chow Chow and also contains several gumbo recipes. In 1884 with the publication of *La Cuisine Creole* Lafcadio Hearn named the collective cuisine of the city in a book that reached the visitors to the city during the World Cotton Exposition. It took Hearn, a journalist—an outsider—to realize that the food prepared and eaten in the city was unlike the food eaten in the rest of the United States. For those who grew up eating the food, it was just their familiar food—the food that they found both inside and outside of their homes. Later in 1938 Lyle Saxon, another writer published the *WPA Guide to New Orleans*. In this volume, complete with recipes, Saxon pointed out that eating the food of the city was just as important as seeing its architectural and historic sites. Since then eating the food has been an important experience for visitors. One hundred years after the 1884 World Exposition at what is now Audubon Park, the city hosted the 1984 Louisiana World Exposition. That event brought in food writers and journalists to eat the food of the city, once again recognizing the preeminence of food in the cultural life of the city.

So many cultural traditions in New Orleans include food as a central component, making food and kitchen the standard bearers of the culture. Will H. Coleman, in 1885, published a book about New Orleans in which he discussed food and food traditions with affection. Both men and women today cook with their children as a way to pass down tradition and a bit of civilization with it. Families eat together as a way to share their love. Fathers cook with sons and daughters at fishing camps and in backyards. Cooking is a respected skill. Good home cooks are honored and recognized, competing with each other to make the best gumbo or best red beans and rice at festival competitions.

People take their cooking seriously. From eating at home everyone at all levels of culinary training, all levels of academic accomplishment, and all levels of financial status and employment has an opinion about food and taste and flavor in New Orleans. And everyone feels the impulse to share their opinion. And the opinions of others are considered valid regardless of the status of others. People know how to make the food of the city, because they continue to make it and eat it at home. Even when going out to eat food in restaurants prepared by renowned chefs, the standard set for the best gumbo or the best red beans and rice or the best whatever is what they would eat at home. Trying gumbo and having someone say, "This isn't as good as Aunt Sally's," is a feature of conversation that reinforces the prominence and importance of home cooking.

Making cookies for a St. Joseph's Altar, frying a turkey for Thanksgiving, bringing food to someone's home after a funeral, making food for a Mardi Gras celebration, having a crab boil in the backyard—these are all special cultural activities supported by food. This food is made at home. But in addition the people of New Orleans eat at home on an everyday basis. They frugally keep from wasting food by using stale bread for pain perdu. They turn a big turkey dinner into turkey bone gumbo the next day. Stale cornbread becomes an oyster dressing. Nothing is wasted—Sunday's ham bone flavors Monday's red beans and rice.

After the failure of the federal levee system in August 2005, all of the boxes, notebooks, and files of personal recipes were lost when 80 percent of the city was flooded. Even those who did not have personal recipe collections had collections of cookbooks. These were lost too. The people turned to the *Times Picayune*, the city newspaper, to rebuild their recipe collections. Judy Walker, the food editor of the newspaper, and a food writer for the paper, Marcelle Bienvenu, cowrote the 2008 book, *Cooking up a Storm*, based on all of the recipes requested by the readers to help them recreate their former tables. Fortunately the archives of the newspaper were not lost and the quest of the returning residents to restore their kitchens to what had been could be satisfied. The dramatic experience of loss borne by the city, and the desire to return to Creole cooking and to normalcy, document how important recipes and home cooking are to the city's culinary life. Cooking is still regularly happening in people's homes. Not having their personal collections of recipes was something that made home cooks seek to replace particular recipes, not just buy a new cookbook. Their personal tastes and habits were specific and definite, further affirming the assertion that the city has a cuisine and a deep gastronomic heritage.

Moving into the Present

Despite its unique cuisine and its French and Spanish governing traditions—as opposed to the often English traditions of the developing eighteenth-century America—present-day New Orleans is just as influenced by general food and beverage trends in the United States as the rest of the country. The role of food has allowed for the development of media food personalities—newspaper columnists, cooking school teachers, radio and television personalities, and cookbook writers—long before the advent of the Food Network, but the number of personalities has increased with the popularity of food as an American cultural phenomenon. In the same way Creole cuisine is being influenced by such trends as the locavore movement and the development of convenience foods. The modern day also reflects the cultural importance of teaching children and teens, using food as a way to teach culture and train teens to join the workforce.

Using the Food Culture

The growth of children's cooking programs all continue to support home cooking in the city. Youth chef programs in local high schools and children's cooking camps, all modern reflections of the way heritage has been passed down through the generations, abound in the city. These phenomena bode well for the future of the city's continued respect for its common heritage of food. Several programs have sprung up in the city which use food and the food culture to help at-risk youth find their way back to the mainstream. They work in several ways, but are all based on the strong tie between the culture of the people of New Orleans and its food. Food provides an anchor for these programs to help youth find structure, job training, and a way to relate to others. These programs, like the one at Café Reconcile, serve traditional Creole food to the community in a café setting. The students in the program, looking for direction in their lives, learn to cook, to serve, and to work with each other grounded in a cultural identity reflected in Creole cuisine. Other programs, also based on traditional foods, include Liberty's Kitchen and Café Hope.

Another use of the pervasive nature of the cuisine in the culture of the city is its use in advertising and as a simple way to represent the city. After it was established and recognized at the end of the nineteenth century, Creole cuisine was promoted in a number of ways within and without the city. Of course it was promoted by tourism officials, who also made sure that restaurateurs offered appropriate dishes in their restaurants to satisfy tourists. Tourism officials also advertised the unique nature of the cuisine in magazines. At the same time travel writers were telling the rest of the country about the special attraction of the food of New Orleans. Since the mid-twentieth century, the businesses of New Orleans recognized that tourism was an important aspect of the city's economy. In deciding to attempt to increase tourism the businesses determined that they should actively promote the culinary experience of a visit to New Orleans. This is not to say that the culinary experience of the city had not been remarked upon for years—by Lafcadio Hearn with his cookbook, by the WPA in the 1930s in its guidebook, by various travelers in their diaries and other writings. Finally the city government itself, as well as the business leaders, concluded that it should promote this phenomenon. The various city marketing and business organizations talked about the food of the city as a lure to entice tourists to visit New Orleans.

This decision by the city and its businesses took the idea of a culinary city to another level. Now instead of the cuisine of the city being something that was observed and experienced by tourists while they visited the city, tourists were being encouraged to visit the city to experience the cuisine. The city recognized itself as a culinary city. This recognition did not make New Orleans a culinary city. It did not create the cuisine. The decision to promote the culinary aspects of the city has made restaurants, cookbook writers, and chefs into the city's ambassadors. The news media—from television to blogs—provided new ways to share the culinary message of New Orleans with outsiders and with each other.

Personalities, the Arts, and Cookbook Writers

In the modern era the people who represented the people of New Orleans—in the newspaper, in the arts like literature and music, on the radio, on television, and on the Internet—could do so with the city of New Orleans as the primary audience. These personalities were and are popular because the cuisine of New Orleans is still a home cuisine enjoyed every day. They shaped the cuisine by reinterpreting the cuisine for their viewers, listeners, and readers. Not only does this keep the cuisine fresh, but it continues to train new home cooks and maintains all of the cuisine's cultural connections. These people were not just cookbook authors, they were cultural leaders. These people influenced how the people of the city cooked at home, how and what they ate in restaurants, and how they thought about their food and their identity.

Food and the Arts in the City

Chefs and scholars have taken the connection between food and literature seriously. Writers who lived in the city, both locals and transplants, also spread the gospel of the food of New Orleans. They used the city's attitude toward food as a synecdoche to describe the city. In doing this they reinforce the understanding and the belief that the city has a special cuisine. But they can use the cuisine to represent the city precisely because the cuisine exists and is different from the food of the rest of the country. Besides O'Toole's *Confederacy of Dunces*, which captures the eating and drinking culture of the city, many other writers reflect the mood through food. *Dinner with Tennessee Williams: Recipes and Stories Inspired by America's Southern Playwright*, by Troy Gilbert and Greg Picolo, is a culinary tribute to Williams, but at the same time explains all of the food references that Williams uses in his plays, especially those set in New Orleans. In *A Streetcar Named Desire*, Williams references the tamales sold on the streets of New Orleans at that time. Kenneth Holditch, a Williams scholar, added essays to the book about the food references in Williams's play to the book. He also wrote about Williams and his love of food and drink in his book, *Tennessee Williams and the South*.

In 1947 Francis Parkinson Keyes, in her book *Dinner at Antoine's*, set the tone of a certain class of New Orleanian through this first restaurant and the dishes invented there. Antoine's as a setting establishes an attitude that Keyes is trying to establish about the city. Food and elegant eating reflect not only class but exoticism and mystery. Keyes lived in New Orleans only a few blocks from Antoine's. Food and Antoine's were mentioned in several other books by Keyes, including *Once on Esplanade: A Cycle between Two Creole Weddings* and *Crescent Carnival*.

Holditch himself is a literary scholar who recognizes the place of food in the city and its literature. He also cowrote the book about the role that Galatoire's Restaurant plays in the city. Holditch and Marda Burdon wrote the book, *Galatoire's: The Biography of a Bistro*, which recounts over many years the importance of the restaurant in setting and reflecting the tone of the city. It does that through food and its service and its culture.

Musicians write about many things they love. Not all songs about food come from New Orleans. But many do. Kermit Ruffins and the Barbecue Swingers actually cook and serve barbecue during many of their performances. Songs about the waffle man, gumbo, crawfish, and jambalaya are indicators of how important food is to the local culture. The monthly music magazine, *OffBeat*, has a regular and popular column featuring a musician and his or her favorite recipes. In April 2012 the Smithsonian released a download of a Louis Armstrong concert at the National Press Club. The food at the event was prepared by Christopher Blake, named Gourmet Laureate by then-Mayor Dutch Morial. Together Armstrong and Blake made a list of favorite dishes while Armstrong waited to perform. The recipes for those dishes were published as a booklet called *Red Beans and Rice-ly Yours*, after the unique way that Armstrong signed his letters.

The New Orleans Jazz and Heritage Festival, known as Jazz Fest, has become almost as popular for its great food and popular food demonstrations as it has for its music. The food tent is carefully curated and Fest-goers look forward to Crawfish Monica, crawfish bread, yaka mein, and other great food throughout the festival.

Television

Television has been a documenter and a transmitter of Creole cuisine. In the early days of television many stations presented cooking demonstrations. From 1949 to 1950, WDSU, the city's first television station, presented *Lena Richard's Cookbook*. Richard was a celebrated cook with a restaurant and a cookbook. Upon her death in 1950, Marie Matthews, Amanda Lee, and Scoop Kennedy presented cooking shows. There were cooking segments on the Midday Show with Terry Flettrich and also on the morning show. Alec Gifford, a longtime reporter, anchor, and commentator on various New Orleans stations, was a part of many years of programs featuring Leah Chase, cooking Creole cuisine. WWL-TV has an early morning show that regularly hosts chefs who hold demonstrations in the mornings. Most stations in the city have provided some form of cooking on the air.

Through the years the local commercial television stations in New Orleans continued to present locally produced cooking programs which were not only popular, but also ensured that Creole cuisine remained a staple in the homes of television watchers. Public television stations produced cooking programs that were seen in New Orleans and also around America. Justin Wilson hosted Cajun cooking shows produced by PBS station WYES in the early 1980s. Some of his shows were produced in Mississippi, but were aired on the public stations in New Orleans. The cooking was not Creole, but it exposed New Orleanians to Cajun food in the comfort of their own homes.

Paul Prudhomme began his television career on WYES. His series began in 1995 with *Fork in the Road*. There are four other series, including his most recent production called *Always Cooking* (2007). These series include more than one hundred episodes of Chef Paul Prudhomme presenting his personal and creative take on the food of Louisiana, including Creole food. His reputation for building flavor and his playful personality contributed to the spread of that most interesting fusion of Creole and Cajun cuisine which he embodies.

The Great Chefs series began in New Orleans with Great Chefs of New Orleans created by John Shoup. The Great Chefs of New Orleans series includes twenty-six episodes. The series expanded to include Great Chefs programs from other major food cities in America as well as around the world. Many chefs from New Orleans were captured early in their careers by the Great Chefs series. This series brought restaurant cooking into people's homes. The cooking was not done in a studio, but in restaurant kitchens. This innovation in presentation of cooking shows changed the way many people perceived the restaurant, paving the way for cooking shows set on location in restaurants by many cable channels today.

Earl Peyroux

Earl Peyroux was born in New Orleans. He was an important television food teacher—he appeared in more than 600 public television programs—although he did not produce his shows in New Orleans. He was a graduate of Le Cordon Bleu in Paris. He taught at the Pensacola Junior College as a culinary instructor, which is where his broadcasts originated. Even from Florida Peyroux was an ambassador for Creole cuisine. He began hosting the television show, *Gourmet Cooking*, in 1977. He wrote seven cookbooks.

Emeril Lagasse

Emeril Lagasse is not from New Orleans or even from Louisiana. He is from Massachusetts. But he is one of the most important modern ambassadors of Creole cuisine who has ever appeared on television. His mentor at Commander's Palace was Paul Prudhomme, the man who sparked the explosion of Cajun cuisine into America. Lagasse is more identified with Creole cuisine than Cajun. He has been an important influence in establishing the prominence of the Food Network, creating cooking shows which have live audiences and live music, and using the buzz words "Bam"—when using seasonings—and "Kick it up a notch"—when adding other flavor elements. In his role as a daily fixture on the Food Network, Lagasse appeared in the homes of hundreds of thousands of viewers. On a daily basis he exposed viewers to secrets and flavors of Creole food. Lagasse also established a number of Creole restaurants, at first in New Orleans, and later in other cities in the United States.

NOPSI

New Orleans Public Service, or NOPSI, was the enterprise that combined being the utility company and the public transit company of the city. NOPSI was highly regulated by the City Council of New Orleans. NOPSI provided reading material on a periodic basis for riders on the city's streetcars and buses. This material always included recipes. When riding on public transportation the company expected its riders to take the pamphlet that also contained information about the company because New Orleanians would read recipes. These recipes have been collected into cookbooks. Many people found the recipes to be important enough to save informally in their own recipe collections.

The work of spreading the word about the food of New Orleans continues through the work of a number of important blogs that concentrate on New Orleans food and the food scene. They make what happens on the streets and tables of New Orleans accessible to the world. They are written by people who live in New Orleans or who are from New Orleans and live elsewhere. In the latter case the bloggers prove that the food is a stronger tie to the city of New Orleans than geography.

One New Orleans blog is Native Palate. There are many, many blogs about New Orleans food and drink, for example, Haute Plates, Gumbo Pages, NOJuju, NOLA Cuisine, Mr. Lakes Nonpompous New Orleans Food Forum, Yat Cuisine, to name just some. Many national food sites have regular New Orleans contributors. These sites are often linked to Twitter and there are many Tweets, making it easy to follow the opinions and experiences of the bloggers in many formats. Twitter is particularly useful to find the best food and festivals, like Jazz Fest, the Tomato Festival, Oyster Festival, or French Quarter Festival. The Road Food Festival, which happens annually in New Orleans, brings out the need for using Twitter to find the best food fast when there are so many choices and large crowds.

Lena Richard

Lena Richard was an ambassador of New Orleans cuisine for the home cook on television, through writing her cookbook and by cooking at restaurants around the country. She was born in New Roads, Louisiana. When Richard was young she worked with her mother for Nugent B. Vairin. Vairin hired Richard when she finished high school. She was even sent to the Fanny Farmer Cooking School in Boston by Vairin, who recognized her talent. Richard found that she had little to learn and much to teach to her instructors at the Fanny Farmer School. This experience led her to understand her talent and to appreciate the special nature of the food of her home.

Richard wrote a book, *New Orleans Cook Book*, which she self-published. Later it was republished by Houghton Mifflin in 1939. She was a culinary Renaissance woman. She ran a cooking school in 1937. She starred in a cooking show demonstrating Creole cuisine on television in 1948 to 1949. The show was called *Lena Richard's Cookbook*. WDSU was an early television station, the earliest one in Louisiana and the sixth in the South. Richard was likely one of the first, if not the first, African American with her own television show in America. The show appeared on WDSU on Tuesdays and Thursdays at 5:00 p.m. In addition to her show she was running a restaurant in New Orleans, Gumbo House, when she died in 1950.

Although the documentation is sketchy regarding the exact dates, it is known that Richard ran the kitchen at Bird & Bottle Inn, a restaurant in Garrison, New York. Later in the 1940s Richard was the chef who opened Travis House in Williamsburg, Virginia. She had been recruited for Travis House by the Rockefeller Foundation based on her culinary reputation. No less a commentator than Clementine Paddleford, the food editor of the *New York Herald Tribune*, sang the praises of Richard.

Mary Land

Mary Land published her cookbook, *Louisiana Cookery*, in 1954. It is a very Louisiana cookbook, which covers the food of the entire state. She wrote *New Orleans Cuisine* in 1969. Especially when read together they are encyclopedic in scope and help explain the subtle differences between traditional Cajun and traditional Creole cuisine. By reading her gumbo recipes, for example, one can discern the differences in technique and ingredients between the two area cuisines. Her cookbook tells tales and documents cultural food practices and food history that span more than 1,000 recipes. Land was a hunter and an avid fisherwoman. From these activities she became a supporter of conservation and wrote for *Louisiana Conservation Review*.

Leon E. Soniat Jr.

Leon E. Soniat Jr. is the author of two books, *La Bouche Creole* and *La Bouche Creole II*. He was also a columnist for the *Times Picayune/States-Item*. His weekly column, "The Creole Kitchen," sustained the kitchens of many New Orleanians. He taught cooking classes and was the highly respected host of both a radio show and a television show about food. He died shortly before his second book was released. It was his grandmother, Memere, with his mother, who taught him about *la bouche Creole*.

His two books, the second cowritten with his wife, June, are full of authentic recipes with wonderful stories about his grandmother's and his mother's kitchen. There is plenty of kitchen lore and good advice about the pitfalls of untended roux and heated filé. Soniat also espoused and perpetuated many myths about Creole cooking and food in New Orleans as though they were truth. Considered such an authority on preparing the food, his historical statements may also seem true. His delivery of the history is full of charm and the pleasure of the story is delivered in true Creole style.

Lee Barnes

Lee Barnes was born in Natchez, Mississippi. She graduated from Newcomb College in New Orleans in 1973 and from Cordon Bleu in Paris. She ran the

Lee Barnes Cooking School and Gourmet Shop in New Orleans from 1974 to 1986 where she greatly influenced many home cooks. Her school was said to be the first real culinary school ever run in New Orleans. She introduced the city to the cooking of renowned chefs both local and international whom she sponsored as guest instructors. By hosting guest chefs from outside the city, Ms. Barnes introduced many chefs to the cuisine of the city. She died on November 3, 1992, of cancer.

Richard H. Collin and Rima Collin

Also known as the New Orleans Underground Gourmet, this husband and wife team ranked restaurants. They were the first writers who attempted to comprehensively cover the restaurants of the city. In doing so Richard Collin, a native of Philadelphia, introduced people to the neighborhood gems that were usually unknown outside of their neighborhoods. Collin insisted on including traditionally African American restaurants in the Underground Gourmet books (first published in 1970), which meant that many white New Orleanians explored restaurants that they had not known. Collin held poboy (those New Orleans overstuffed sandwiches) counters to the same high expectations—an excellent poboy—that he did the bastions of Creole tradition. Richard and Rima were rigorous scholars who worked at the University of New Orleans. Their explorations of the cuisine of the city reawakened an awareness of Creole cuisine in the people of New Orleans, as well as introducing yet another generation of outsiders to the cuisine.

Collin was a restaurant critic for the *States-Item* beginning in 1972—the first restaurant critic at a city newspaper. He had high expectations of the restaurants in the city, and he was not afraid to express his opinion. He has been credited with raising the bar on restaurants in the city by holding them accountable in print for their service and food. Rima Reck Collin was the cook half of the team. They collaborated on *The New Orleans Cookbook* in 1975, an extremely popular and influential Creole cookbook. The husband and wife team collaborated on several other books, notably, *The Pleasures of Seafood*. Because of the Collins, New Orleanians were reminded that to be a citizen of the city meant that a person must appreciate the food and demand that even the lowliest foods rise to a standard of excellence. Even home-cooked meals should be excellent and memorable.

Poppy Tooker

One of the most vocal and enthusiastic ambassadors of the food of New Orleans today is native daughter, Poppy Tooker. She teaches classes to locals and tourists. She is an author, having penned in 2009 a cookbook for the

CCFM, the *Crescent City Farmer's Market Cookbook*. She is also the host of a local weekly radio show, *Louisiana Eats!*, and she appears regularly on a local public television program which discusses the culinary cultural happenings of the week. She received a master chef's diploma from Madeleine Kamman's school, and she uses her training to teach and promote the traditional foods of the city.

Tooker was active with the Slow Food movement, once serving on the board of Slow Food USA. In that position she enshrined several important foods in the Ark of Taste. When Creole cream cheese was no longer produced commercially, Tooker made it her crusade to teach New Orleanians how to make their own cream cheese. She talked about Creole cream cheese until it became unthinkable that it not be made commercially. She single-handedly created the demand. It is now made regularly again by several local dairies.

In addition to Creole cream cheese Tooker has revived calas. Once a standard breakfast item made by frugal Creoles to make use of leftover rice, fried into a fritter and dusted with powdered sugar, calas had become less and less frequently eaten. Even at parties, a second popular time to eat calas, they were becoming rare. In her role as cooking teacher, both to locals and tourists, Tooker began to tell the story of the calas. She sang the street cry of the cala vendor while she demonstrated making the fritters. She made them sweet and she made them savory. Today calas can be found on the menus of several restaurants in the city; some are sweet and some are savory. Tooker also ensured that Roman Candy was included in the Ark of Taste. She currently encourages people to make the labor-intensive dish, crawfish bisque.

Tooker has been publically representing the food of New Orleans for years. She has cooked gumbo against Bobby Flay in a televised gumbo throw down—and won. She has cooked New Orleans food all over the world. Her motto, "Eat it to save it," reflects her philosophy that if the city stops eating a traditional dish, it will disappear. So she encourages people to keep eating traditional foods. Tooker is also an active supporter of the Edible Schoolyard. This is a program that was started by Chez Panisse owner and activist Alice Waters. The Edible Schoolyard at Green School in New Orleans is the only other official Edible Schoolyard endorsed by Waters.

Tom Fitzmorris
This radio, print, and Internet journalist holds a unique place among the food journalists in the city. He has been hosting a radio show about food since 1975. His newsletter *New Orleans Menu*, which he has published since 1977, began as a traditional print newsletter and has transitioned to a website, nomenu.com.

He writes and talks about the restaurants of New Orleans and the surrounding area. He eats at different restaurants and discusses his experiences with his listeners. His listeners also call in to ask his advice about where to eat and what to order. He has guided the city when new restaurants have opened and encourages dining out. He hosts regular visits to restaurants through his Eat Club. He chooses a restaurant and arranges for a special menu for the Eat Club visit. Those who wish to attend prepay a fixed price and enjoy the meal. Fitzmorris attends these events and the opportunity to share a meal with him is, of course, in large part the reason that people attend. But these events provide a social outlet for unattached people. It is a small adventure supported by a group, with a leader and a chance to taste many parts of a restaurant's offerings.

In addition to his broadcast and web outlets he has written a number of books. The books include restaurant guides, histories, as well as cookbooks—all about the food of New Orleans. He has written a memoir, *Hungry Town*, that is partly about his life, especially after Hurricane Katrina, and partly recent history of the restaurants of New Orleans. He also coauthored a book with Peggy Scott Laborde, *The Lost Restaurants of New Orleans*, which laments the loss of many restaurants in the city and discusses their history and influence. The book includes profiles of the restaurants, special menu items and signature aspects of each place, and occasional interviews about the restaurants with former owners, the children of former owners, and former employees. Fitzmorris is important because he makes sure that all restaurants are appreciated, not just the fancy ones or the ones that advertise to tourists. His very presence on the air and his commitment to the restaurants of the city after Hurricane Katrina contributed to the return of the spirit of the city as much as the return of the restaurants did. His chronicle of the return and reopening of restaurants was an important documentation of the healing and restoration of the city. It was both reality and analogy.

Publications
Judy Walker, the Food Editor of the *Times Picayune*, the daily newspaper of New Orleans, is not a New Orleanian. She observes the city and its attitudes about food as an outsider, but one who loves food. She has said that readers of the food section of the paper are more passionate about local food than readers from other parts of the country. After Hurricane Katrina when so many people lost their cookbooks and recipe collections to the floodwaters, Walker and food writer and teacher Marcelle Bienvenu wrote a cookbook that contained the most requested recipes of readers after the storm. The book, *Cooking Up a Storm*, illustrates how traditional New Orleans readers

and cooks are. Those old recipes represented a comfort to cooks and the families they cooked for. The cuisine is so ingrained and so natural that it represents identity and a return to self that was missing when people were temporarily resettled after the storm.

Brett Anderson, restaurant critic of the *Times Picayune*, has especially since Hurricane Katrina become a great defender of the food of the city. Only recently has he returned to actual restaurant reviewing as the city is truly functioning again. For a city as small as New Orleans, it is notable that there is a restaurant critic and a food editor at the daily newspaper. Other writers regularly write about the cocktail scene and most weekly newspapers also have a food writer or restaurant critic.

Louisiana Cookin' magazine, founded by New Orleanian Romney Richard, is devoted to exploring the food of Louisiana. It not only creates a forum that documents the current state of New Orleans cuisine, along with the food of the rest of Louisiana, but it also takes this information beyond the city and state into the mailboxes of people all over the country. Much of its content revolves around recipes from chefs as well as from well-respected home cooks. The recipes are designed to be cooked in home kitchens. Besides the photos of the food and the chefs, there are ads of local producers and manufacturers. This disseminates the word about advertisers as well as the recipes.

Culinary Concierge, a quarterly, is another food-related publication that is widely available. A new monthly magazine, *Louisiana Kitchen*, began publication in 2012. No newspaper or magazine can avoid writing about food—*Gambit Weekly*, *Where Y'at*, the *Tribune*, and other publications all contain at least occasional food or restaurant sections. Even radio is involved. WWOZ and WWNO, both local public radio stations, have produced food-related weekly shows, such as *Louisiana Eats!* with Poppy Tooker on WWNO and extended segments of *New Orleans All the Way Live* with George Ingmire on WWOZ, which exploits the connections between food and music in the city. The long-running radio show of Tom Fitzmorris keeps listeners up to date on new restaurants and changes in menus and staff in established restaurants.

~

CHAPTER TEN

Signature Foods and Dishes

The food of New Orleans is made up of signature dishes easily identified as part of the canon of Creole cuisine. Certain raw products are so fundamental to these dishes and to the economy of the city that they need to be examined so that their importance in the dishes themselves and in how the dishes developed becomes apparent. Sugar, for example, has been available in New Orleans almost since its founding, making the candies and desserts of the city available from the early days. Rice became the common starch of the city. From gumbo to stuffing to beans, it is everywhere the partner of some other thing.

Sugar

Sugar has been grown in Louisiana during four centuries. Though sugar was cultivated in Louisiana from first settlement, no commercially profitable crop was made until Etienne de Boré's success in 1797. After the slave revolt in Haiti, sugar makers left Haiti and began growing sugar in New Orleans commercially. In 1812 Louisiana became a state. Thus tariffs were removed from its products, leading to tremendous financial success for the planters along the Mississippi River, for the traders and brokers who lived in the city, and for everyone else who worked in the industry. Success, that is, for everyone except the slaves.

Historian Sidney Mintz argues that sugar created slavery in the New World. Slaves were always present in Louisiana, but after it became apparent how much money there was in sugar, their numbers soared. Prior to mecha-nization, sugar making was backbreaking labor at every step from planting, weeding, and harvesting to grinding and boiling. Limbs and lives were often lost. The grinding or rolling season required unending labor. Teams of slaves worked in shifts; the boiler fires were always lit.

The invention of the steam-powered mill in 1822 revolutionized sugar production. Steam mills yielded a higher volume of cane juice than mills turned by mules, and this sped the processing of sugar. The vacuum pan evaporator, invented in 1846 by Norbert Rillieux, a free man of color from New Orleans, cousin to Edgar Degas, drew 25 percent more sugar from the molasses than kettle cooking, and minimized the risk of scorching the sugar. Finally, in 1850, steam rail lines connected the bayou sugar parishes with New Orleans to ship much of Louisiana's sugar products to northern markets. By 1853, Louisiana was producing one-quarter of the world's sugar.

Today's sugar industry does not resemble the antebellum industry. The 1,400 sugar mills have dwindled to thirteen. Louisiana currently supplies 20 percent of the domestic market. Mechanization has reduced the workforce to 27,000, less than half of what it was in 1950. The Domino Sugar Refinery in Arabi, just over the St. Bernard Parish line from New Orleans, is the largest sugar refinery in the Western hemisphere. It receives raw sugar from Texas, Florida, Louisiana, and Mexico, it refines and transports the sugar via river and rail.

New Orleanians eat pralines and other candies made with sugar. Beignets and pain perdu and waffles are liberally sprinkled with powdered sugar. Sweet king cake is iced and sugared and sweetly stuffed. Of course New Orleanians are known for drinking that sugar in a bottle—rum. Coffee with sugar and many a soda are all drunk by those in New Orleans. But sweet tea, the ubiq-uitous drink of the South, has not been a staple in the city.

Rice

According to Hall, in 1718 the Company of the West ordered the captains of *L'Aurore* and *Le Duc du Maine*—the first two slave ships traveling from Sene-gal to New Orleans—to "purchase several blacks who knew how to cultivate rice and three or four barrels of rice for seeding." From its beginning rice was considered an important crop. Rice became a staple in Creole cuisine.

After statehood rice was grown increasingly and on a large scale in Loui-siana. The Southern Pacific Railroad made rice growing even more efficient. At the end of the nineteenth century into the twentieth, rice growing blossomed. Today rice and crawfish are often grown together, each crop symbiotically nourishing the other. Although other states may outproduce Louisiana rice growers, it is hard to imagine any other city eating more rice per capita. Rice eating in New Orleans is about double the national average at almost thirty pounds per person. Whether it is in gumbo, jambalaya, shrimp creole, various etouffes, stuffed peppers or other vegetables, or calas, rice is the starch of choice in Creole cuisine. The Creole table includes sweet and white potatoes and pastas, but rice is the king of the Creole starches.

BUSTER HOLMES HANDMADE FRIED CHICKEN

New Orleans Handmade Cookin'

Red Beans & Rice   1.39
Red Beans & Rice with Sausage 2.49
Red Beans & Rice with Chicken 2.49
Red Beans & Rice with Ribs   2.59

Fried Chicken 2 Pc. 1.69
Fried Chicken 3 Pc. 2.19
Fried Chicken 4 Pc. 2.69

Shrimp ½ Doz. 2.29   Bar-B Qued Ribs 2.59 With Fried Potatoes or Creole Rice & French Bread

Buster's Donuts Available Anytime

Family Size Chicken

10 pieces 5.89
12 pieces 6.89
16 pieces 8.39
20 pieces 10.39
24 pieces 11.39

Small Drink .45
Medium   .55
Large   .65
Coffee   .40
Milk   .40

Buster's Hot Bread Pudding .59

On the Side

Creole Rice .49
Fried potatoes .49
Cole Slaw .49
Potato Salad .49
Baked beans   .49
Turnip Greens .49
Corn on the Cob   .79
Jalapeno Pepper .10

Buster Holmes T-Shirt   5.99

Buster Holmes Cookbooks 6.99

Buster Holmes menu, c. 1990.

An entire book could be written about the important dishes that make up the canon of Creole cuisine. Many cookbooks have been written about this very thing since 1885. But this discussion will give some background on the foods discussed in other parts of the book. Most of these dishes and foods have been selected because they are either so fundamental that they must be included or because they represent foods that are ubiquitous, however they may be cooked. No doubt the favorite dishes of many people are not discussed here.

Red Beans and Rice

Red beans and rice is a dish that forms one of the mainstays of the Creole canon. It derives from the African tradition of beans or peas and rice. It is made with red kidney beans, simply called red beans in New Orleans. Traditionally in New Orleans red beans and rice is eaten on Mondays. According to the traditional story Monday was a traditional wash day. It was also the day when a ham bone from a Sunday ham would be available to flavor a pot of beans. A person who has to tend a washtub and heat hot water all day could tend a pot of red beans without difficulty. It would also allow the efficient use of fuel, for when else would there be a time when a fire would be tended all day? Today red beans are often served with smoked sausage, a pork chop, or a side of fried chicken, but more traditional recipes were made with ham.

Eating red beans and rice on Monday is such a tradition that it is served weekly in schools, public and parochial, on Mondays. Buster Holmes, a chef who was famous for his red beans and rice, served red beans every day. Contemporary chef Susan Spicer served a *stage*, a chef's apprenticeship, with Buster Holmes to learn his technique for cooking red beans. Louis Armstrong, famous New Orleans musician, signed his letters with a reference to his favorite dish. He signed his letters "Red Beans and Rice-ly Yours."

A Mardi Gras walking club that walks the city on Lundi Gras, the Monday before the Tuesday of Mardi Gras, decorates its costumes each year with red beans, rice, and the seasonings traditionally used in cooking red beans, like bay leaves. The predominant brand of red beans in New Orleans is Camellia. It is dominant enough that a reference to Camellia beans in conversation is understood to mean red beans.

Red Beans and Rice

1 pound dried red beans (red kidney beans, preferably Camellia brand)
3 tablespoons oil (can be bacon fat or butter or other oil)

1 ham bone with some meat left on it
2 yellow or white onions chopped in a medium dice
3 stalks of celery (including leaves), chopped in a medium dice
1 seeded green bell pepper, chopped in a medium dice
Bunch of flat leaf parsley, chopped
3 bay leaves
2 teaspoons fresh thyme or a teaspoon of dried thyme
1 to 2 pounds of sliced smoked sausage or ham hocks, or a combination of
    the two
10 cups chicken stock or water
1 teaspoon cayenne, more or less to taste
Salt and pepper to taste
4 cups cooked white rice
1/4 cup chopped green onions, garnish

Allow the beans to soak in water overnight in a large ceramic, glass, or stainless bowl. The water should cover the beans by several inches, as the beans will swell. Drain and discard the water.

Heat the preferred fat in a large pot. Add the onions, celery and bell pepper and allow to sauté at medium heat for about 5 minutes, stirring to distribute the vegetables. Add half of the parsley, the bay leaves and the ham bone. Stir. Add the meat and brown it. Add the liquid and the beans. Heat to a boil and then simmer. It will take about 2 hours for the beans to soften. Stir occasionally. Check the level of liquid since the beans will absorb the liquid and add more as needed.

With a large spoon, mash about a quarter of the beans against the side of the pot. Stir this creamy part of the beans back into the liquid so that the beans are both whole and creamy. Stir in the cayenne and black pepper. Check the salt level by tasting the beans. The ham and sausage will have added salt, so checking the salt level is important. Cook about 30 minutes more. Remove from heat. Discard bay leaves.

Serve over rice and garnish with green onions.

Roux

A roux is a cooked mixture of a fat and a like amount of flour. References to roux can be found in French receipts in the seventeenth century. A white roux, the classic French thickener of béchamel, a veloute, and other sauces, is quite different from the roux of Creole cuisine. The early cookbooks of Lafcadio Hearn and the Christian Woman's Exchange contain gumbos that begin with a roux. Not all of the gumbos in the early cookbooks were thickened with roux. The current belief that "first you make a roux" represents a historic methodology basic to Creole cooking is not substantiated. However, in the modern Creole kitchen every gumbo, every red gravy, and many sauces begin with a roux.

A roux is a slowly cooked and stirred base that results in a toasted flour flavoring agent. A roux can take a long time to toast and should be cooked over a very low fire and stirred constantly. A burned roux cannot be saved, but has to be tossed out. The more the flour is cooked the less thickening power it has, so a dark roux is a poor thickener. However, it lends a unique flavor and smoothness to a dish. While a roux is a European aspect of Creole dishes, a proper modern Creole roux is not the same as a modern French roux. A French roux is cooked long enough to cook past the raw taste of flour, and for an Espangnole sauce (a spicy light brown, tomato-flavored sauce, one of Escoffier's mother sauces that forms the basis for many other sauces) can be a light brown. But it is not considered properly done if it is as dark as most Creole roux. A Creole roux can vary in color from a light brown to a dark coffee color. The color that the Creole cook uses depends on taste and on what is being made. A red gravy might, for example, take a lighter roux than a duck gumbo. A Creole roux is likely to be made with lard or bacon fat, as opposed to butter.

Health concerns today have led people to develop roux either with less fat or without any fat. Some people place dry flour on a cookie sheet and toast it in a low oven. Others use the microwave to toast dry flour. Grocery stores now stock roux in jars with various proportions of oil and different degrees of darkness.

The Trinity

Today Creole cooks talk about the trinity, sometimes called the holy trinity, in reference to the Creole mirepoix of chopped celery, onions, and bell peppers. The name reflects the Roman Catholic heritage of the city. Garlic, often added to the trinity, is called the "pope." In his book, *A Feast Made for Laughter*, Craig Claiborne attributes the phrase "holy trinity" to Paul Prudhomme. The turn-of-the-twentieth-century cookbooks do not call this mixture the trinity. Often the vegetable mixture that is called for in early cookbooks includes scallions (often called shallots in New Orleans) and other vegetables. The phrase isn't found in mid-twentieth-century cookbooks either. The phrases "first you made roux" and then sauté the "holy trinity" have made cooking Creole food have a magic formula that has made New Orleanians feel that they have the secret to the cuisine—just as the phrases "making groceries" and "saving groceries" have unified them. These fairly modern phrases provide a common vocabulary that only insiders can interpret, making the food inaccessible to the uninitiated.

Gumbo

Gumbo is the dish that most people associate with Creole cuisine. There is probably no single gumbo. In fact each person will recognize another's gumbo but knows that only the family gumbo is real gumbo. The word gumbo probably derives from the word for okra in the Bantu language, *ki ngombo*. It is certainly possible that early versions of this thick soup or stew was merely made with okra. We do not recognize stewed okra alone as gumbo today. Kevin McCaffrey, filmmaker and Louisiana food historian, notes a reference to gumbo in the research of Gwendolyn Midlo Hall, a historian specializing in African influences in New Orleans, at the archives of the Louisiana State Museum. The reference is located in testimony at a hearing in 1764 regarding aid given to an alleged runaway slave. That aid was in the form of *gombeau*. This being a court record there was no recipe accompanying the reference, thus we cannot know whether the food was merely stewed okra or a stew with meat and okra.

Today gumbo is a stew or thick soup made with almost anything. There are traditional combinations of ingredients, such as chicken and sausage or seafood, but there are really no rules. There is duck gumbo, squirrel gumbo, and turkey gumbo, just to begin the list. Today we usually begin a gumbo with a roux. The roux can be as light or as dark according to one's taste. A check of early cookbooks indicates that in the late nineteenth century not all gumbos were made with a roux. In New Orleans Creole gumbo was made with the addition of chopped tomatoes as well as the trinity. It is traditionally seasoned with thyme, bay leaf, and cayenne.

Traditionally there were thickeners for a gumbo: filé, okra, or roux. Gumbo truly represents the history of New Orleans in a bowl. Filé is the Native American contribution. Okra is the African contribution. Roux is the European contribution. Gumbo that was made with okra was made when okra was in season. One wouldn't use filé in an okra gumbo. It would be superfluous. But when okra wasn't in season, one could use a roux or filé to make gumbo. Today a roux, and the flavor that toasted flour lends to the gumbo, is used in gumbo even with okra or filé. There are traditional rules about whether to add okra to certain types of gumbo. These rules derive from a time when certain seafoods were available and okra wasn't in season, thus they were not traditionally used together. However, today these rules can be broken—frozen okra is available year round.

Gumbo Z'herbes, which derives from *gumbo aux herbes*, or gumbo of greens, is a meatless gumbo. In Roman Catholic New Orleans, where traditional Lenten fasting was observed, on some days eating meat was forbidden. But that didn't stop Creoles from wanting to eat something tasty. So Gumbo Z'herbes made it possible to be religiously observant and eat well. Traditional cookbooks make Gumbo Z'herbes of an odd number of mixed greens—usually either seven or nine. The greens can include mustard, turnip, spinach, and other greens that might be available. In the earliest cookbooks this gumbo passed the cooked greens through a sieve for a smooth consistency. It is usually made without a roux, with water and not a meat stock. It is said that the cook will make a friend for each type of greens used.

As Lenten rules have relaxed it has become common to continue to make Gumbo Z'herbes with many greens, but to add meat or seafood (or both) for additional flavor. Chef Leah Chase has become known for her Gumbo Z'herbes, which she serves on Holy Thursday at her restaurant, Dooky Chase. Her version is rich and delicious, with veal and other nonfasting meats.

Calas

"Calas, belles calas, tout chauds" is the street cry associated with the sweet and creamy rice fritter known as the cala. The rice fritter was sold by street vendors in Congo Square and in the French Quarter. Part of the allure of the story of calas is that slaves, cooking and selling rice fritters on their Sunday off, were said to be such successful entrepreneurs that they could buy their freedom.

The origin of calas is a matter of dispute with various camps being established to claim the crown of originator. Calas, cooked and sold by people of African descent, are surely descendants of a cooked rice fritter found in West Africa. The name "calas" is similar to rice fritters named in West African languages, for example, called *kárá* in the Nupe language. Rice fritters were not unknown even in France—they were found in old French receipt books—which might explain their acceptance by those of French heritage in the city. If their popularity might have waned, the Italian presence on either side of the twentieth century could have expanded their place at the city's table, as the cousin of the savory *arancini*, the Sicilian rice fritter. Calas were made and distributed in New Orleans primarily by people of African descent, and regardless of written references to rice fritters in very early sources, they were popularized here by those of African descent, whether prepared on the street or in the kitchen. Their place in New Orleans is clearly creditable to Africa.

Calas were not totally gone, but they were fast being lost. Thanks to noted cooking teacher and media personality Poppy Tooker, calas are once again eaten, not only remembered.

These rice fritters were the stuff of frugality and legend. The fritters are made of a batter of leftover rice. The tradition is that the rice was prepared the evening before and the fritters enjoyed for breakfast dusted with powdered sugar. The fritters were also a very popular street food. They were sold by street vendors, African American women, *vendeuses*, who sold the hot fritters from baskets in Congo Square and the French Quarter. They often sang out street cries that let potential customers know what they were selling.

According to the *Code Noir* slaves could buy their freedom if they had sufficient money to pay when their price was declared by their owner. Calas are said to have been the source of freedom for many slaves and their families. While it is clear that African slaves and free people of color sold calas—they were observed by many sources—that calas alone were the regular source of this freedom is a wonderful story. It is difficult to imagine that calas could produce sufficient funds for such release.

Pralines

The spread of sugar to Europe as well as its accessibility in the seventeenth century allowed for the experimentation with sugar's malleability and its attraction. Cesar du Plessis-Praslin was a French sugar grower whose cook coated individual almonds in caramelized sugar. The confection was brought to New Orleans where cooks used available nuts—pecans and peanuts—to make them. In New Orleans the name "praline" has come to refer exclusively to a candy made of sugar and pecans. Unlike the sugared nut that was the original praslin. The Creole praline is a disk made with caramelized sugar and pecans. Some versions today include cream or butter, as well as other flavorings, such as chocolate, coffee, or bourbon.

Pralines are another product sold by street vendors, primarily African Americans, who, according to popular belief, were said to earn their freedom from the sale of these sweets, although the actual documentation of this enterprise is difficult to establish. Early street vendors sold many types of candies made with a variety of nuts, including peanuts and coconuts. A brittle of peanuts, small candies cut into rectangles and wrapped into paper boxes, and coconut candy made pink with beetle shells, could be found in the baskets of the *vendeuses* or *pralinieres*. Most of the candies lost favor, leaving the praline, known also as pecan candy, as the final object of the candy maker's labor.

The praline makers, whose photos could be found on postcards for tourists, were dressed in long skirts and aprons with *tignons*, a cloth headscarf tied in a distinctive manner, in a parody of the Mammy figure. In the 1930s Lyle Saxon, Works Progress Administration (WPA) writer and cultural observer, wrote about the praline vendors carrying palmetto fans against the heat in his book, *Gumbo Ya-Ya*. The older African American women were referred to by their first names with "Aunt" used as an honorific. Stuffed Mammy mannequins were used like tobacco store Indians to mark the shops that sold pralines. There are candy companies in New Orleans today, like Aunt Sally's, that represent the third generation of African American women candy makers. The fact that the companies can continue to be viable gives credence to the stories about the successful women vendors.

A note about pralines—it is pronounced "prawleen" in New Orleans, even if it is "prayleen" in other places.

New Orleans Pralines

    1 cup packed light brown sugar
    1 cup granulated sugar
    1/2 cup half and half
    1/8 teaspoon salt
    1 1/2 cups pecan halves
    2 tablespoons butter

Whisk the two sugars together in a heavy bottomed pan or a copper sugar kettle. Add the cream and bring the mixture to a boil over medium heat. Stir with a wooden spoon until the mixture thickens. Heat to the soft ball stage, 236 degrees. Add the salt and pecans and butter. Remove from heat and let stand for 10 minutes. Drop by the tablespoon onto a marble surface with room for the candies to spread. They are ready when cool. This will make about a dozen pralines.

Poboys

These sandwiches are a twentieth-century addition to the Creole menu. They are one of few foods almost only eaten out and not fixed at home. As the story goes, there was a turbulent streetcar strike in 1929 that lasted for months. The strikers were picketing in front of Martin Brothers Coffee Stand on St. Claude Avenue. The Martin brothers, Benny and Clovis, had been streetcar workers themselves, so they were sympathetic to the strikers.

Knowing that the strikers were not earning money while they were striking, the Martin Brothers made sandwiches out of the ends of roast beef for the strikers. The Martin Brothers called the strikers poor boys who needed the support of the community. The reference to the strikers became the name of the sandwiches fed to them.

The story is further embellished by the explanation that the shape of the French bread in the city was not the familiar baguette, but a shape called the gigot, a shape that had a tail. When using the gigot to make a sandwich, the tail would have to be cut off. To stop the waste and to make the sandwich more efficient, the loaf—now the poboy loaf—was made the same shape from one end to the other.

Poboys are part of the overstuffed sandwich phenomenon of the Depression. What are served today as poboys are probably much more substantial than what may have been served to streetcar strikers. It is said that those sandwiches were either gravy sandwiches which might have had bits of meat in it or perhaps potato sandwiches. The 1901 version of the *Picayune's Creole Cook Book* has a recipe for a Mediatrice (Mediator or peacemaker) or an oyster loaf made from French bread partially hollowed out. The bread taken from the inside of the loaf is cooked with oysters and cream in a pan. When hot it is spooned back into the loaf and served. It was called the Mediatrice to be given as a peace offering to the wife of a penitent, but late, husband. The idea of a sandwich was not new in the twentieth century.

There was a time it was said that franchise sandwich shops like Subway or Quiznos could not get a toehold in the city, because the city was so bound to its poboys. But finally the forces of homogenization made the people of the city allow room for franchise sandwich shops. Using preserved meats is cheaper than making poboys by starting with raw roasts and fresh seafood. But traditional poboys are holding their own. Traditional poboys include roast beef, fried shrimp, fried oysters, fried catfish, fried soft shell crab, ham, meatball, and sausage. Today Vietnamese poboys—banh mi—and vegan poboys and many more creative poboys are sold at poboy shops. The annual Poboy Festival boasts creative and traditional poboys.

The spelling of poboy or poorboy is a matter of some controversy. The initial reference was to the poor boys on the picket line. The change in pronunciation when referring to the sandwich causes grammarians to gnash their teeth.

Another quirk in the city is the reference to being dressed. When a poboy is being ordered, the clerk is likely to ask if you want the sandwich dressed. This refers to shredded lettuce, thinly sliced tomatoes, mayonnaise, and

Oyster lugger unloading in New Orleans, c. 1906. Courtesy of Library of Congress, LC-D4-19315.

sometimes pickles. If you want any variation of this combination of adorn-ments, you must speak quickly, or you will receive them anyway.

Oysters Rockefeller

Oysters Rockefeller was invented at Antoine's Restaurant by Jules Alciatore in 1899. The story goes that the very French restaurant routinely served snails baked or broiled in a sauce in snail dishes. There was a shortage of snails and the restaurateur substituted plentiful, local, fresh oysters for snails, but treated them in a manner akin to broiling snails. The sauce is rich and was named after the richest person of the day, John D. Rockefeller. The recipe is still a secret and is never printed in cookbooks that are penned by members of the Antoine's Restaurant family. The controversy revolves around the question of whether the recipe contains spinach, which members of the family have claimed it does not.

Other popular oyster dishes that followed the creation of Oysters Rock-efeller include Oysters Bienville, Oysters en Brochette, and Charbroiled Oysters. These dishes are served at home and in restaurants around the city.

Mirliton

This American squash, known in Spanish-speaking areas as *chayote*, is very popular in New Orleans. Mirliton is also eaten in the Caribbean where it is called christophine or vegetable pear. The fruit is served pickled, can be served raw in salads, or is cooked. Because of its bland flavor and the frugal Creole practice of using leftover rice and small bits of seafood and meat, mirliton is often served stuffed and baked with a seasoned rice mixture.

Réveillon Dinner

Eating a late night dinner at especially Christmas or New Year's Eve is a common older Creole practice that has been revived by restaurants in recent years. The meals were often finished in time for families to attend midnight mass. Réveillon dinners are usually associated with the special foods of the holidays, so the dinners are multicoursed and more elaborate than regular meals. Midnight dinners are still celebrated in people's homes for these holidays. But Creoles were also known to entertain very late on other special occasions and personal celebrations, somehow finding the night more festive than the evening.

Grillades and Grits

Grillades are a veal or pounded round steak stewed in a roux-based tomato sauce with onions and green peppers. Traditionally served with grits, the dish is one which is associated with suppers, usually called the queen's supper, after the end of traditional Mardi Gras balls. Often grillades and grits are served as an early breakfast or a late supper, as they hold well and can be prepared in quantity. Grillades can be prepared with pork or even thinly sliced turkey breast. Although this dish derived from the need to stretch meat to serve many, it is now considered a familiar traditional food served as a special meal. Like many slow-cooked foods made with delicious and tough cuts of meat, busy families may not take the time to prepare them, so grillades have become a traditional treat.

Shrimp Remoulade

Arnaud's Restaurant claims invention of this dish by its founder, Arnaud Cazenave. It is on that menu as Shrimp Arnaud. It is a cold appetizer of boiled shrimp in a spicy remoulade sauce, which is bottled and sold by the restaurant. The restaurant has opened a casual component called Remoulade. The dish still finds its way on many other menus as Shrimp Remoulade. Besides requiring perfectly cooked shrimp, which must be slightly undercooked before being tossed in a slightly acid sauce, further "cooking" the shrimp in a process similar to ceviche, the sauce must also be perfect. The sauce is not a mayonnaise-based sauce, as is the French remoulade. Creole remoulade is a lemony sauce made with Creole mustard, horseradish, capers, parsley, onions, celery, cayenne pepper, and oil. The Upperline Restaurant serves a very popular version of the dish over fried green tomatoes. Several poboy restaurants offer a shrimp remoulade with fried green tomato poboys.

Shrimp Remoulade

Make the sauce the day before to allow the flavors to meld together.

>   2 cups Creole mustard
>   1 cup minced flat leaf parsley
>   1 cup finely diced celery
>   1 cup finely diced green onions (scallions, also called shallots in older recipes)
>   2 tablespoons minced garlic
>   3 tablespoons grated horseradish
>   1/3 cup lemon juice
>   Grated zest of one lemon
>   1 cup olive oil

Mix all ingredients well. Store in refrigerator overnight. Add 12 to 18 peeled boiled shrimp. Allow the shrimp to marinate for a few hours in the sauce. Serve cold on shredded lettuce. Garnish with lemon wedges.

Creole Mustard

Creole mustard is used in many poboys, in Creole remoulade sauce, and in many other dishes. It is a coarsely ground preparation of brown mustard seeds and vinegar similar to the French moutarde à l'ancienne or German mustard. It was probably popularized by early German immigrants to the colony.

Daube Glacé

As electric refrigeration became virtually universal in the twentieth century, daube glacé began to decline. Jellied meat was a delicious form of preservation, like hogs head cheese, allowing meat to be kept in an environment without air. Refrigeration made preservation easy and efficient. Daube glacé required the cook to create a gelatin from bones and ligaments of meat, cooking down beef with seasonings. It was allowed to become firm. Today it is made from prepared gelatin. It is not a dish generally prepared at home today. Rather it is usually served as party food prepared by certain grocers and caterers.

Turtle Soup

Terrapin or cowan or snapping turtle form the basis of a traditional soup, once popular wherever turtle was available, that is still popular in New Orleans. The soup is made with the meat of the turtle and served with sherry. Sherry is often found in cruets on the table for patrons at a restaurant that serves turtle soup. A mock turtle version of the soup is often made from veal. Because of the decline in many wild turtle populations, the soup is often made today from farm-raised turtles.

Stuffed Artichokes

These delightful vegetables reflect the habit of the Sicilians to stuff things with bread crumbs. Stuffed artichokes have made their way to restaurant tables as well as home tables. They are rather elaborate and labor intensive— seasoned bread stuffing is placed in each leaf. They are very often a part of St. Joseph Altars.

King Cakes

The king cake is one of the seasonal foods associated with Mardi Gras. The cake is derived from the cake eaten on Three Kings Day or Twelfth Night (the twelfth day after Christmas) in which a bean was baked. Twelfth Night is the first day of the carnival season and a day of celebration in its own right. Originally when the cake was served, whomever received the bean was the king or queen for the party. This tradition was brought from France to New Orleans. The king cake eaten in New Orleans was derived from the cake eaten in southern France, which is a brioche ring called *gateau des rois*. The French version of the cake used a dried fava bean (*féve*) in the cake. Today in France the small porcelain favors found in the cakes are still called *féves*. Haydel's Bakery has revived the tradition of putting small porcelain figures in the cakes. These figures were made by Alberta Lewis, a local porcelain artist. They reflect different themes of carnival, like floats and marchers, or city themes, like post-Katrina houses covered with blue tarp. Cochon Butcher serves an individual king cake that contains a small plastic pig instead of a baby. Hubig Pies made a short-lived attempt to sell individual king cakes during the carnival season, when the sales of their pies is depressed in favor of king cake. During the season, there are king cake taste-offs and many variations on the cake as bakers try to outdo each other.

Beans were used in New Orleans king cakes which came to be decorated in patches with sugar colored green, purple, and yellow. The brioche dough slightly flavored with cinnamon and vanilla was very similar from bakery to bakery. One bakery, McKenzie's, distinguished itself, not by selling a better cake, but by substituting bisque dolls called "frozen Charlottes" for the beans. (The dolls were used to test the evenness of heat in kilns.) These dolls were referred to as baby dolls, as in "Did you get the baby doll?" This was shortened to "Did you get the baby?" The bean had become a baby doll or just a baby.

On the first day of the carnival season, January 6 each year, king cakes begin to be served. They are served throughout the season until Mardi Gras Day (Fat Tuesday). Eventually frozen Charlottes were no longer available and were substituted by small plastic babies. Because of concerns over liability for a person biting the plastic, some bakeries no longer bake the baby into the dough, but include it in the package.

The role of the baby changed over the years, reflecting a cultural shift. *The Picayune Creole Cook Book* describes the tradition of the king cake at the turn of the twentieth century, explaining that the king (who might receive a bejeweled ring instead of a bean) would have to pay for the costs of the ball where the king cake was served. If a woman received the bean or other trinket, she would select her king. Later the recipient of the baby, instead of being the king or queen of the party, had to give the next party. Or if the cake was brought to work or a regular gathering, the recipient had to purchase the next cake. In the past king cakes were eaten at king cake parties during the carnival season and other celebrations during the season. For example, if your birthday fell during that time, you might have a king cake and a birthday cake at a party. Today they are eaten all the time during the season.

The king cake itself has also changed recently. According to interviews appearing in the *Times Picayune*, bakers have noted that the simple brioche ring decorated with sugar grew sweeter and sweeter, and the dough became more like Danish in the 1980s. It became iced and then sugared, instead of just sugared. Now it is rare to find the old brioche cake. Most king cakes today are filled with cream cheese, fruit, and other toppings such as praline. The practice of filling the king cake followed logically from the use of Danish dough. Several bakeries will ship king cakes around the country to ex-patriot

New Orleanians or as presents from New Orleanians who want to share a bit of Mardi Gras with those not in the city.

Other Mardi Gras foods are also important. Coconuts are shaved and decorated and now handed out during the Zulu parade. (They were thrown from floats until this practice was prohibited as too dangerous.) The coconuts are highly prized and collectable. They represent another example of the city using food to represent itself and its revelry.

Crab Boil and Boiled Shellfish

Many informal meals of boiled seafood are seasoned with one mixture or another of spices placed in muslin bags and boiled with the seafood. The spice mixture, called crab boil, is commercially available in a bag and as a concentrated liquid. A popular version is made by Zatarain's. The spice mix can include coriander, cloves, cayenne, and other spices according to personal taste. Large pots of water are brought to a boil with the bag of crab boil. Other seasonings may also be added, such as lemons, celery, and whole onions. People can add salt and cayenne pepper to taste. In addition to the seafood which is added whole (after being cleaned and purged) to the pot, other vegetables are often added to be eaten with the boiled seafood. These vegetables can include whole garlic, which is spread on French bread, corn,

Eating crabs at a crab boil, 1938. Courtesy of Library of Congress, LC-USF33-011654-M1.

artichokes, potatoes, mushrooms, and whatever else strikes people's fancy. After the shellfish is cooked, it is usually taken off the heat and allowed to soak up seasonings for a while. It is drained and served on newspaper-covered tables. Most people learn to pick their crabs, shrimp, and crawfish when they are children at these tables. Some people eat as they pick. Others pick their shellfish and put the meat on a plate and eat it with a fork. Both methods are acceptable.

Leftover shellfish is usually picked to be made into other dishes. That means that the seafood in it will be well seasoned and not bland. This blend of spices was likely a flavor introduced by the Spanish, who had developed a particular taste for spices during the period they were ruled by the Moors. The Spanish explored the world searching for those spices. They still linger in New Orleans in crab boil.

Seasonings are not sprinkled on the shells of plain boiled or steamed seafood, as might be found in Maryland or San Francisco. The spices in the crab boil bag are usually whole.

Crawfish

Crawfish, in season, were eaten by Native Americans. Drawings and symbols created by Native Americans have represented crawfish, demonstrating how important the crustaceans have been to them. The crawfish were most plentiful in the areas around Lafayette and Crowley, where rice also grows. As the Cajuns settled in these areas they developed dishes made with crawfish, notably crawfish étoufée and crawfish bisque. They were also eaten boiled in the shell at informal meals where the group would peel and eat crawfish on a table covered with newspaper. Crawfish could also be found around New Orleans. As the city grew and expanded, and as bayous and marshes filled in, crawfish were only available further from the city. It was a food that anyone could gather, but it was not reliably available. It was originally considered a food of poverty and was not universally found on restaurant menus.

Recipes for crawfish dishes can be found in older cookbooks. The bisque is of particular interest. Because crawfish were often caught one at a time on a string, they were time-consuming to catch. Each crawfish only yields a small bit of meat. To capture the flavor and stretch the crawfish, a bisque was made by stuffing the cleaned body or head of the crawfish shell with a corn bread stuffing flavored with chopped crawfish meat from the tail and larger claws. The soup was intensely flavored by use of a stock of crawfish shells. The stuffed heads were placed into the soup and served. This was a delicious, but highly labor-intensive dish. It has almost been lost because crawfish have become plentiful, and the need to stretch the delicacy in such a labor-intensive manner has greatly diminished.

From the 1960s to late 1970s crawfish farming as a commercial enterprise was becoming perfected. Crawfish were farmed in coordination with rice farming, resulting in more predictable yields. That meant that restaurants in New Orleans, which had previously not been able to rely on the availability of crawfish, could add crawfish dishes to their menus. Crawfish boils joined the informal gatherings of the folks of New Orleans along with crab and shrimp boils.

Shortly after crawfish became available, the country was looking for Cajun cuisine because of Paul Prudhomme and because of the 1984 World's Fair. They came to New Orleans and asked for Cajun food. The restaurants of New Orleans began to include crawfish dishes on their menus, because they could obtain a reliable supply and because there was demand. The traditional Cajun preparations were made with a Creole twist—crawfish etouffe in New Orleans is not the same as that prepared in Cajun country. Crawfish was substituted for shrimp in a number of traditional Creole dishes in preparations never eaten in Cajun country. These new dishes include crawfish Creole, soft shell crawfish, and fried crawfish tail poboys.

Crabs

Crabs have been enjoyed by people in the New Orleans area from the time of the Native Americans. Unlike in some places, like Maryland or San Francisco, crabs are boiled in New Orleans. They are boiled in highly seasoned water and allowed to stand in the water until they absorb the seasoning. Picked at this point and served picked, the meat is flavorful and can be used in crab dishes such as crabmeat au gratin. Boiled crabs are informally served while still in their shells on tables covered with newspaper. These crabs are cracked and eaten directly from the shell from a communal pile on the table.

Another crab delicacy is the soft-shell crab. When the crab sheds its shell every year to grow, it reveals a soft, as yet unhardened shell underneath. These crabs, called busters as they "busted" out of their shells, are a delicacy. They can be fried or sautéed and prepared with a meuniére sauce. During the molting season, when they are plentiful, they can also be found on poboys.

Shrimp

Both brown and white shrimp are eaten in New Orleans, depending upon the season. Even small shrimp, called grass shrimp, can be fished along shorelines. Shrimp are plentiful enough that dishes made with shrimp can be found everywhere, whether on the home table or on the table in a fine restaurant. They can be fried, boiled, baked, blackened, broiled, and barbequed. While shrimp may be a company dish in other parts of the United States, shrimp can be eaten every day in New Orleans.

Besides shrimp remoulade, notable is shrimp creole. This is a simple but delicious dish of sautéed shrimp cooked with a sauce of fresh tomatoes and the trinity, served over rice. The fresh tomato sauce is known as a Creole sauce. It can be used with chicken and other foods, including crawfish, but it is most commonly paired with shrimp.

Pascal's Manale Restaurant invented another dish called barbequed shrimp. This shrimp spends no time on a grill. It is a highly seasoned sauté of unpeeled shrimp in butter or margarine (margarine allows for a higher heat without burning) and lots of black pepper, garlic, and Worcestershire sauce. The shrimp with heads on are served sizzling in the pan. The diner peels and eats the shrimp at the table, sopping up the sauce with all of the shrimp flavor on pieces of French bread. New Orleanians would prefer the flavor of unpeeled heads on shrimp to a blander but daintier version that is peeled, ready to eat with a fork.

Alligator

This is another food eaten by Native Americans. The French wrote with fear about these beasts, which were controlled by the Native Americans. Alligator recipes were found in the early cookbooks, along with recipes for other game. However, alligators were over hunted for their hides until they were threatened, making them unavailable for their meat for many years. They are once again available and are usually farm raised. They are primarily eaten as a tourist attraction at fairs and festivals, although alligator sausage is available in groceries. In recent times the meat is also available frozen in grocery stores.

Pampano en papalliote

This classic dish was often found in New Orleans Creole restaurants. The dish was prepared in packets of parchment paper with the fish and herbs cooked in a poaching liquid in which the food in the packets steams. It is found on the menus of several old-line Creole restaurants like Antoine's and Arnaud's.

Filé

When the European explorers began to search for a route to the Indies by traveling west, they were looking for spices like nutmeg and cinnamon. When the explorers came to the area that was to become Louisiana they found a spice in New Orleans. They found filé. Unlike the other spices this New World spice was not heralded as a new sensation and introduced into the courts of Europe. It was not recognized. It was ignored.

Native Americans used filé as both a seasoning and a thickener. Filé was made from the dried leaves of the native sassafras tree and made into a powder. They also ate the new shoots of the sassafras tree. The thick soups or ragouts that have collectively become known as gumbo had to be thickened with something and filé became one of those thickeners. Before the widespread availability of flour in Louisiana, filé was likely a welcome way for Europeans to make a gravy.

Jambalaya

Jambalaya is really a Cajun dish that was adopted by the Creoles. As can be found in many rice eating cultures, it is a frugal dish using the bits and pieces that are leftover to make a new and delicious dish. As is usual with Creole and Cajun the jambalayas were not the same, or at least in modern time a distinction is recognized. Classic Cajun jambalaya—brown jambalaya—is made without tomatoes. Red jambalaya, made with tomatoes, is the Creole version. Creoles use tomatoes in many dishes.

One of the myths about jambalaya is the story of the origin of the word. It is said that the word for ham, *jamón* in Spanish or *jambon* in French, was agglutinated with a supposed African phrase for rice, yaya, "jamonyaya." It was then corrupted into jambalaya. This myth seems to establish a European origin for the dish, say, from paella, while acknowledging the African preparation or the African growing of the rice. The African dish, jollof rice, is traditionally made with tomatoes.

The excruciating etymological analysis applied to the word jambalaya, as well as the theories and analysis about the origin of the dish, indicate how important, on several levels, the food is to people in New Orleans. People want to understand the food by explaining it. They feel that they will know it better if its origins are revealed. They can feel closer to it, if their ancestors contributed to it. Like other art forms, there seems to be no end to the possibilities of intellectual as well as sensory analysis.

It is interesting that the early recipes for jambalaya from Hearn's book and the Christian Woman's Exchange (spelled jumballaya) do not include tomatoes. Andrew Sigal did a thorough historical search for early references of jambalaya. He found the word jambalaya in a French-Provencal dictionary. It was defined as a food of rice mixed with fowl and vegetables. An earlier meaning was defined as a mish mash. Sigal found an American reference to jambalaya in an 1849 journal from Alabama, *American Agriculturalist*. This recipe was also prepared without tomatoes and also referenced Hopping Johnny (jambalaya). Several other references to the dish from Alabama call the dish jambalaya and by Low Country names, like pilou.

Early restaurateur and cook Mrs. Begue, for example, had more than one recipe for jambalaya. One used tomatoes and the other did not. One explanation of this tomato mystery is that jambalaya had a fluid list of ingredients. It could contain tomatoes, if they were available. It would not if they were not. If chicken and ham were available year-round, this version of jambalaya might not include tomatoes since they were not available year-round. One could always add tomatoes if they were available. But the version with shrimp or crab or oysters might be seasonal, made when tomatoes were usually available. Early cookbooks assumed that readers knew how to cook. Seasonality was obvious at that time. A definitive recipe was not the goal. Recipes were suggestions.

Jambalaya

1/3 cup oil, bacon fat or butter
1 onion, chopped in a medium dice
3 stalks celery, chopped in a medium dice
1 bell pepper, chopped in a medium dice
1 bunch of green onions, chopped
2 cloves garlic, minced
1/2 pound peeled shrimp
1 cup cooked chicken, chopped
1 pound sausage, sliced, or ham, chopped
1 pint oysters
2 cups chopped tomatoes
2 cups chicken stock
2 bay leaves
2 teaspoons dried thyme
1 teaspoon cayenne
2 cups raw white rice
Salt and pepper to taste

In a large skillet heat the oil over medium heat. Sauté the first 5 ingredients. Cook for 5 minutes. Add all ingredients except rice. Simmer for about 10 minutes. Add rice, salt and pepper. Stir well. Cover and simmer for about 30 minutes until rice is cooked and all liquid is absorbed. Serves 6 to 8.

French Bread

Although this bread would not be recognized by anyone as French, it is called French bread in New Orleans. When wheat flour was often not easily obtained, the Alsatian bakers were able to create a light, airy bread with the meager supplies of flour that were available. This bread becomes stale very quickly and must be salvaged as either bread pudding, pain perdu, or bread crumbs. As generations became used to this bread, it became the bread of choice, even when more flour was available. It seems to be the perfect bread for poboys. It absorbs the gravy and juices of the sandwich fillings, it mashes down for easy eating, and it does not seriously interfere with the flavors of the filling.

New Orleans French bread was once shaped into a loaf with a sort of tail, called a gigot, after a leg of lamb. After the invention of the poboy, most loaves are uniformly shaped in a long baguette. Traditional loaves are still baked by companies with names that reflect their German heritage.

Coffee and Chicory

Coffee was imported from the Caribbean in the eighteenth century. After being established there, coffee plantations arose in Central America and Brazil. New Orleans became a major port of importation of coffee beans, a major center of roasting and grinding, and a significant point of distribution of coffee to the rest of America. It also developed its own coffee culture along the way. Drinking café au lait in the French manner from large bowls was a common breakfast practice. There were coffee houses around the city during the nineteenth century and early twentieth centuries. (The poboy was invented at the Martin Brothers Coffee House.) New Orleanians drank coffee all day. In Parisian style demitasses of dark black coffee were served after evening meals.

Chicory, made from the root of the Belgian endive, is roasted and ground. It was originally sold separately as a coffee substitute. It was blended at home with roasted coffee. The taste for chicory coffee developed in New Orleans and persisted even after coffee was abundant enough to be affordable. Today local coffee companies sell a coffee and chicory blend, containing one-third chicory.

Bibliography

Airriess, Christopher A. "Creating Vietnamese Landscapes and Place in New Orleans" in *Geographical Identities of Ethnic America: Race, Space, and Place*, edited by Kate A. Berry and Martha L. Henderson. Reno: University of Nevada Press, 2002.

Allen, Carol. *Leah Chase: Listen I Say Like This*. New Orleans: Pelican Publishing Company, 2002.

Anderson, E. N. *Everyone Eats: Understanding Food and Culture*. New York: New York University Press, 2005.

Beaumont, Gustave de. *Marie; ou, L'esclavage aux États Unis, tableau de moeurs américaines* [Marie; or, slavery in the United States: A novel of Jacksonian America], 1835. Translated by Barbara Chapman. Stanford, CA: Stanford University Press, 1958.

Bell, Caryn Cossé. *Revolution, Romanticism, and the Afro-Creole Protest Tradition in Louisiana, 1718–1868*. Baton Rouge: Louisiana State University, 1997.

Bell, David, and Gill Valentine. *Consuming Geographies: We Are Where We Eat*. New York: Routledge, 1997.

Beriss, David. "Authentic Creole: Tourism, Style, and Calamity in New Orleans Restaurants" Chapter 10 in *The Restaurants Book: Ethnographies of Where We Eat*, edited by David Beriss and David Evan Sutton. New York: Berg, 2007.

Bernard, Shane. *The Cajuns: Americanization of a People*. Jackson: University Press of Mississippi, 2003.

Bienvenu, Marcelle, Carl A. Brasseaux, and Ryan A. Brasseaux. *Stir the Pot: The History of Cajun Cuisine*. New York: Hippocrene Books, 2005.

Bienvenu, Marcelle, and Judy Walker. *Cooking Up a Storm: Recipes Lost and Found from the Times Picayune of New Orleans*. San Francisco: Chronicle Books, 2008.

Bienvenu, Marcelle. *Who's Your Mama, Are You Catholic, and Can You Make a Roux? A Cajun/Creole Family Album Cookbook.* Lafayette, LA: Acadian House Publishing, 2006.

Black, Jane. "By Freezing His Catch at Sea, Louisiana Shrimper Turns the Tide on His Business." *Washington Post,* December 13, 2011.

Bouciault, Dion. *The Octoroon.* 1866. Cambridge, UK: Chadwyck-Healey, 1996.

Bourdieu, Pierre. *Distinction: A Social Critique of the Judgement of Taste.* Cambridge: Harvard University Press, 1984.

Brasseaux, Carl A. *The Founding of New Acadia.* Baton Rouge: Louisiana State University Press, 1987.

Brite, Poppy Z. *Second Line: Two Short Novels of Love and Cooking in New Orleans.* East Hampton, MA: Small Beer Press, 2009.

Bultman, Bethany Ewald. "A True and Delectable History of Creole Cooking." *American Heritage* 38(1) (December 1986): 66–73.

Bronner, Simon. "'Gombo' Folkloristics: Lafcadio Hearn's Creolization and Hybridization in the Formative Period of Folklore Studies." *Journal of Folklore Research* 42, no. 2 (2005): 141–184.

Bryan, Violet Harrington. *The Myth of New Orleans in Literature: Dialogues of Race and Gender.* Knoxville: University of Tennessee Press, 1993.

Burns, John Jr. "Makin' Groceries," *Edible New Orleans* no. 6 (Spring 2011): 9–10.

Burton, Marda, and Kenneth Holditch. *Galatoire's: Biography of a Bistro.* Athens, GA: Hill Street Press, 2004.

Burton, Nathaniel, and Rudy Lombard. *Creole Feast: Fifteen Master Chefs of New Orleans Reveal Their Secrets.* New York: Random House, 1978.

Cable, George Washington. *The Creoles of Louisiana.* Gretna, LA: Pelican Publishing, 2000. First published in 1884 by Scribners.

———. *The Grandissimes: A Story of Creole Life.* New York: Scribners, 1880.

Campanella, Richard. *Bienville's Dilemma: A Historical Geography of New Orleans.* Lafayette: Center for Louisiana Studies, University of Louisiana, 2008.

———. *Geographies of New Orleans: Urban Fabrics before the Storm.* Lafayette: Center for Louisiana Studies, University of Louisiana, 2006.

Child, Lydia Maria. *A Romance of the Republic.* Boston: Ticknor and Fields, 1867.

Christian Woman's Exchange of New Orleans, Louisiana, ed. *The Creole Cookery Book.* New Orleans: T. H. Thomason, Printer, 1885.

Claiborne, Craig. "French Chef, New Orleans Style." *New York Times,* April 22, 1981, Section C, p. 1, col. 3.

Claiborne, Craig. *A Feast Made for Laughter: A Memoir with Recipes.* New York: Henry Holt, 1983.

Cohen, Hennig. "The History of 'Poor Boy,' the New Orleans Bargain Sandwich." *American Speech* 25, no. 1 (February 1950): 67–69.

Coleman, William Head. *Historical Sketch Book and Guide to New Orleans and Environs.* New York: Astor House, 1885.

Collin, Richard H. *The New Orleans Underground Gourmet*. New York: Simon & Schuster, 1970.

Collin, Richard H., and Rima Collin. *The New Orleans Restaurant Guide*. New Orleans: Strether and Swan, 1976.

Covert, Mildred L., and Sylvia P. Gerson. *Kosher Cajun Cookbook*. Gretna, LA: Pelican Publishing Co., 1989 and 2006.

Crosby, Alfred W. Jr. *The Columbian Exchange: Biological and Cultural Consequences of 1492*. Westport, CT: Greenwood Press, 1972.

Dalton, Susan. *Engendering the Republic of Letters: Reconnecting Public and Private Spaces*. Montreal: McGill Queens University Press, 2004.

Davidson, Alan, and Tom Jaine, eds. *The Oxford Companion to Food*. Oxford: Oxford University Press, 2006.

Dawdy, Shannon Lee. *Building the Devil's Empire: French Colonial New Orleans*. Chicago: University of Chicago Press, 2008.

DeJean, Joan. *The Essence of Style: How the French Invented High Fashion, Fine Food, Chic Cafes, Style, Sophistication and Glamour*. New York: Free Press, 2005.

Delehanty, Randolph. *The Ultimate Guide to New Orleans*. San Francisco: Chronicle Books, 1998.

Derven, Daphne, and Natalie Jayroe. "Transforming Hunger in New Orleans." NOLA Loyola "Live to Eat" Symposium, Sept. 2011.

Deutsch, Hermann B. *Brennan's New Orleans Cookbook and the Story of the Fabulous New Orleans Restaurant*. New Orleans: Robert L. Crager and Company, 1964.

Din, Gilbert C. "Cimarrones and the San Malo Band in Spanish Louisiana," *Louisiana History* 21 (Summer 1980): 237–262.

Douglas, Lake. *Public Spaces, Private Gardens: A History of Designed Landscapes in New Orleans*. Baton Rouge: Louisiana University Press, 2011.

Dyson, Michael Eric. *Come Hell or High Water: Hurricane Katrina and the Color of Disaster*. New York: Basic Civitas, 2006.

Edge, John T. "Saving New Orleans Culture, One Sandwich at a Time." *New York Times*, November 10, 2009.

Edge, John T. "Shuck and jive." Excerpted from *Gourmet* 2002.

Elie, Lolis Eric. "A Letter from New Orleans." *Gourmet*, February 2006.

———. "A New Orleans Original." *Gourmet*, Feb. 2000. *[Dooky Chase]*.

———. "Lolis Eric Elie Explores the Origin Myth of New Orleans Cuisine." *Oxford American: Southern Food 2010*. No. 68, April 5, 2010.

Elliot, Shanti. "Carnival and Dialogue in Bakhtin's Poetics of Folklore." *Folklore Forum* 30, no. 1/2 (1999): 129–139.

Eustis, Celestine. *Cooking in Old Creole Days*. New York: R.H. Russell, 1904.

Evans, Freddi Williams. "Congo Square: African Roots in New Orleans," *Louisiana Cultural Vistas* 22, no. 3 (Fall 2011): 10–21.

Feldman, Nina. "'On the House': The Peculiar Tradition of Free Food in New Orleans," *Edible New Orleans* no. 6 (Spring 2011): 20–21.

Ferris, Marcie Cohen. *Matzoh Ball Gumbo: Culinary Tales of the Jewish South*. Chapel Hill: University of North Carolina Press, 2005.

Fertel, Randy. "The BP Oil Spill and the Bounty of Plaquemines Parish." *Gastronomica* 11, no. 1 (Spring 2011): **[AU: Please supply page ranges of article]**.

Fertel, Rien. "Creole Cookbook, Creole Cookery, Creole Identity in 1885 New Orleans," (paper presented at the first annual "Words in Food Symposium," New Orleans, Louisiana, October 10, 2009.

Fisher, Abby. *What Mrs. Fisher Knows about Old Southern Cooking*. San Francisco, CA: Women's Cooperative Printing Office, 1881.

Fitzmorris, Tom. *Hungry Town: A Culinary History of New Orleans, The City Where Food Is Almost Everything*. New York: Stewart, Tabori & Chang, 2010.

Fussell, Betty. *I Hear America Cooking*. New York: Viking, 1986.

Gaudet, Marsha, and James McDonald, eds. *Mardi Gras, Gumbo, and Zydeco: An Introduction to Louisiana Culture*. Jackson: University Press of Mississippi, 2003.

Gayarré, Charles. *History of Louisiana*. New York: Redfield, 1854; W. J. Widdleton, 1866.

Gehman, Mary. *The Free People of Color of New Orleans: An Introduction*. New Orleans: Margaret Media, 1994.

Gilbert, Troy, Greg Picolo, and Kenneth Holditch. *Dinner with Tennessee Williams: Recipes and Stories Inspired by America's Southern Playwright*. Layton, UT: Gibbs Smith Publishers, 2011.

Goodman, Dena. *The Republic of Letters: A Cultural History of the French Enlightenment*. Ithaca, NY: Cornell University Press, 2002.

Gopnik, Adam. *The Table Comes First: Family, France, and the Meaning of Food*. New York: Knopf, 2011.

Gutierrez, C. Paige. *Cajun Foodways*. Jackson: University Press of Mississippi, 1992.

Haggerty, Mary Loyola. *Margaret Gaffney Haughery of New Orleans: Social Worker*. Washington, D.C.: Catholic University of America, 1945.

Hall, Gwendolyn Midlo. *Africans in Colonial Louisiana: The Development of Afro-Creole Culture in the Eighteenth Century*. Baton Rouge: Louisiana State University Press, 1992.

Hancock, David. *Oceans of Wine: Madeira and the Emergence of American Trade and Taste*. New Haven, CT: Yale University Press, 2009.

Harris, Jessica B. *Beyond Gumbo: Creole Fusion Food from the Atlantic Rim*. New York: Simon & Schuster, 2003.

———. "Oysters: The Gulf's Bountiful Bivalves Face a Challenge from the Oil Spill of 2010," *Louisiana Cultural Vistas* 21, no. 4 (Winter 2010–2011): 68–69.

Hearn, Lafcadio. *Lafcadio Hearn's Creole Cook Book*. Gretna, LA: Pelican, 1990 (first published in 1885).

Hirsch, Arnold, and Joseph Logsdon. *Creole New Orleans: Race and Americanization*. Baton Rouge: Louisiana State University Press, 1992.

Holditch, Kenneth, and Marda Burdon. *Galatoire's: The Biography of a Bistro*. New Orleans: Garrett County Press, 2011.

Holditch, Kenneth, and Richard Freemen Leavitt. *Tennessee Williams and the South.* Jackson: University of Mississippi Press, 2009.

Jackson, Joy J. "Prohibition in New Orleans: The Unlikeliest Crusade," *Louisiana History* 19, no. 3 (1978): 261–284.

Johnson, Jerah. "New Orleans's Congo Square: An Urban Setting for Early Afro-American Culture Formation," *Louisiana History* 32 (Spring 1991): 117–157.

Johnson, Walter. *Soul by Soul: Life inside the Antebellum Slave Market.* Cambridge, MA: Harvard University Press, 1999.

Keyes, Frances Parkinson. *Dinner at Antoine's.* New York: Julian Messner, 1948.

———. *Once on Esplanade: A Cycle between Two Creole Weddings.* New York: Julian Messner, 1947.

———. *Crescent Carnival.* New York: Julian Messner, 1946.

Kukla, Jon. *A Wilderness So Immense: The Louisiana Purchase and the Destiny of America (Lewis & Clark Expedition).* New York: Knopf, 2003.

Laborde, Peggy Scott, and Tom Fitzmorris. *Lost Restaurants of New Orleans.* Gretna, LA: Pelican Publishing, 2011.

Land, Mary. *Louisiana Cookery.* New York: A. S. Barnes, 1954.

———. *New Orleans Cuisine.* New York: A. S. Barnes, 1969.

Langley, Linda, Claude Oubre, and Jay Precht. "Louisa Williams Robinson, Her Daughters and Granddaughters," *Louisiana Cultural Vistas* 20, no. 4 (Winter 2009–2010): 26–35.

Lanusse, Armand. *Les Cenelles: A Collection of Poems of Creole Writers of the Early Nineteenth Century.* Translated by Regine Latortue and Gleason Rex Adams. Boston: G. K. Hall, 1979.

Larson, Susan. "The Pursuit of Pleasure and Perfection," *Louisiana Cultural Vistas* 21, no. 4 (Winter 2010–2011): 70–77.

Lawrence, John H. *What's Cooking in New Orleans? Culinary Traditions of the Crescent City.* The Historic New Orleans Collection, exhibition guide January 16–July 7, 2007.

Leathen, Karen Trahan. "Three Women and Their Restaurants: Elizabeth Begué, Marie Esparbé, and Corinne Dunbar: An Exhibition Guide." New Orleans: Newcomb Center for Research on Women, 2001.

———. "Two Women and Their Cookbooks: Lena Richard and Mary Land." New Orleans: Newcomb Center for Research on Women, 2001.

Lelièvre, Jacques-Felix, *New Louisiana Gardener.* Translated, with an Introduction, by Sally Kittredge Reeves. Baton Rouge: Louisiana University Press, 2001.

Leong, Karen J., et al. "Resilient History and the Rebuilding of a Community: The Vietnamese American Community in New Orleans East." *Journal of American History,* 94 (December 2007, 770–79).

Le Page du Pratz, and Antoine Simon. *The History of Louisiana,* edited by Joseph G. Tregle Jr. Reprinted from 1758. Baton Rouge: Louisiana American Revolution Bicentennial Commission and Louisiana University Press, 1974.

Leavitt, Richard Freeman, and Kenneth Holditch. *Tennessee Williams and the South.* Oxford: University Press of Mississippi, 2009.

Lockwood, Yvonne, and Lucy Long. "Key Ingredients: America by Food" Exhibition Review. *Journal of American Folklore* 122, no. 483 (Winter 2009): 92–96.

Long, Lucy. "Introduction." In *Culinary Tourism*, edited by Lucy Long, 2–19. Lexington: University of Kentucky Press, 2004.

Magnaghi, Russell M. "Louisiana's Italian Immigrants Prior to 1870." *Louisiana History* 27, no. 1 (1986): 43–68.

Mann, Charles, *1491: New Revelations of the Americas before Columbus.* New York: Knopf, 2005.

Mayo, H. M. *Mme. Begué and Her Recipes: Old Creole Cookery.* New Orleans: Southern Pacific Co., Sunset Route Passenger Dept., c. 1900.

McCaffety, Kerri. *Saint Joseph Altars.* Gretna, LA. Pelican Publishing Company, 2003.

McCaffrey, Kevin. "We Are What We Ate," *Louisiana Cultural Vistas* 23, no. 1 (Spring 2012): 80–81.

Merrill, Ellen C. *Germans of Louisiana.* New Orleans: Pelican Publishing, 2005.

Mitchell, Patricia B. *French Cooking in Early America.* Self-published, 1991.

Mintz, Sidney. *Tasting Food, Tasting Freedom: Excursions into Eating, Culture, and the Past.* Boston: Beacon Press, 1996.

Nabhan, Gary, Leigh Belanger, and Regina Fitzsimmons. "Food Producers and Their Place-Based Foods at Risk in the Gulf Coast." RAFT (Renewing America's Food Traditions), June 2010.

Neufeld, Josh. *A.D.: New Orleans after the Deluge.* New York: Pantheon Books, 2009.

Northup, Solomon. *Twelve Years a Slave.* London: Auburn, Derby, and Miller, 1853.

Nott, Josiah, and George Glidden. *Types of Mankind; or, Ethnological Researches, Based upon the Ancient Monuments, Paintings, Sculptures, and Crania of Races.* 1854. Philadelphia: J. B. Lippincott; London: Trubner, 1865.

Olopade, Dayo. "Green Shoots in New Orleans: A Frustrating Quest for Food Security Has Led Some Residents to Grow Their Own." *The Nation* (September 21, 2009), pp. 23–26. (New Orleans Food & Farm Network, Market Umbrella, Viet Village).

O'Toole, John Kennedy. *A Confederacy of Dunces.* Baton Rouge: Louisiana State University Press, 1980.

Paddleford, Clementine. *How America Eats.* New York: Charles Scribner & Sons, 1960.

Perrin, Warren. *Acadian Redemption: From Beausoleil Brossard to the Queen's Royal Proclamation.* Opelousas, LA: Andrepont Publishing, 2005.

Peters, Erica J. *Appetites and Aspirations in Vietnam: Food and Drink in the Long Nineteenth Century.* Lanham, MD: AltaMira Press, 2011.

The Picayune Creole Cook Book. New Orleans: The Times-Picayune, 1987 [1901].

Pillsbury, Richard. "Cuisine Regions: Concept and Content." Chapter 10 in *No Foreign Food: The American Diet in Time and Place.* Boulder, CO: Westview Press, 1988.

Pinkard, Susan. *A Revolution in Taste: The Rise of French Cuisine*. Cambridge: Cambridge University Press, 2009.

Powers, Madelon. *Faces along the Bar: Lore and Order in the Workingman's Saloon, 1870–1920*. Chicago: University of Chicago Press, 1999.

Reinders, Robert. *The End of an Era: New Orleans 1850–1860*. New Orleans: Pelican Press, 1964.

Reizenstein, Baron Ludwig von. *The Mysteries of New Orleans*. Translated and edited by Steven Rowan. Baltimore: Johns Hopkins University Press, 2002.

Richard, Lena. *New Orleans Cook Book*. Boston: Houghton Mifflin, 1940.

Roach, Joseph. *Cities of the Dead: Circum-Atlantic Performance*. New York: Columbia University Press, 1996.

Roahen, Sara. *Gumbo Tales: Finding My Place at the New Orleans Table*. New York: W. W. Norton & Company, 2008.

Rosofsky, Meryl. "Food to the Rescue! The Restorative Role of Food-Related Organizations in Post-Katrina New Orleans." Paper presented at the Association for the Study of Food and Society Conference, June 2008.

Rowan, Steve. "Introduction." In *The Mysteries of New Orleans*, by Baron Ludwig von Reizenstein, edited by Steven Rowan, pp. xiii–xxxiii. Baltimore: Johns Hopkins University Press, 2002.

Ryan, Mary. *Civic Wars: Democracy and Public Life in the American City during the Nineteenth Century*. Berkeley: University of California Press, 1997.

St. John, Warren. "Greens in Black and White." *New York Times*, Section F, p. 1, October 6, 2004.

St. Joseph Guild. *Viva San Giuseppe: A Guide to Saint Joseph Altars*. New Orleans, St. Joseph Guild, no date.

Sauder, Robert A., "The Origin and Spread of the Public Market System in New Orleans," *Louisiana History: The Journal of the Louisiana Historical Association* 22, no. 3 (Summer 1981): 281–297.

Saxon, Lyle, Edward Dreyer, and Robert Tallant. *Gumbo Ya-Ya: Folk Tales of Louisiana*. Gretna, LA: Pelican Publishing Company, 1987.

Schell, Heather. "Gendered Feasts: A Feminist Reflects on Dining in New Orleans." Chapter 11 in *Pilaf, Pozole, and Pad Thai: American Women and Ethnic Food*, edited by Sherrie Inness. Amherst: University of Massachusetts Press, 2001.

Scott, Natalie, and Caroline Merrick Jones. *Gourmet's Guide to New Orleans*. New Orleans: Scott & Jones, 1933.

Scott, Natalie V. *Mandy's Favorite Louisiana Recipes*. New York: Jonathan Cape and Harrison Smith, 1929.

Scott, Natalie V. *Two Hundred Years of New Orleans Cooking*. New York: Jonathan Cape and Harrison Smith, 1931.

Séjour, Victor. "Le Mûlatre." In *The Multilingual Anthology of American Literature: A Reader of Original Texts with English Translations*, edited by Marc Shell and Werner Sollors. New York: New York University Press, 2000.

Severson, Kim. "A Brighter View Astern Than over the Bow." *New York Times*, December 21, 2005. (Shrimping industry post-Katrina.)

——. "Can New Orleans Save the Soul of Its Food?" *New York Times*, January 11, 2006.

——. "In New Orleans, Knives, Forks, and Hammers." *New York Times*, August 23, 2006.

Soniat, Leon. *La Bouche Creole*, Gretna, LA: Pelican Publishing Company, 1981.

Southern Food and Beverage Museum. "Gulf Coast Oil Spill Data Collecting Clearing House: Cultural Impact Research." http://southernfood.org/sofab/?p=1156 (compendium of ongoing research efforts to catalogue and analyze the cultural impact of the oil spill).

Stanforth, Deirdre. *Creole! The Legendary Cuisine of New Orleans: Gumbo, jambalaya, Grillades, Fricassee; The Great Seafood Specialties, the Most Opulent Sweets, Fifty-five Authentic Recipes Plus Fascinating Lore for the Cook*. New York: Simon & Schuster, 1969.

——. *The New Orleans Restaurant Cookbook*. Garden City, NY: Doubleday, 1967.

Stanonis, Anthony J. *Creating the Big Easy: New Orleans and the Emergence of Modern Tourism, 1918–1945*. Athens: University of Georgia Press, 2006.

——. "The Triumph of Epicure: A Global History of New Orleans Culinary Tourism." *Southern Quarterly* 46, no. 3 (Spring 2009): 145–161.

Starr, S. Frederick, ed. *Inventing New Orleans: Writings of Lafcadio Hearn*. Jackson: University Press of Mississippi, 2001.

Stowe, Harriet Beecher. *Uncle Tom's Cabin; or, Life among the Lowly*. 1851–1852. Oxford: Oxford University Press, 1998.

Strahan, Jerry E. *Managing Ignatius: The Lunacy of Lucky Dogs and Life in the Quarter*. Baton Rouge: Louisiana State University Press, 1998.

Sublette, Ned. *The World That Made New Orleans: From Spanish Silver to Congo Square*. Chicago: Lawrence Hill Books, 2009.

Theriot, Jude. *La Meilleure de la Louisiane: The Best of Louisiana*. Cambridge: Cambridge University Press, 1990.

Thomas, Jerry. *How to Mix Drinks*. New York: self-published, 1862.

Toledano, Roulhac. *The National Trust Guide to New Orleans*. New Orleans, LA: Wiley, 1996.

Tooker, Poppy. *The Crescent City Farmers Market Cookbook*. New Orleans: Market Umbrella, 2009.

Tucker, Susan, ed. *New Orleans Cuisine: Fourteen Signature Dishes and Their Histories*, University Press of Mississippi, 2009.

Twain, Mark. *Life on the Mississippi*. New York: Oxford University Press, 1996 [1883].

Urry, John. "The Tourist Gaze 'Revisited.'" *American Behavioral Scientist* 36, no. 2 (November 1992): 172–186.

Usner, Daniel H. Jr., "The Facility Offered by the Country: The Creolization of Agriculture in the Lower Mississippi Valley," in *Creolization in the Americas*, edited by David Buisseret and Steven G. Reinhardt. Walter Prescott Webb Memorial Lectures. College Station: Texas A&M University Press, 2000.

Van Wey, Adelaide. Singing *Street Cries and Creole Songs of New Orleans*. Washington, D.C.: Smithsonian Institute, 1956.

Varisco, Tom. *Spoiled: The Refrigerators of New Orleans*. New Orleans: self-published, 2005.

Vujnovich, Milos. *Yugoslavs in Louisiana*. Gretna, Louisiana: Pelican Publishing Company, 1974.

Wilds, John, Charles L. Dufour, and Walter G. Cowan. *Louisiana Yesterday and Today: A Historical Guide to the State*. Baton Rouge: Louisiana State University Press, 1996.

Williams, Elizabeth M., with others. *Crawfish Farming in Louisiana*, monograph published by Sea Grant Legal Program, Louisiana State University Law Center, Baton Rouge, Louisiana, 1975.

Williams, Elizabeth M. "Red Gravy," *Southern Culture* (Winter 2009), 133–136.

Wilson, Nancy Tregre. *Louisiana's Italian, Food, Recipes, and Folkways*. New Orleans: Pelican Publishing Company, 2005.

Wolnik, Dar. "Food Will Save Us." In *Do You Know What It Means to Miss New Orleans?* edited by David Rutledge, 110–114. Seattle: Chin Music Press, 2006.

Wondrich, David. *Imbibe! From Absinthe Cocktail to Whiskey Smash, a Salute in Stories and Drinks to "Professor" Jerry Thomas, Pioneer of the American Bar*. New York: Perigee, 2007.

Young, Ashley. "Cooking in the Old Creole Days: An Exploration of Late Nineteenth and Early Twentieth Century Creole Culture and Society through the Study of Creole Cookbooks." Unpublished Senior Thesis, Yale University, 2010.

Zacherie, James S. *New Orleans Guide*. New Orleans: *New Orleans News*, 1885.

Zimmerman, Jordan. "Bayou *Bánh Mì*: The Food Practices of the Vietnamese in New Orleans East." Unpublished Senior Thesis, Yale University, 2011.

Index

About the Author

Elizabeth M. Williams, a native of New Orleans, is founder and president of the Southern Food and Beverage Museum in New Orleans, which celebrates the food of the American South, with exhibits, a library, archives, collections, and programming. SoFab is one of *Saveur's* "5 Great Museums Devoted to Food" (May 2011). Williams is also consulting professor at the Kabacoff School of Hotel, Restaurant and Tourism, University of New Orleans. Her roles there include teaching, writing, and researching issues in hospitality law, culinary history and culture, and nonprofit administration. She has contributed a number of articles on aspects of Southern food to journals. She has a law degree and coauthored the *A to Z of Food Controversies and the Law* (2010).